ANIMATING CIVIL PROCEDURE

ANIMATING CIVIL PROCEDURE

SECOND EDITION

Michael Vitiello
Distinguished Professor of Law
University of the Pacific, McGeorge School of Law

CAROLINA ACADEMIC PRESS
Durham, North Carolina

Library of Congress Cataloging-in-Publication Data

Names: Vitiello, Michael author
Title: Animating civil procedure / by Michael Vitiello.
Description: Second edition. | Durham, North Carolina : Carolina Academic Press, LLC, 2025. | Includes bibliographical references and index.
Identifiers: LCCN 2025032777 | ISBN 9781531034276 paperback | ISBN 9781531034283 ebook
Subjects: LCSH: Civil procedure—United States | Trial practice—United States
Classification: LCC KF8840 .V58 2025 | DDC 347.73/5—dc23/eng/20250728
LC record available at https://lccn.loc.gov/2025032777

Carolina Academic Press, LLC
700 Kent Street
Durham, North Carolina 27701
(919) 489-7486
www.cap-press.com

Printed in the United States of America

To my wife, Erie P. Vitiello,
a Civil Procedure professor's dream come true

Contents

Acknowledgments for the Second Edition

This book project is rooted in almost fifty years of teaching Civil Procedure. During that time, so many colleagues and students have helped me refine my understanding of how to animate teaching Civil Procedure. Indeed, there are far too many to acknowledge here. However, several people deserve special recognition. I am especially grateful to my acquisitions editor Roberta O'Meara for ushering my book proposal through the original selection process and to David Herzig for his encouragement to do a second edition of this book. In addition, I want to thank the Carolina Academic Press staff members, including Tasha Gervais, Grace Pledger, Keith Moore, Steve Oliva, and Ryland Bowman for their help.

I am also extremely appreciative of the work that my research assistants have done to help prepare this edition of the book. I have had the great fortune to work with a wonderful group of research assistants, including Sabina Bagdasarova, Khalil Ferguson, Brandon Rizotto, and Krista Simpson. Also, I want to thank my colleague Daniel Croxall for his helpful comments about this edition of the book and for sharing my enthusiasm for Civil Procedure. Finally, I want to extend special thanks to my colleague Professor MaryBeth Moylan for organizing a symposium about the first edition of the book and to the contributors to that symposium. They were Professor Donald L. Doernberg, Professor (now Dean) Richard D. Freer, Professor Thomas O. Main, and Professor Linda S. Mullenix.

INTRODUCTION

Animating Civil Procedure

I will be in my forty-ninth year of teaching when this edition of the book is published. For most of that time, I have taught Civil Procedure. I continue to love to teach the course despite its many challenges. Some of these challenges include the need to animate arcane principles of law and to overcome students' misperceptions that the course involves a series of dry concepts. If students have thoughts about the subject matter before they begin the course, they are more likely to believe that they will be learning about where the courthouse is and how many days they have in which to file an answer to a complaint than they are to believe that the course is about some of the most important and exciting concepts in the law.

Students entering law school usually want to discuss broad themes about justice. For example, they may have strong opinions about whether the Constitution includes a right to privacy, encompassing the right to abortion. Indeed, many commentators believe that the Supreme Court's decision overruling *Roe v. Wade*[1] almost certainly prevented a Republican landslide in the 2022 midterm congressional election.[2] Similarly, students often have unequivocal views about whether the Second Amendment creates a personal right to own weapons.

---

1. Dobbs v. Jackson Women's Health Org., 597 U.S. 215 (2022).

2. Diana C. Mutz & Edward D. Mansfield, *Inflation in 2022 Did Not Affect Congressional Voting, But Abortion Did*, PNAS (May 13, 2024), https://www.pnas.org/doi/10.1073/pnas.2319512121.

By contrast, few students have much interest in whether the Supreme Court expands or narrows the interpretation of the Due Process Clause as it relates to personal jurisdiction. Nor are many likely to understand what is at stake if the Court heightens pleading requirements, narrows the scope of discovery, or alters the interpretation of a statute governing transfer of venue. And yet, many procedural lawyers and professors know that procedure is more important than is substantive law.

My memory is hazy about my law school experience; but I suspect that I did not recognize the power of procedure as a 1L. Indeed, I doubt that I did when I began teaching Civil Procedure in 1977. When my first associate dean told me that I would be teaching Civil Procedure, I accepted the assignment willingly enough because I was also able to teach Criminal Law and Criminal Procedure, the courses that dovetailed with my scholarly interest in the early part of my career. It took me several years to learn how to bring Civil Procedure to life. A bit self-serving, I believe that I have done so for many of my students. Doing so required me to develop a much deeper understanding of the power of procedure and then to find ways to communicate that to my students. Animating procedure is the major theme of this book. My hope is that if you are a law professor teaching Civil Procedure or a law student taking Civil Procedure, you will find the insights in this book helpful in enhancing the course.

This book also has a second theme that supports my first theme. Often, members of the public become engaged (or enraged) when they read about Supreme Court decisions involving substantive rights. Examples are easy to come by: *Obergefell v. Hodges*,[3] the same-sex marriage case, produced a flood of comments on many websites including the *New York Times*' page. So, too, did the Supreme Court's decision in *District of Columbia v. Heller*,[4] one of the cases involving gun rights. Yet another example is the response to *Citizens United v. Federal Election Commission*,[5] which struck down provisions of the campaign finance law. As indicated above, the Court's *Dobbs* decision produced concrete

3. Obergefell v. Hodges, 576 U.S. 644 (2015).
4. District of Colombia v. Heller, 554 U.S. 570 (2008).
5. Citizens United v. Fed. Election Comm'n, 558 U.S. 310 (2010).

results in the 2022 congressional election. But members of the public are far less likely to understand the impact of procedural decisions.[6]

Few readers reacted passionately or otherwise to the Supreme Court's decisions narrowing personal jurisdiction. Nor did they call for changes in the rules governing pleading when the Court rewrote Federal Rule of Civil Procedure 8(a)(2) in *Bell Atlantic Corp. v. Twombly*[7] and *Ashcroft v. Iqbal*.[8] Few members of the public understand decisions like *Mallory v. Norfolk Southern Railway*,[9] a case that upheld the assertion of jurisdiction over an out-of-state corporation, which opened the courthouse door for an injured plaintiff. And yet these decisions are critically important to whether plaintiffs have access to court.

This book focuses on a series of Supreme Court decisions and changes to the Federal Rules of Civil Procedure that demonstrate the Court's erosion of rules originally designed to allow plaintiffs access to court. Many of the Court's decisions unravel rules developed during the height of the Progressive Movement and the postwar era when courts created

---

6. Linda Mullenix, *Federal Class Actions: A Near-Death Experience in a Shady Grove*, 79 Geo. Wash. L. Rev. 448 (2011). To make this point more fully, I asked one of my research assistants to look at online comments about major Supreme Court cases. The results support the point in the text. Members of the public respond (often passionately) in large numbers about cases where the Court renders a substantive decision, but far less frequently when the Court renders a procedural decision. Using the Google news search, my research assistant found about 25,000 comments about *Citizens United*, 558 U.S. 310 (dealing with campaign finance laws); almost 20,000 comments about *Heller*, 554 U.S. 570 (the Second Amendment right to bear arms); about 12,000 comments about *Obergefell*, 135 S. Ct. 2584 (same sex marriage equality); and about 1,400 comments about *Snyder v. Phelps*, 562 U.S. 443 (2011) (the First Amendment rights of protesters who demonstrated at the funeral of a deceased soldier). By comparison, only 190 readers commented on *Ledbetter v. Goodyear Tire & Rubber Co.*, 550 U.S. 618 (2007) (dealing with statute of limitations for an employment discrimination case); fewer than 120 readers commented on *J. McIntyre Mach., Ltd. v. Nicastro*, 564 U.S. 873 (2011) (denying personal jurisdiction to an injured plaintiff in a specific jurisdiction case), and only 106 readers commented on *Daimler AG v. Bauman*, 134 S. Ct. 746 (2014) (same, in a general jurisdiction case). One of my research assistants updated this informal research, the results of which are reported in Chapter 1. As you will see there, the results of that research are similar to those reported in the first edition: members of the public care about Court decisions dealing with substantive rights, while they seem not to appreciate the implications of procedural decisions.

7. Bell Atlantic Corp. v. Twombly, 550 U.S. 544 (2007).

8. Ashcroft v. Iqbal, 556 U.S. 662 (2009).

9. Mallory v. Norfolk Southern Railway, 600 U.S. 122 (2023).

rules favoring plaintiffs' access to court.[10] The Court's decisions are eroding one of the foundational principles of American law—that the rule of law depends upon ready access to court, where litigants have a fair chance to bring their claims before a neutral arbiter.[11] Narrowing the opportunity to get into a convenient forum with other important procedural rights erodes that fundamental concept.

Many of the cases and other changes in the law covered in chapters below invite a discussion of underlying policies that support decisions to narrow access to our courts. When former President Obama nominated Sonia Sotomayor to serve as a justice on the Supreme Court, he commented about the importance of her life experiences. Critics argued that a justice's life experiences are irrelevant. They were either dishonest or naïve. Any observer of the system knows that judges' life experiences influence their views of the law. Indeed, in one famous case discussed in this book, former Justice Kennedy referred explicitly to the need for judges to rely on their common sense and life experiences.[12] Given the makeup of the current Court—one of the most right-wing lineups in history, even more so than when I wrote the first edition of this book, one should not be surprised that the Court has adopted positions advanced by corporate and other business interests, not just on hot button social issues like access to guns and abortion rights. In most of these cases, the right wing of the Court has taken the lead in narrowing access to our judicial system.[13]

By focusing on the policy implications of the Court's procedural case law, one can animate the importance of procedure. Thus, in addition to teaching students doctrine, I focus on the important policy implications in the Court's case law and rulemaking. The Court has limited ability to alter substantive law. Some statutes create rights found to be unconstitutional, but such decisions are relatively rare. In addition, when the Court

---

10. *See infra* Chapters 3 and 4.

11. *See* Steven H. Goldberg, *Putting the Supreme Court Back in Place: Ideology, Yes; Agenda, No*, 17 Geo. J. Legal Ethics 175, 176–77 (2004).

12. *See infra* Chapter 6.

13. *See, e.g.*, McCutcheon v. Fed. Election Comm'n, 572 U.S. 185 (2014); Shelby County v. Holder, 570 U.S. 529 (2013); United States v. Windsor, 570 U.S. 744 (2013). Some commentators already see a shift in the direction of the Court since Justice Scalia's death. *See* Adam Liptak, *The Right-Wing Supreme Court That Wasn't*, New York Times (June 28, 2016), http://nyti.ms/29oGmqU.

renders substantive decisions, it faces intense public scrutiny. At times, such decisions have influenced presidential elections.[14] By comparison, as I develop in this book, the Court can achieve many of its policy goals by deciding cases on procedural grounds. A person with a host of substantive rights may not prevail unless that person has access to a convenient forum with rules allowing liberal discovery.

One might ask fairly whether there is a need for a second edition of this book. Obviously, the editors at Carolina Academic Press agree with me that there is such a need. Witness the Supreme Court's further movement towards the extreme right wing since Justice Scalia's death and then-Senate Majority leader Mitch McConnell's questionable moves to prevent then-President Obama's nominee Merrick Garland's appointment to the Court, followed by his success in ramming Amy Coney Barrett's selection through the Senate after the 2020 Presidential election.

In some areas, my earlier assessment may have been too dire. Or as University of Texas Law Professor Linda Mullenix suggested in a paper delivered as part of a symposium about the first edition of *Animating Civil Procedure,* perhaps I am a "procedural Cassandra[]" who believes that "the Court's procedural pronouncements have been headed on a consistently downward arc."[15] For example, the Supreme Court's efforts to rachet up pleading requirements have produced mixed results. But in other areas, the Court's use of procedure has masked significant substantive reforms, largely unnoticed by the public. Most notably, the Court's use of its "shadow docket" has had profound and largely invisible impacts on substantive rights. Indeed, Georgetown University Law Professor Stephen Vladeck has argued that the Court's unprincipled use of its shadow docket allowed Republicans to retain control of the House of Representatives in the 2022 midterm elections.[16] Perhaps a good way to understand an underlying theme in this second edition is to assess where

14. *See, e.g.*, Roe v. Wade, 410 U.S. 113 (1973); *see also* Nadja Popovich, *Roe v. Wade at 40: Republicans More Conservative Than Ever About Abortion*, The Guardian (Jan. 22, 2013), https://www.theguardian.com/world/2013/jan/22/roe-v-wade-republican-radicalisation (describing how upholding or overturning the case is often a platform for Democrats and Republicans, respectively).

15. Linda Mullenix, *Is the Arc of Procedure Bending Towards Injustice?* 50 U. Pac. L. Rev. 611, 614 (2019).

16. Stephen Vladeck, The Shadow Dockets: How the Supreme Court Uses Stealth Rulings to Amass Power and Undermine the Republic (2023).

the first edition demonstrated too dire a view of the Court's work and where my earlier assessment remains as an important warning about the Court's role in narrowing plaintiffs' access to our courts.

Here is a list of specific topics covered in this book: Chapter One explores the overall theme of this book that the Court's procedural holdings seldom evoke a public outcry, making political backlash against the Court for such decisions unlikely. Although the Court's shadow docket is not typically discussed in basic Civil Procedure courses, the Court's use of the shadow docket presents an especially powerful example of the Court's use of procedure to advance a political agenda with relatively little risk that members of the public will understand how an arcane procedural device impacts our rights. Chapter Two explains the shadow docket and describes its impact on our body politic. Chapter Three discusses the Supreme Court's recent personal jurisdiction case law. When I wrote the first edition, I argued that the Court's personal jurisdiction case law demonstrated how the Court follows its pro-corporate bias at the expense of injured plaintiffs. Since then, the Court has upheld state courts' assertion of jurisdiction over corporate defendants in two cases. The Court's pro-defendant bias has not been as obvious as it was prior to those recent cases. But as explored in Chapter Three, at least some justices have suggested new arguments that would favor corporate defendants and limit plaintiffs' ability to sue in their preferred forum. Chapter Four highlights the Court's rewriting of its pleading rules that, when drafted, originally reflected the Court's intent to encourage access to the judicial system through simplified pleading. Instead, in *Bell Atlantic Corp. v. Twombly*[17] and *Ashcroft v. Iqbal*,[18] the Court reintroduced arcane concepts of pleading that limited access to court. Since the first edition, the Court seems to have backed away from its holdings in *Twiqbal*. As explored in Chapter Four, lower courts have divided on how broadly or narrowly to read those cases. Empirical data support my earlier contention that a judge's political views help to explain how broadly to read those cases. Chapter Five focuses on discovery, including a review of its importance in leveling the playing field for plaintiffs facing wealthy corporate defendants. The goal of discovery, to achieve just results based on the merits after full disclosure of all relevant material, is likely to be

17. *Twombly*, 550 U.S. 544.

18. *Iqbal*, 556 U.S. 662.

undercut by recent amendments to Rule 26(b), which now invites courts to limit discovery based on the overall value of the suit. Notably, the right wing and business interests have attempted to narrow the scope of discovery. In 2015, the Advisory Committee proposed a modest reform to the scope of discovery. The Court and Congress signed off on that reform. Despite Chief Justice Roberts' attempt to portray efforts to address two kinds of discovery abuse, over-discovery and evasion, the 2015 reform addressed only over-discovery, typically an abuse associated with plaintiffs. Chapter Five explores how the 2015 change to Rule 26(b)(1) has played out in lower federal court decisions. Chapter Six examines the controversy surrounding former President Obama's appointment of Justice Sotomayor when the President referenced the importance of a judge's life experience and empathy in deciding cases. Not only does the chapter explore that controversy, but it examines instances in which the members of the right wing of the Court have substituted their views for those of juries and demonstrated their own kind of empathy—favoring the interests of the powerful over the interests of injured plaintiffs. Chapter Seven examines what appears to be a minor, noncontroversial transfer of venue case. *Atlantic Marine Construction Co. v. U.S. District Court*,[19] decided by a unanimous Court, demonstrates how a seemingly minor procedural decision may give corporations a less than obvious, but nonetheless real, advantage over less powerful parties. Chapter Eight considers how the Court's class action case law has undercut many litigants' substantive rights. It begins with a discussion of *Shady Grove Orthopedic Associates, P.A. v. Allstate Insurance, Co.*,[20] an opinion written by Justice Scalia that seems to undercut my thesis about the right wing of the Court closing the courthouse door. After exploring that case, the chapter focuses more fully on the drift of most of the Roberts Court's class action case law, where the trend has been to limit the availability of class actions. This results in denial of meaningful access to court for plaintiffs who possess claims too small to be litigated on their own.

Chapters Three through Eight largely focus on the broad theme that the net effect of the Court's case law has been to narrow access to our courts for many potential plaintiffs. Chapter Nine discusses the Court's arbitration case law, which also has the same effect. In the first edition of

19. Atl. Marine Constr. Co. v. United States Dist. Court, 571 U.S. 49 (2013).

20. Shady Grove Orthopedic Assocs., P.A. v. Allstate Ins. Co., 559 U.S. 393 (2010).

the book, I described what appeared to be significant political will to unravel some of the Supreme Court's anti-consumer arbitration case law. Chapter Nine updates those efforts and, perhaps not surprisingly given other political developments in recent years, those efforts have failed. That chapter reviews concerns raised by several scholars, including Professor Mullenix, about the Court's continued use of procedure to close the courthouse door for injured plaintiffs. The politics of procedure are clearly in evidence. I should offer a caveat: as I finish this manuscript in the summer of 2025, President Trump has shown a willingness to upset basic norms in government that may challenge the rule of law. How the Supreme Court will respond is open to question at this point.[21] But given recent history, I may have to write a third edition in the not-too-distant future.

Read on. My hope is that you will come to share my enthusiasm for the subject matter even if you do not share my policy preferences. By the time you have finished reading this book, I hope that you recognize that understanding procedure is the most important thing that you can do to become a good lawyer.

---

21. For example, at the end of the 2024 term, the Court ruled that nationwide injunctions or "universal" injunctions may be unconstitutional absent a showing that it is necessary to give the plaintiff complete relief. The Court remanded the case for further proceedings. Trump v. CASA, Inc., 145 S. Ct. 2540 (2025).

ANIMATING CIVIL PROCEDURE

ONE

Procedural Reform and Staying Under the Radar

A. Introduction

As I explained in the Introduction, one of the central themes of this book is how the right wing of the Court is closing the courthouse door through its procedural decisions. Corporate and other interests have pushed for substantive reform in many areas of the law, and on occasion, those efforts have succeeded. But a full frontal attack on many substantive rights produces pushback from other interest groups and makes change more difficult. Central to my thesis is that members of the public and even many law students and lawyers may not understand how interest groups can achieve their political goals by advancing procedural reform without similar pushback from the public. That is the topic of this chapter.

To explore that theme, I briefly discuss a few substantive changes in the law in this century and share some public reactions to those changes. Thereafter, I compare the reaction, or lack thereof, when the Court decides a case on arcane procedural grounds. Despite that, such decisions have enormous implications for advancement of individual rights. Instead of using a contemporary example, this chapter discusses one of the most famous cases in the Court's history, *Erie Railroad Co. v. Tompkins*,[1] as a way to explore that point.

1. Erie R.R. v. Tompkins, 304 U.S. 64 (1938).

I have chosen to use *Erie* for a number of reasons. Over my almost 50-year teaching career, I have taught *Erie* repeatedly and seen students' eyes glaze over when they read the decision. Even before beginning Civil Procedure, some of them have heard about the *Erie* doctrine as something to dread, not to love. Properly understood, *Erie* is not mystifying.

Even more important than hoping to demystify *Erie*, I have chosen to focus on the case because it produced almost no public response when the Court announced the decision. On the surface, the case was about a conflict between two bodies of tort law.

Despite the lack of public response, *Erie* was a case about political power, corporate forum-shopping, the role of judges and legislatures, and the interplay of federal and state law.[2] One of the most progressive justices to serve on the Court, Louis Brandeis, vindicated many of his views in an opinion that stayed under the public's radar.[3]

As I write this chapter in 2025, I predict that major law reviews throughout the country will conduct symposia in 2028 dedicated to *Erie* to mark its 90th anniversary. The case continues to produce exciting scholarly debates about its meaning and lasting effect. The continuing fascination with the case has nothing to do with the underlying tort law. Instead, it is a case about a procedural revolution.[4]

2. Edward A. Purcell, Jr., Brandeis and the Progressive Constitution (2000).

3. Ruth Bader Ginsburg, Address, *Informing the Public about the U.S. Supreme Court's Work*, 29 Loy. U. Chi. L.J. 275, 278 (1998).

4. Purcell, *supra* note 2; Jay Tidmarsh, Erie *Under Advisement: The Doctrine After* Shady Grove—*Foreword:* Erie's *Gift*, 44 Akron L. Rev. 897 (2011).

B. Substantive Law and Public Sentiment

In the first edition of the book, I invited readers to conduct the following experiment: Google the following case names: *District of Columbia v. Heller*;[5] *Obergefell v. Hodges*;[6] *Citizens United v. Federal Election Commission*;[7] *Snyder v. Phelps*;[8] *Ledbetter v. Goodyear Tire & Rubber Co., Inc.*;[9] *Daimler AG v. Bauman*;[10] and *J. McIntyre Machinery v. Nicastro*.[11] Also Google "new civil discovery rules" (or similar language focusing on the 2015 changes to the Federal Rules of Civil Procedure). Compare the number of results you get for each case.

I then suggested a second experiment: Find newspaper articles reporting on those cases and look at the number of reader responses to each case. No doubt, you get a sense of the purpose of this unscientific sampling: *Heller* found that the Second Amendment created an individual right to possess a firearm.[12] *Snyder* found that members of the Phelps family had a First Amendment right to demonstrate at a funeral of a deceased member of the military.[13] *Citizens United* held that a corporation had a First Amendment right that cannot be limited when it was funding an independent political broadcast in a candidate election.[14] *Obergefell* held that a state law ban on same-sex marriage violated the Equal Protection Clause of the Fourteenth Amendment.[15] *Ledbetter* held that the plaintiff, a woman whose employer discriminated against her based on her gender (as found by a jury), had to bring suit under Title VII for discrimination within a 180-day period from when the discrimination took place.[16] The net effect of the majority's reading of Title VII

---

5. District of Columbia v. Heller, 554 U.S. 570 (2008).
6. Obergefell v. Hodges, 576 U.S. 644 (2015).
7. Citizens United v. Fed. Election Comm'n, 558 U.S. 310 (2010).
8. Snyder v. Phelps, 562 U.S. 443 (2011).
9. Ledbetter v. Goodyear Tire & Rubber Co., 550 U.S. 618 (2007).
10. Daimler AG v. Bauman, 134 S. Ct. 746 (2014).
11. J. McIntyre Mach., Ltd. v. Nicastro, 564 U.S. 873 (2011).
12. District of Columbia v. Heller, 554 U.S. 570 (2008).
13. Snyder v. Phelps, 562 U.S. 443 (2011).
14. Citizens United v. Fed. Election Comm'n, 558 U.S. 310 (2010).
15. Obergefell v. Hodges, 576 U.S. 644 (2015).
16. Ledbetter v. Goodyear Tire & Rubber Co., 550 U.S. 618 (2007).

was that Ledbetter lost a significant verdict based on harm that took place over years of being underpaid.[17] *Bauman* and *Nicastro* involved personal jurisdiction; in both, the Court found that the lower court lacked personal jurisdiction over the defendant.[18]

As you read this edition of the book, try a similar experiment. Google *Dobbs v. Jackson Women's Health Organization*,[19] *New York Pistol & Rifle Association v. Bruen*,[20] and *Mallory v. Norfolk Southern Railway*[21] to see how many citations you get for each Supreme Court case. Then conduct the second experiment that I described above: look for newspaper articles about those cases and examine reader responses to those cases. As you will see, cases involving substantive rights generate frequent and passionate responses. Procedural decisions elicit an occasional response but typically any comments are made without great passion.

In the Introduction, I described my research assistant's original findings that demonstrate the lack of public interest, at least as measured by the frequency of their comments, when the Court renders a procedural decision. The frequency of comments about substantive decisions is far greater than for procedural decisions, as summarized in the Introduction. As I stated there, using the Google news search, my research assistant found about 25,000 comments on *Citizens United*, 20,000 on *Heller*, 12,000 on *Obergefell*, and about 1,400 on *Snyder v. Phelps*. By comparison, only 190 readers commented on *Ledbetter*, fewer than 120 on *Nicastro*, and only 106 on *Daimler*.[22]

Similarly, the tone of the comments was far more strident when readers discussed substantive decisions than when they commented about procedural decisions. Several examples make that point. Commenting on the 2016 *New York Times* piece on *Citizens United*, one reader described the decision as "revolting" and "one of the worst Court decisions," ranking it as such alongside *Plessy v. Ferguson* and *Dred Scott v.*

17. *Id.*

18. Daimler AG v. Bauman, 134 S. Ct. 746 (2014); J. McIntyre Mach., Ltd. v. Nicastro, 564 U.S. 873 (2011).

19. 597 U.S. 215 (2022).

20. 597 U.S. 1 (2022).

21. 600 U.S. 122 (2023).

22. *See supra* Introduction n.6 and accompanying text.

Sandford.[23] In commenting on *Obergefell,* one reader of the *Wall Street Journal* stated, "I can't wait until a pair of fanny bandits decide [sic] they want to be married in the local mosque."[24] Yet another reader wrote of Justice Kennedy's arrogance for all but telling those who opposed homosexuality that they are haters, while a Catholic who supported the decision accused Justice Scalia of the sin of pride.[25] The same article included a long string of comments, filled with colorful commentary. One must keep in mind that the *Wall Street Journal* has a policy that limits particularly crass dialogue and occasionally deletes such comments.

A 2010 *Wall Street Journal* article on how the Court's gun rights cases have shifted the debate about weapons included a series of thinly veiled racist comments. For example, one writer commented that the left distorts the truth about cross racial crimes; another commented that if one annoys a neighborhood hoodlum, one is committing suicide. After describing what he saw as the clear meaning of the Second Amendment (the right of all citizens to bear arms), a third asked, "What is it that these ANTI-US CONSTITUTION LEFTWING NUTS don't understand?"[26] By comparison, a *Wall Street Journal* article on *McIntyre* and *Goodyear* produced only one comment. That comment did discuss the politics of the Court, but without much of the acerb found in discussions of same-sex marriage or Second Amendment rights.[27] Consider what one of my research assistants uncovered about impactful cases decided since the first edition of this book. He focused on three decisions: the first was *Dobbs v. Jackson Women's Health Organization;*[28] the second

23. Meredith, Comment to *Taking on Citizens United,* New York Times (Mar. 30, 2016), http://www.nytimes.com/2016/03/30/opinion/taking-n-citizens-united.html.

24. Anthony Swenson, Comment to *After Obergefell,* Wall Street Journal (June 26, 2015), http://www.wsj.com/articles/after-obergefell-1435341928#livefyre-comment. According to Urban Dictionary, "fanny bandit" is the Spanish term for a homosexual. *Fanny Bandit,* Urban Dictionary, http://www.urbandictionary.com/define.php?term=-fanny%20bandit.

25. Chaz Palm, Comment to *After Obergefell, supra* note 24 (June 29, 2015); Guillermo Reyes, Comment to *id.* (June 28, 2015).

26. Michael Manella, Comment to *Washington's New Gun Rules Shift Constitutional Debate,* Wall Street Journal (May 17, 2010), http://www.wsj.com/articles/SB10001424052748704093204575216680860962548.

27. Roger Baker, Comment to *Supreme Court Bars U.S. Suit Against Goodyear Units Over French Crash,* Wall Street Journal (June 27, 2011), http://www.wsj.com/articles/SB10001424052702304447804576411650063028560.

28. 597 U.S. 215 (2022).

was *New York State Rifle & Pistol Association v. Bruen*;[29] the third was *Mallory v. Norfolk Southern Railway*.[30] I suspect that most readers know what the Court held in *Dobbs* and *Bruen*, but that few readers are familiar with *Mallory*.

My research assistant used various search techniques and terms to see how many comments he could find on major news outlets for those three cases. Here are a few of his findings: after searching on the *New York Times* and *Washington Post* webpages, he found almost 200,000 comments about those cases over about a three-and-a-half-year period. While not as provocative as *Dobbs*, *Bruen* resulted in 56,174 comments over about a three-year period.

As with the earlier decisions, the recent cases produced colorful commentary. Here are just a few comments that give a sense of the anger that readers have about controversial substantive rights cases. One writer said of the *Dobbs* decision, "It's interesting that you have to pass a basic mental health assessment to be a Private in the U.S. Army, but not to be a Supreme Court Justice or President of the United States."[31] Another commentator praised the *New York Times* for an article on the case and added, "Brilliant work NYT. It was really important to showcase the shenanigans of this court. These are nothing but a bunch of ultra conservative politicians masquerading as judges. There are so many grave issues facing our country and it's almost impossible to believe that justice will ever be served fairly, with integrity and only in the best interests of the US citizenry. What a tragedy!"[32]

Commentary about *Bruen* was similar. This comment captures the reader's disgust with the right wing of the Court: "I do not expect this court to provide substantial guidance. The big 6 are lazy, willful and arrogant. They appear not to care, and they don't care that we all know they don't care. It is just sick at this point."[33] Yet another reader added this

---

29. 597 U.S. 1 (2022).

30. 600 U.S. 122 (2023).

31. Cowboy Marine, Comment to *Behind the Scenes at the Dismantling of Roe v. Wade*, New York Times (Dec. 15, 2023), https://www.nytimes.com/shared/comment/3rptls?rsrc=cshare&smid=url-share.

32. *Id.* at 31.

33. CAB, Comment to *Supreme Court's Gun Rulings Leave Baffled Judges Asking for Help*, New York Times (Sept. 23, 2024), https://www.nytimes.com/shared/comment/422ft0?rsrc=cshare&smid=url-share.

sentiment: "The Robert's Court is appalling. 6 justices are far below average in terms of legal knowledge or common sense. America's Senate needs to impeach 5 of these mediocre justices, for nomination violations, bribery, and sexual assaults."[34]

Mallory generated almost no commentary, as we expected. The *New York Times* ran three articles discussing *Mallory*, but the articles did not allow comments. My research assistant found no results when he searched the *Washington Post* website. Searching elsewhere, he found fewer than 40 comments dealing with that case.

Not only did the public respond frequently and with passion to the two substantive rights cases, but, as cited earlier, at least the *Dobbs* case is credited with getting many more voters to the polls in the 2022 midterm election and the 2024 election. As developed earlier, the public takes note of the Court's substantive rights decisions.

Compare the importance of *Mallory*. As developed in Chapter 3, dealing with personal jurisdiction, the Court's decision has the potential to open the courthouse door to many injured plaintiffs who are seeking a convenient forum in which to bring their suits. Only a few members of the public (probably proceduralists) seem to have noticed the power that the case has had on access to justice.

The next section turns to one of the most famous Supreme Court cases. Like modern procedural decisions whose significance is lost on members of the public and many lawyers, the *Erie* case was largely ignored and yet brought about a dramatic revolution in the Court's approach to social issues.

C. *Erie Railroad Co. v. Tompkins*

In July 1934, Harry J. Tompkins was walking along a well-worn path parallel to railroad tracks near his home in Pennsylvania. He heard a train but by the time he looked up, he had no time to react to a black object coming right at him, an object swinging from a train car. The object slammed into him, rendering him unconscious. He lived but lost his right arm.[35]

---

34. *Id.*

35. Erie R.R. v. Tompkins, 304 U.S. 64, 69 (1938); PURCELL, *supra* note 2, at 95.

Tompkins consulted a lawyer about suing the railroad company. The substantive law differed depending on where Tompkins filed his lawsuit, but the two rules that might have applied were straightforward enough. If Tompkins was a trespasser, then the railroad's only responsibility was to avoid willfully injuring him. However, if he was a licensee, the railroad could be found liable for its negligence.[36] Interesting policies may support one rule or another, but a debate about those policy questions would not give *Erie* much staying power.

Instead, *Erie* was a case about forum-shopping with a vengeance and much more as well. Almost a hundred years before *Erie*, the Court held that when a federal court had diversity subject matter jurisdiction, the governing law under certain circumstances should be general federal common law, not state common law. In *Swift v. Tyson*,[37] the Court gave a narrow interpretation to the Rules of Decision Act's[38] language that in diversity jurisdiction, "the laws of the several states" shall provide the rule of decision. Consistent with natural law, the then-prevailing jurisprudential philosophy was that judge-made common law decisions were not law, but merely reflections of the natural law. As a result, a federal court sitting in diversity did not have to follow state common law in most cases.

Tompkins' lawyers understood *Swift*'s implications. Personal jurisdiction would have been proper in either New York or Pennsylvania. More importantly, they had a choice between filing in a federal or a state court. A New York federal court would apply federal common law, which, consistent with case law as applied within the federal Second Circuit, would allow Tompkins to prevail if he could show that the railroad was negligent. Filing in a state court in Pennsylvania would have been fatal to their case because its courts would have applied Pennsylvania tort law, making Tompkins a trespasser. Filing in a federal court in Pennsylvania would probably have had the same result. Although that court would apply federal common law, federal courts within the Third Circuit took a narrower view of the applicable common law than did the Second Circuit.[39]

---

36. *Erie*, 304 U.S. at 69–70.

37. Swift v. Tyson, 41 U.S. 1 (1842).

38. Rules of Decision Act, 28 U.S.C.S. § 1652.

39. PURCELL, *supra* note 2, at 96–97.

Tompkins' lawyers seemed to have found a successful strategy. The New York jury awarded Tompkins $30,000 in damages and the Second Circuit affirmed the judgment. But the Supreme Court took certiorari, reversed the judgment, and remanded the case to the lower court.[40]

As developed in *Brandeis and the Progressive Constitution*, Justice Brandeis held together a precarious majority supporting his opinion. Two of the five justices who joined his opinion would later express doubts about the most important aspect of the opinion, specifically, the suggestion that the Constitution dictated the result in the case.[41] Justice Reed's concurring opinion avoided the discussion of any constitutional basis for the decision. He argued that the Court needed only to reinterpret the Rules of Decision Act, in effect, admitting that its earlier interpretation of the "laws of the several states" language was misguided.[42]

Had Justice Reed prevailed, generations of students would have been spared the fear and loathing of the *Erie* doctrine. Reed's approach was straightforward: the *Swift* Court's interpretation of the statutory language was wrong.

Generations of scholars have debated *Erie*'s constitutional basis and its continued vitality as a decision of constitutional dimensions. Justice Brandeis' opinion did not state explicitly what provision of the Constitution he believed was at play. He did state explicitly that the Court did not find that the Rules of Decision Act was unconstitutional. (Indeed, had that been the case, the Court would have to give notice to the Attorney General to allow the Attorney General to intervene to defend the federal law.) Instead, Brandeis stated that the course that *Swift* put the courts on was unconstitutional.[43] Thus, *Erie* presents two intriguing questions: (1) what does it mean to put the courts on an unconstitutional path? And (2) what provision of the Constitution was implicated?

Surely, the way in which *Swift* put the lower courts on an unconstitutional path was that somehow, its interpretation of "the laws of the several states" was improper. But how is that different from Justice Reed's position? My best explanation of Justice Brandeis' position is to refer students to a position that the Court has adhered to elsewhere:

---

40. *Erie*, 304 U.S. at 80.

41. PURCELL, *supra* note 2, at 105–09.

42. *Erie*, 304 U.S. at 90–92 (Reed, J., concurring).

43. *Id.* at 77–78 (majority opinion).

when a court faces two plausible interpretations of a statute, and one interpretation would render the statute unconstitutional, the court should adopt the alternative interpretation.[44] Perhaps that is the best defense of *Erie* that one can offer. That, of course, shifts the discussion to how *Swift*'s interpretation of the Rules of Decision Act might have violated the Constitution.

One aspect of *Erie* is beyond question—the policy that drove the result in the case. A decade earlier, the Court applied *Swift* in a case that demonstrated the power of intra-jurisdictional forum shopping. In *Black & White Taxicab Co. v. Brown & Yellow Taxicab Co.*,[45] Brown & Yellow, a Kentucky corporation, entered into a contract with the Louisville and Nashville Railroad, also a Kentucky corporation. The contract gave Brown & Yellow exclusive rights to pick up passengers at one of Louisville and Nashville's railway stations. Aware that Kentucky common law would not enforce such contracts, Brown & Yellow reincorporated in Tennessee. After the parties entered the contract, Brown & Yellow sued in federal court to enjoin Black & White from competing for business at the station. The federal court, following general federal common law, found in favor of Brown & Yellow and enjoined Black & White from competing. The Supreme Court upheld the lower court decision, over Justice Oliver Wendell Holmes' strong dissent.[46] Justices Brandeis and Stone joined Holmes' dissent, in which he suggested that *Swift* was unconstitutional.[47] Apart from the constitutional question, one can see problems with such obvious forum-shopping where justice, or at least the result of a particular suit presenting identical facts, turns simply on the expedient of being able to sue in federal or state court.[48]

Finding a constitutional theory is more difficult. One theory should be easily dismissed: that somehow, *Swift*'s reading of the Rules of Deci-

---

44. *E.g.*, Ashwander v. Tenn. Valley Authority, 297 U.S. 288, 346–48 (1936) (Brandeis, J., concurring) (noting that if a case can be decided on either of two plausible grounds and one implicates a constitutional question, the court will decide the case only on the non-constitutional basis).

45. Black & White Taxicab Co. v. Brown & Yellow Taxicab Co., 276 U.S. 518 (1928).

46. *Id.* at 531.

47. *Id.* at 532 (Holmes, J., dissenting).

48. *See id.* at 518 (majority opinion); Jack H. Friedenthal, Mary Kay Kane & Arthur R. Miller, Civil Procedure 199–200 (5th ed. 2015); Purcell, *supra* note 2, at 66.

sion Act violated the Equal Protection Clause of the Constitution. Justice Brandeis stated as follows, "Thus, the [*Swift*] doctrine rendered impossible equal protection of the law. In attempting to promote uniformity of law throughout the United States, the doctrine had prevented uniformity in the administration of the law of the State."[49] Presumably, the federal court system was discriminating against a litigant sued in federal court by treating the defendant differently from the way in which the litigant would have been treated in state court. Or the discrimination may have been the disparate treatment given to a non-diverse party who could not sue in federal court in comparison to a litigant who was diverse and could choose federal court to secure a favorable result. In either case, the federal entity—its court system—was discriminating against one of the parties. But the Fourteenth Amendment, where the Equal Protection Clause appears, limits state power, not federal power. The Fifth Amendment, which limits federal power, contains a Due Process Clause, but no equal protection clause. Not until the mid-1960s did the Court find that equal protection was implicit in the Fifth Amendment's Due Process Clause.[50]

Equal protection analysis also turns on the kind of discrimination involved in a particular case. Statutes often, if not always, create different categories of individuals. If a legislature allows ophthalmologists to perform certain procedures but does not allow optometrists to do so, the legislature is treating two groups differently. Surely, not all such disparate treatment implicates the Equal Protection Clause. Apart from arcane distinctions that the Court's Equal Protection Clause case law has engendered, the Court has held repeatedly that the kind of analysis required depends on the class of people affected by the legislation or other governmental action. Thus, a court examines racial classifications strictly and upholds disparate treatment only upon a very strong showing by the state that the disparate treatment is necessary for some com-

49. Erie R.R. v. Tompkins, 304 U.S. 64, 75 (1938).

50. *See, e.g.*, Buckley v. Valeo, 424 U.S. 1, 93 (1976) ("Equal protection analysis in the Fifth Amendment area is the same as that under the Fourteenth Amendment."); Schneider v. Rusk, 377 U.S. 163, 168 (1964) ("[W]hile the Fifth Amendment contains no equal protection clause, it does forbid discrimination that is 'so unjustifiable as to be violative of due process.'" (quoting Bolling v. Sharpe, 347 U.S. 497, 499 (1954))).

pelling governmental interest.[51] If the government creates two categories of citizens who do not come within any protected class, however, that entity must only demonstrate that the government had a rational basis for the disparate treatment.[52] Most of the Court's jurisprudence dealing with strict scrutiny postdates *Swift*. But finding a form of discrimination that requires a heightened standard of review is difficult.[53]

Many readers believe that Justice Brandeis grounded *Erie* in the Tenth Amendment.[54] That is, when the federal court applied federal common law in Tompkins' trial against the Erie Railroad, it intruded on the state's right to state the rule of law. In 1938, one might have made a plausible argument for such a reading of *Erie*. Presumably, the Tenth Amendment reserved authority in the states over tort law. Some scholarship supports such a reading of *Erie* and the Tenth Amendment.[55]

Today, I doubt any serious scholar would advance such an argument. In the past several decades, various business interests have urged Congress to adopt national standards for products liability. Challenging such a law on Tenth Amendment grounds today would almost certainly be a

---

51. *See, e.g.*, Korematsu v. United States, 323 U.S. 214 (1944) (holding that an order excluding Japanese people from certain military areas during World War II was constitutional because war time constituted a compelling state interest).

52. *See, e.g.*, Armour v. Indianapolis, 132 S. Ct. 2073 (2012) (holding that saving administrative costs was a rational basis for the city of Indianapolis when it forgave unpaid assessments for sewer construction for those who paid in installments but refused to refund the money for those who paid for the sewer construction in a lump sum).

53. *See* United States v. Carolene Prod. Co., 304 U.S. 144, 152 n.4 (1938) ("There may be narrower scope for operation of the presumption of constitutionality when legislation appears on its face to be within a specific prohibition of the Constitution, such as those of the first ten amendments."); Colo. River Water Conservation Dist. v. United States, 424 U.S. 800, 814 (1976) ("Abstention is ... appropriate where there have been presented difficult questions of state law bearing on policy problems of substantial public import whose importance transcends the result in the case then at bar.").

54. U.S. Const. amend. X.

55. *See, e.g.*, Gregory Gelfand & Howard B. Abrams, *Putting Erie on the Right Track*, 49 U. Pitt. L. Rev. 937, 949 (1988) (noting that Justice Brandeis' constitutional reference in *Erie* was an "almost literal echo of the Tenth Amendment"); Alfred Hill, *The Erie Doctrine and the Constitution* (pt. 1), 53 Nw. U. L. Rev. 427, 427–28 (1958) (suggesting that a federal court's disregard for appropriate vertical choice of law, as implicated in *Erie*, disrupts constitutionally-based notions of federalism).

losing battle. Even in 1938, that argument was beginning to lose its force.[56]

For most of the twentieth century prior to *Erie*, the Court's right-wing majority struck down a variety of progressive state laws. Those laws included regulations of working conditions. Similarly, the Court struck down a number of important pieces of New Deal legislation early in Franklin D. Roosevelt's first term. While Justice Brandeis did join some of those holdings, most of the decisions striking down state and New Deal legislation divided along political lines, with the Court's right wing routinely winning the battle. President Roosevelt proposed legislation that would have allowed the President to appoint a new justice (up to a total of six new justices) for each justice over 70 years of age.[57] Not coincidentally, the Justices on the right were over 70.[58]

Even though Roosevelt's "court-packing" scheme backfired, causing him the loss of support of many members of his own party (and Brandeis was particularly offended by the scheme), Roosevelt was about to win the larger battle. In 1937, Justice Owen Roberts, often a swing vote in battles between the right and left wings of the Court, joined the liberal wing of the Court to uphold progressive legislation. In *West Coast Hotel Co. v. Parrish*,[59] the Court upheld a Washington state law establishing a minimum wage. Some modern scholars have raised questions about the extent to which Roberts' shift really reflected a reaction to the President's court-packing scheme. But it reflected an important trend that was afoot.[60]

---

56. *E.g.*, Hon. Joseph C. Hutcheson, Jr., *The Erie-Tompkins Case and the Doctrine of Precedent, Advance or Retreat? Address at the University of Cincinnati Law Review Conference: Status of the Rule of Judicial Precedent* (Feb. 17, 1940), *in* 14 U. Cin. L. Rev. 243, 271 (1940) (describing Justice Brandeis' constitutional argument in *Erie* as both "wholly unnecessary" and "wholly untenable"); *see* Craig Green, *Turning the Kaleidoscope: Toward a Theory of Interpreting Precedents*, 94 N. C. L. Rev. 379, 436–37 (2016) (quoting a 1938 letter by then-Professor Frankfurter, expressing his view that *Erie* was incorrectly based on the Tenth Amendment).

57. *See* Arthur Krock, *Roosevelt Asks Power to Reform Courts, Increasing the Supreme Bench to 15 Judges; Congress Startled, But Expected to Approve*, New York Times (Feb. 5, 1937), http://www.nytimes.com/learning/general/onthisday/big/0205.html#article.

58. Purcell, *supra* note 2, at 34–35.

59. West Coast Hotel Co. v. Parrish, 300 U.S. 379 (1937).

60. Purcell, *supra* note 2, at 35–36.

Over the next several years, the Court began upholding legislation aimed at ending the Depression, legislation that the right-wing Justices would have struck down prior to 1937. In a number of important decisions, Justice Roberts joined the increasingly progressive majority in reliance on the Commerce Clause.[61]

In addition to Roberts' switch, President Roosevelt was able to make five appointments to the Court between 1937 and 1939. *Wickard v. Filburn*[62] may represent the furthest extent of the Court's use of the Commerce Clause. There, a unanimous Court, including Justice Roberts, upheld federal farm legislation aimed at stabilizing wheat prices. After accepting a farm subsidy to reduce his wheat crop, Filburn, an Ohio farmer, harvested acreage in excess of his allotment and used it to feed his livestock. The Court upheld the federal law. The Court's theory, in effect, was that the farmer's use of grain on his farm would have an effect on interstate commerce even if his crop was consumed entirely on his own farm.[63]

During the Rehnquist Court years, the Court signaled that it might cut back on such a liberal reading of the Commerce Clause. But by 2005, it seemed to re-endorse a broad reading of the Commerce Clause in *Gonzales v. Raich*,[64] a case in which the Court rejected Ms. Raich's claim that the federal government could not criminalize her use of marijuana for medical purposes (lawful under California law) because the production was entirely local.[65]

In *Erie*, had Congress enacted a statute regulating activity along an interstate railway, certainly by the time of *Filburn*, the Court would have upheld the law as a proper exercise of Congress's power under the Commerce Clause. While *Filburn* was still four years in the future when *Erie* was decided, the Court, especially its progressive wing, had already begun the expansion of Congressional power and implicitly narrowed the Tenth Amendment.[66]

---

61. U.S. Const. art. I, § 8, cl. 3.
62. Wickard v. Filburn, 317 U.S. 111 (1942).
63. *Id.* at 118–19.
64. Gonzalez v. Raich, 545 U.S. 1 (2005).
65. *Id.* at 17–18, 32–33.
66. *See, e.g.*, Adam N. Steinman, *What Is the* Erie *Doctrine? (And What Does It Mean For the Contemporary Politics of Judicial Federalism?)*, 84 Notre Dame L. Rev. 245, 313 (explaining that, since the *Erie* doctrine generally applies to cases in federal court based

A third constitutional right could have been at play in *Erie*: separation of powers. Many students and certainly many listeners of radio talk shows believe that the idea that legislatures make laws and courts interpret laws is a principle ingrained in our Constitution. It is not. As was obvious for many years, consistent with *Swift*, federal courts had the power to create common law. That almost certainly would not have surprised the Constitution's framers, who included a number of common law lawyers.[67]

Some of Justice Brandeis' discussion suggests that the constitutional problem with *Swift*'s reading of the Rules of Decision Act was that the courts, not Congress, created the governing substantive law. But in *Hinderlider v. La Plata River and Cherry Creek River Co.*,[68] a second Brandeis opinion announced the same day as *Erie*, he made clear that federal courts, at least under certain circumstances, have constitutional power to create common law. No doubt, one can distinguish the cases. *La Plata* involved an interstate water dispute where reliance on state law would be singularly inappropriate. But apart from distinct policies that may justify a different result, even under Brandeis' view, the Constitution does not contain a bright line rule against judicial law-making.[69]

Whether a majority of the Court still believes that *Erie* is grounded in the Constitution is open to debate. As a law professor, Felix Frankfurter expressed doubts about its constitutional moorings. As a Justice, he suggested as much in *Guaranty Trust Co. v. York*.[70] So, too, did Chief Justice Earl Warren in *Hanna v. Plumer*.[71] Some scholars have argued that we should consider *Erie* as constitutionally based because the Court said as much. An occasional scholar offers a plausible explanation for what one might call a "soft" constitutional theory. As one scholar explained, one can read *Erie* to mean that, if the federal government enters

---

on diversity jurisdiction, Congress can avoid the potential application of state law by "enacting statutes sufficient to create federal question jurisdiction," where federal common law applies and choice of law is not an issue).

67. *E.g.*, Irah Donner, *The Copyright Clause of the U.S. Constitution: Why Did the Framers Include It with Unanimous Approval?*, 36 AM. J. LEGAL HIST. 361, 374 (1992) ("[T]hirty-one of the fifty-five framers were lawyers.").

68. Hinderlider v. La Plata River and Cherry Creek River Co., 304 U.S. 92 (1938).

69. *See* PURCELL, *supra* note 2, at 182–83.

70. Guaranty Trust Co. v. York, 326 U.S. 99 (1945).

71. Hanna v. Plumer, 380 U.S. 460 (1965).

a field traditionally within the province of state regulation, Congress, not the courts, should lead the way. In the *Erie* context, tort law was historically state law. And while the federal government would have the authority to regulate activity along an interstate railway under an expanded interpretation of the Commerce Clause, Congress should legislate, not the courts.[72]

Surely, this is technical stuff that would not interest members of the public. Not surprisingly, no newspaper found it fit to print the news of *Swift*'s demise. A week after the Court announced its decision, according to Justice Stone's biographer, Stone wrote to Arthur Krock at the *New York Times*. He explained that *Erie* was "the most important opinion since I have been on the court."[73] That is saying something. Justice Stone, later Chief Justice Stone, served on the Court for over 20 years and did so during the period of time when the Court waged major battles over important social policies.[74]

So why were news reporters and members of the public not attuned to *Erie*'s importance? It seems like the driest of procedural decisions. As you read my discussion above, even including the discussion of the uncertainty about the constitutional basis of the decision, were you stirred to action? Did you find anything inherently exciting about the discussion? (If so, you should consider a career in the legal academy!) And yet, a great deal was at stake in *Erie*, reflective of one of the great battles between the left wing and right wing of the Court.

Whether empowering judges to make law is a good thing is debatable. Federal judges have lifetime tenure; in theory, that makes them less easily influenced by the politics of the day than judges who may face election or reelection. As a result, they may be more able to protect rights of unpopular litigants. At the same time, granting too much power to unelected officials can erode democracy, a criticism increasingly leveled against the current Supreme Court. Many lawyers of my generation who came of age during the heyday of the Warren Court saw federal judges

---

72. *See* Thomas W. Merrill, *Common Law Powers of Federal Courts*, 52 U. Chi. L. Rev. 1, 15 (1985) ("The issue [in *Erie*] is one that Congress today could clearly resolve by legislation enacted pursuant to its power to regulate interstate commerce.").

73. Ginsburg, *supra* note 3, at 278.

74. *See generally* John Fox, *The Supreme Court Biographies of the Robes: Harlan Fiske Stone*, PBS (Dec. 2006), http://www.pbs.org/wnet/supremecourt/capitalism/robes_stone.html.

as protectors of liberty and the rights of minorities. Indeed, most listeners of radio talk shows associate activism with liberal judges. But that was certainly not the case beginning in the late nineteenth and early twentieth centuries.[75]

For much of the period between the late nineteenth and early twentieth centuries, the Court used various provisions of the Constitution, including the Due Process Clause,[76] to protect business interests and limit socially progressive legislation.[77] In effect, the right wing of the Court believed that the Constitution included a particular laissez-faire economic structure, quite in tune with Social Darwinism. The Court's substantive due process case law allowed the right wing of the Court to strike down legislative efforts to regulate business if the Court found the regulations unreasonable. As stated by the Court in one such case, the question of reasonableness "is eminently a question for judicial investigation."[78]

The Court did not only use substantive due process to expand its power. As summarized by Professor Purcell,

> The Court also employed the long-used Contract Clause to check governmental actions and in 1905 enlarged the range of rights that the clause protected. It incorporated the Fifth Amendment Takings Clause into the Fourteenth Amendment, thereby making the clause applicable to the states, and extended corporations Fourth Amendment protections against unlawful searches and seizures. Throughout the period, too, the Court applied the Commerce Clause to police both state and federal governments.[79]

Similarly, the Court used substantive due process to prevent Congress or state legislatures from outlawing "yellow dog" contracts (contracts allowing an employer to make an employee agree not to become a member of a union as a condition of employment). But for purposes of this

---

75. *See* Purcell, *supra* note 2, at 39–40.

76. U.S. Const. amend. V; *id.* amend. XIV § 2.

77. Purcell, *supra* note 2, at 41.

78. Chicago, Milwaukee and St. Paul Railway Co. v. Minnesota (Minnesota Rate Case), 134 U.S. 418, 458 (1890), *quoted in* Purcell, *supra* note 2, at 41.

79. Purcell, *supra* note 2, at 41.

discussion, the Court also used federal common law to do so in a parallel fashion.[80]

When written, *Swift* may have been defensible. Its interpretation of the Rules of Decision Act is more than plausible. Its author, Justice Story, was a highly regarded member of the Court. *Swift* aimed to produce national uniformity in business matters that would encourage interstate commerce. Thus, under *Swift*, a federal court sitting in diversity could follow federal common law if the matter was not local in nature. But, by the end of the nineteenth century, federal courts ignored local law with increasing frequency.[81]

Even in tort cases, the Court rejected state law favorable to plaintiffs. In *Baltimore v. Baugh*,[82] for example, the Court applied the federal common law rule that denied an injured plaintiff a tort recovery against the employer if a fellow employee caused the plaintiff's injury. *Baugh* was hardly unique.[83]

Prior to *Erie*, corporate defendants began to seek removal from state to federal courts in a wide variety of cases. In theory, they did so out of fear of local prejudice, which was a justification for the framers' inclusion of diversity jurisdiction in Article III. In addition, *Swift* promised greater uniformity of applicable law in diversity actions when the Court applied federal common law. As legitimate as those explanations are, corporations had other reasons to seek access to federal court.[84]

Litigation in federal as opposed to state court often added expense for plaintiffs who frequently had to travel from their home venues to cities where federal district courts are typically located. More importantly, federal courts were pro-corporate. As a result, not surprisingly, "[T]he substantive rules of the federal common law tended to favor national corporations."[85]

Although in the short term, Justice Brandeis' decision in *Erie* denied an injured plaintiff a substantial recovery, in the long term, the decision was consistent with progressive and populist positions of the era. Ironi-

80. *Id.* at 74, 76–77.

81. Friedenthal, Kane & Miller, *supra* note 48, at 197–200; Purcell, *supra* note 2, at 66.

82. Baltimore & Ohio Railroad Co. v. Baugh, 149 U.S. 368 (1893).

83. Purcell, *supra* note 2, at 66.

84. *Id.*

85. *Id.*

cally, in light of the association of "states' rights" with segregationist efforts in the late twentieth century, at the time, conservatives feared radical state legislatures. Populists and progressives supported states' rights where they had greater success in advancing their agendas than they did in federal courts.[86]

In context, one can see what was at stake in *Erie* and, nonetheless, understand why the news media and general public would not have an intuitive feel for its importance. But *Erie*'s procedural importance far exceeded the substantive law involved in the case. Members of the public, like students in Torts classes, may have an intuitive feel for which rules should apply in torts cases, but they are not likely to have an intuitive feel for *Erie*'s importance. And yet, it established a new rule governing the relationship between state and federal law; it limited judicial power and expanded legislative power. It advanced progressive political goals at the expense of corporate interests. It eliminated a pro-defendant forum shopping device whereby a defendant could dictate governing substantive law by deciding whether to remove an action to federal court.[87]

D. Concluding Thoughts

As developed in Section B, the public responds passionately to cases involving substantive rights. Thus, when right-wing commentator Peggy Noonan wrote disparagingly about *Obergefell* in the *Wall Street Journal*, almost 1100 readers commented. Those comments are indicative of strongly felt sentiments generated when the Court decides cases on substantive grounds. Readers accuse one another and the members of the Court of a variety of sins. For example, one commentator accuses the Chief Justice of being a "bozo," while another accuses the five justices in the *Obergefell* majority of being "Socialists."[88] Follow a Google trail for

86. *See id.* at 160, 295.

87. PURCELL, *supra* note 2, at 160; *cf.* FRIEDENTHAL, KANE & MILLER, *supra* note 48, at 201–22 (noting that *Swift* created an incentive for a plaintiff to engage in forum-shopping; the same motivation applied to a defendant's decision to remove to federal court prior to *Erie*).

88. Peggy Noonan, *The High Court's Disunited State*, WALL STREET JOURNAL (Jul. 2, 2015, 7:12 PM), http://www.wsj.com/articles/the-high-courts-disunited-state-143587401 2#livefyre-comment.

Citizens United and you learn that many political candidates made it a campaign issue, with some calling for its reversal.

A *Washington Post* editorial on *Citizens United* generated sixty-seven comments. Many of them were barbed, including a comment stating that being a lawyer today is an embarrassment;[89] another stating that the justices in the majority were either naïve or malicious;[90] still another suggesting that the Congress should impeach the justices in the majority.[91]

At the same time, one can find editorials and comments about procedural matters. Notably, for example, the *Wall Street Journal* published an article focusing on the changes to the Federal Rules of Civil Procedure with a headline to the effect that the changes are a big win for big business. Unlike Noonan's article in the same publication, Joe Palazzolo and Jess Bravin's article entitled *Businesses Win Lawsuit Curbs With New Rules* generated eight comments (and from only four readers). Some of the language is vituperative, but the theme generated little public interest.[92]

Media coverage of the Court's personal jurisdiction case law is thin at best. And few readers bother to comment on the topic even if they have read the submissions.[93] That is not surprising. As developed above, procedural decisions do not resonate with most readers. Even many law students and lawyers may not grasp the power of a procedural ruling. Often readers may believe procedural rulings are neutral and fail to see the ways in which such rulings favor one class of litigants over another.

---

89. Ferobson, Comment to *The Selective Reading of the Supreme Court's Decision in 'Citizens United,'* The Washington Post (Oct. 12, 2014, 8:42 PM), https://www.washingtonpost.com/opinions/the-selective-reading-of-the-supreme-courts-decision-in-citizens-united/2014/10/12/4b0f39a4-50b4-11e4-babe-e91da079cb8a_story.html.

90. Kirtbhatt, Comment to The Washington Post (Oct. 13, 2014, 5:56 PM), *supra* note 89.

91. TedZeeMan, Comment to The Washington Post (Oct. 13, 2014, 6:02 PM), *supra* note 89.

92. Joe Palazzolo & Jess Bravin, *Businesses Win Lawsuit Curbs with New Rules*, The Wall Street Journal (Mar. 22, 2016, 7:26 PM), http://www.wsj.com/articles/businesses-win-lawsuit-curbs-with-new-rules-1458689192.

93. *E.g.*, Rich Samp, *With* Bauman v. DaimlerChrysler, *High Court May Have Put Brakes on Forum Shopping*, Forbes (Feb. 4, 2014, 9:00 AM), http://www.forbes.com/sites/wlf/2014/02/04/with-bauman-v-daimlerchrysler-high-court-may-have-put-brakes-on-forum-shopping/#58670d0e7aad (the article page shows 5,036 views as of May 19, 2016, with no comments).

To understand that point, consider the *Erie* decision. Typical lawyers and law students view *Erie* as a topic to be avoided.[94] As developed above, *Erie* may seem arcane, but it was hardly a neutral decision. Brandeis' effort to advance progressive policies drove the decision. At stake was a choice between upholding a powerful forum-shopping device that gave an advantage to corporations and eroding that power.

Understanding cases like *Erie* enlivens procedure. But it does more. As developed throughout this book, more is at stake than overcoming one's fear of procedure. The subject of procedure comes alive once one understands the kinds of policies that drive procedural choices. And then beyond that, as I argue in much of the rest of this book, the right wing of the Court has used procedural decisions to limit access to our courts in ways that favor defendants, especially corporate defendants. The right wing of the Court can alter substantive law; doing so often produces strong pushback from the public. By comparison, consciously or unconsciously, members of the Court have been able to achieve major victories for the powerful, including powerful corporations, through a much lower-visibility procedural revolution.

94. *E.g.*, Grad Student, *Erie Doctrine . . .*, Top-Law-Schools.com (Sep. 12, 2009, 2:31 PM), http://www.top-law-schools.com/forums/viewtopic.php?t=85415 (asking "wtf is Erie lol"); AssaultandBattery, *Erie Doctrine, Help Me Master This Sucker Before My Final*, Law School Discussion (Dec. 5, 2007, 11:27 PM), http://www.lawschooldiscussion.org/index.php?topic=3008555.0 (referring to the topic as "that god forsaken Erie doctrine").

TWO

The Shadow Docket

A. Introduction

This chapter focuses on a topic not covered in a basic Civil Procedure course. In fact, as a separate concept, the shadow docket was not the subject of much discussion until the recent use, or more appropriately, misuse of the shadow docket to advance right-wing policies while those decisions stay under the radar. This chapter develops the traditional notion of the appellate process and then compares how emergency orders and other similar procedural steps work. The use of those procedures has come to be known as the shadow docket.

Our system of justice relies on several procedural steps as part of appellate procedure. If a losing party wants to challenge a lower court's ruling, the prevailing party is entitled to fair notice of the appeal. Further, before an appellate court can overrule the lower court's judgment, the litigants have an opportunity to brief the relevant issues. Courts are not required to issue written opinions in all cases.[1] But, especially in cases where an appellate court enjoins a lower court's judgment or reverses the lower court judgment, appellate courts should explain their reasoning. Judicial opinions serve multiple purposes. Litigants deserve an explanation for why the court has ruled as it has. The bar needs written opinions

1. Stephen Vladeck, The Shadow Docket: How the Supreme Court Uses Stealth Rulings to Amass Power and Undermine the Republic 17–18 (Basic Books 2023).

to understand what the law is. Written opinions serve to help the public understand the law, even if they disagree with an appellate court's ruling. Well-reasoned judicial opinions serve an important public educational function.[2] Readers can determine whether the appellate judges are merely substituting their personal policy preferences or, instead, whether they have well-grounded legal justifications for their holdings.

The need for written opinions is especially important when the appellate court is the Supreme Court. That is because it is the most important court in the United States and, if not the most important, one of the most important courts in the world. As the lead opinion in *Planned Parenthood v. Casey* stated, "the Court's legitimacy depends on making legally principled decisions under circumstances in which their principled character is sufficiently plausible to be accepted by the Nation."[3]

At various times in the Court's history, observers have believed that the justices were not following the law, but instead deciding cases based on their personal policy preferences.[4] That has often been the case when the Court experiences turnover on the Court, and the newly constituted Court overturns recent precedent.[5] Members of the public can rightly ask whether justices are following the law or making it up.[6]

The Supreme Court has limited capacity to address every case that litigants present to the Court. Article III of the Constitution gives Con-

---

2. Professor Stephen Vladeck's book *The Shadow Docket* extensively develops the theme developed in this paragraph. *See, e.g.*, *id.*, Chapter 7.

3. 505 U.S. 833, 866 (1992).

4. *See* Barry Friedman, *The History of the Countermajoritarian Difficulty, Part Three: The Lesson of Lochner*, 76 N.Y.U. L. Rev. 1383 (2001) (investigating the "conventional wisdom" that "during the *Lochner* era, Supreme Court Justices failed to adhere to constitutional norms requiring deference to majoritarian decisions and inappropriately struck down laws by substituting their own views for those of legislative bodies").

5. Dobbs v. Jackson Women's Health Org., 597 U.S. 215, 364 (2022) (Breyer, Sotomayor, and Kagan, JJJ., dissenting) ("The Court reverses course today for one reason and one reason only: because the composition of this Court has changed.").

6. Cases like *Dobbs* may explain why a majority of Americans believe that justices put ideology over impartiality. Thomas Beaumont & Linley Sanders, *New poll shows majority of Americans believe Supreme Court justices put ideology over impartiality*, PBS (Jun. 27, 2024), https://www.pbs.org/newshour/nation/new-poll-shows-majority-of-americans-believe-supreme-court-justices-put-ideology-over-impartiality. *See also Do Americans approve or disapprove of the Supreme Court? Supreme Court: Approval Polls*, FiveThirtyEight, https://projects.fivethirtyeight.com/polls/approval/supreme-court/ (last visited Jan. 10, 2025) (showing the historically low rating that Americans give the Supreme Court).

gress the power to shape the Court's jurisdiction. In the Judiciary Act of 1789, Congress created mandatory jurisdiction over cases that came before the Court.[7] As developed in Section B, for various reasons, that changed during the early part of the Twentieth Century. Today, the Court has almost unreviewable discretion to decide which cases it will hear. No one seriously contends that the Court must issue opinions in all cases, for example, denying the writ of certiorari. Instead, the Court has largely limited cases in which it issues full opinions to cases that raise sufficiently important issues to justify the granting of the writ. That set of cases represents a small percentage of the cases that come before the Court.[8]

In 2015, Chicago Law School Professor William Baude coined the phrase "shadow docket" to describe the difference between the "merits docket," those cases where the Court granted review and accompanied its holding with a written opinion, and the less public decisions by the Court. At the time, Professor Baude did not suggest that the "shadow docket" was illegitimate. That has changed.[9]

Today, the term suggests something sinister. That led Justice Alito to object to the use of the term. Subsequently, Justice Amy Coney Barrett has also bristled at the suggestion that Justices are misusing their power.[10] As explored below, serious scholars have argued that the current extreme right-wing Court is misusing the shadow docket. Not only does this chapter explore that question, but it also suggests the Court has misused the shadow docket in ways that have favored the Trump Administration and disadvantaged the Biden Administration. Consistent with the overall theme of this book, the use of the shadow docket is a procedural mechanism not easily understood by members of the public. Like other areas of the law discussed in this book, the right wing of the Court's

---

7. THE JUDICIARY ACT OF 1789, ch. 20, 1 Stat. 73 (1789).

8. VLADECK, *supra* note 1, at *Introduction*, 11–12 (comparing the "small sliver" of the Supreme Court's merits docket to the larger shadow docket, which makes up "almost 99 percent of the Court's actual decisions").

9. Tobias T. Gibson, *The Shadow Docket: How the Supreme Court Uses Stealth Rulings to Amass Power and Undermine the Republic*, LAW AND POLITICS BOOK REVIEW (Nov. 2023) (book review), http://www.lpbr.net/2023/12/the-shadow-docket-how-supreme-court.html.

10. VLADECK, *supra* note 1, at 245 (discussing Justice Barrett's April 2022 speech urging Americans, "before making judgments about whether the Court was acting politically," to first "read the opinion").

use of procedure allows it to achieve policy goals without the same degree of backlash experienced when it makes substantive decisions.

Section B discusses the history of the Court's appellate jurisdiction. It explains how Congress altered the Judiciary Act of 1789 to give the Court discretion over its docket. It then discusses other developments in the Court's handling of appeals. At times, the Court has had to rule on cases on an emergency basis. For example, a lower court's ruling may create the risk of serious harm to one of the parties. In such cases, under certain circumstances, the Court has either stayed the lower court order or lifted a lower court injunction to avoid perceived harm. But until recent changes in the Court personnel, the Court has done so under limited circumstances.

Thereafter, Section C turns to the current use of the shadow docket. Since 2021, not only has the term worked its way into public discourse, but legal scholars have begun publicizing the way in which the Court is using the shadow docket. Most notably, Georgetown University Law Professor Stephen Vladeck has published a widely reviewed book on the shadow docket. Other scholars have weighed in as well. Section C explores important areas where the Court has abandoned previous restraints on the use of the shadow docket to advance right-wing policy preferences.

Section D provides some conclusions about the shadow docket. It also explores how this theme fits into the larger concerns raised by this book.

B. A Historical Perspective

Article III sets out the outer limits of the Court's judicial power. Article III also gives Congress broad power in determining the Court's jurisdiction. But for a few instances in which the Court might have original jurisdiction, Article III largely gives Congress the power to determine the Court's appellate jurisdiction.[11]

11. Article III, section II, provides that, other than in the few cases where the Court has original jurisdiction, "the Supreme Court shall have appellate jurisdiction, both as to law and fact, with such exceptions, and under such regulations as the Congress shall make." U.S. Const. art. 3, § 2.

That Congress has authority to determine the Court's jurisdiction was part of the original argument for creating a Supreme Court. As Alexander Hamilton suggested, given Congress's power over the purse and the Court's ability only to enforce judgments, the Court is the "least dangerous branch."[12] Or so the argument went.

In the Judiciary Act of 1789,[13] Congress did two things that are important for understanding the shadow docket. The first was that Congress mandated that the Court hear various types of appeals from lower federal and state courts. It also included the All Writs Act, which gave the Court the power to enjoin lower court proceedings.[14]

For many years, mandatory jurisdiction did not unduly burden the Court. For example, during the 1840s, the Court had to decide only thirty-five to fifty cases a year.[15] That would change after the Civil War. Congress expanded federal power in several ways, including the passage of laws to enforce the Civil War Amendments. It also increased the reach of federal authority as the United States expanded. For example, Congress authorized the Pacific Railroad and created incentives for states to create public universities. It also allowed the Court for the first time to review state criminal convictions through the writ of habeas corpus. Of course, the Industrial Revolution would also increase federal regulations.[16]

Mandatory jurisdiction became unsustainable. By 1890, the Court had a three-year backlog on its caseload. The Judiciary Act of 1891 was one response to the problem. It created discretionary review. The Act also created stand-alone federal circuits, which would hear most appeals. The creation of the writ of certiorari over a significant number of cases, along with the expansion of the courts of appeals, lessened the Court's docket crisis.[17]

Continued expansion of federal legislation and other aspects of the original grant of mandatory jurisdiction caused the Court's workload to climb back up to unmanageable levels when Robert Taft took over as

12. Vladeck, *supra* note 1, at 32–33.

13. The Judiciary Act of 1789, ch. 20, 1 Stat. 73 (1789).

14. *Id.* at § 14.

15. Vladeck, *supra* note 1, at 36.

16. *Id.* at 38 (discussing the myriad ways Congress regulated "new domains of American life").

17. *Id.* at 39–40 (discussing the impact of the Judiciary Act of 1891).

Chief Justice in 1921. Taft worked behind the scenes to persuade Congress to make the Court's appellate jurisdiction entirely discretionary. During his tenure as Chief Justice, Congress limited the Court's mandatory jurisdiction. But it was not until 1988 when Taft's vision became reality. Thus today, the Court determines which cases it will review via the writ of certiorari.[18]

Many factors contribute to the increased number of cases in which petitioners ask the Court to grant the writ of certiorari. The number of cases is far too great for the Court to provide written explanations for the decision to deny the writ.[19] The Court's failure to explain its reasons for denying review does not suggest agreement with the decision below. Or at least, that is the fair inference from the Court's rules. The Court requires the petitioner to demonstrate that there is, for example, a split between federal circuits or between federal and state courts on the issue presented in the petition for the writ. A dismissal of a petition may be read to mean that the Court does not believe that there is a sufficient split to justify the Court's limited docket.[20]

When Chicago Law Professor Baude used the term "shadow docket" in 2015, he was describing, in part, cases like those described above. He also used that term to describe an additional part of the Court's caseload.[21]

Along with mandatory jurisdiction, the Judiciary Act of 1791 included the All Writs Act, which gave the Court authority to enjoin the enforcement of lower court judgments. The Court retains the power to stay or enjoin lower court proceedings to this day. As with temporary restraining orders and with preliminary injunctions, courts must act

18. *Id.* at 42–54 (discussing Taft's successful efforts to expand the Court's discretion such that "[b]y 1971, the idea that the Supreme Court should have the power to pick and choose which cases it heard... had become an article of faith").

19. *Id.* at 57 ("In its October 2019 Term, for example, the Supreme Court handed down signed rulings in merits cases in only 53 cases (the fewest since the Civil War), representing fewer than 1 percent of the total appeals that it received."). Still, justices may write dissents from denials of cert. For instance, Justice Sotomayor authored ten dissents from denials of certiorari in her first four terms on the Court. Robert M. Yablon, *Justice Sotomayor and the Supreme Court's Certiorari Process*, 123 Yale L.J. F. 551 (2014), https://www.yalelawjournal.org/forum/justice-sotomayor-and-the-supreme-courts-certiorari-process#_ftnref8.

20. Vladeck, *supra* note 1, at 46.

21. *Id.*, *Preface*, at xi.

with caution in granting such relief. Such power should be available to prevent harm from occurring. But in many cases, a court must act before the parties have had a chance to fully brief the merits of the case and to develop a full factual record in the court below.[22] The Court's order typically is issued without explanation as well. Given that reality, until recently, the Court has exercised caution in granting stays or injunctions to prevent action consistent with the lower court's order.[23]

Historically, the Court has cautioned against using its emergency power. As Professor Andrew Koppelman stated in his review of *The Shadow Docket,*

> Cognizant of the danger of uninformed meddling, Justice Potter Stewart declared in 1968 that this power should be utilized "sparingly and only in the most critical and exigent circumstances." Justice William Rehnquist observed in 1972 that the right to emergency relief has to be "indisputably clear." In 1986, Justice Antonin Scalia cited both of these passages with approval. Likewise, in 2001, the full court held that such an order "is appropriate only if the legal rights at issue are indisputably clear."[24]

Of course, at times, legal commentators have criticized the Court's use of its extraordinary power in cases that did not fit the description provided by Professor Koppelman. Think back to *Bush v. Gore,*[25] when then-candidate Bush asked the Court to stay the Florida Supreme Court's order to allow a statewide recount of ballots that voting machines had not tallied. The Court stayed the state court's order. Later, in a 5–4 per curiam decision, the slim majority argued, in part, that the lack of time available for a recount before the need to certify the election

---

22. *Id., Introduction,* at 10.

23. *Id.* at 14–16 (discussing the Court's increasing tendency to grant emergency relief).

24. Andrew Koppelman, *The Law-Breaking Supreme Court: On Stephen Vladeck's "The Shadow Docket"*, Los Angeles Review of Books (Sept. 27, 2023), https://lareviewofbooks.org/article/the-law-breaking-supreme-court-on-stephen-vladecks-the-shadow-docket/.

25. 531 U.S. 98 (2000).

justified its decision in favor of Bush, assuring him the presidency.[26] One would have been hard-pressed to argue at the time of the stay that candidate-Bush's rights were "indisputably clear." Many Election and Constitutional Law scholars question whether the candidate or voters had the novel right that the majority relied on.[27]

Exceptions will always exist. But apart from cases like *Bush v. Gore,* the Court typically limited its use of its extraordinary power. The Court made clear that litigants, including the Solicitor General, had a high bar to clear before the Court would act. Further, most administrations have taken their responsibility seriously and seldom applied for extraordinary relief.[28]

When Professor Baude coined the phrase "shadow docket," these were the kinds of cases that he had in mind as well as the large number of cases denying the writ of certiorari. In that sense, he meant nothing sinister.[29] But as developed in the next section, the term has taken on a darker meaning.

---

26. *Id.* at 110 ("Upon due consideration of the difficulties identified at this point, it is obvious that the recount cannot be conducted in compliance with the requirements of equal protection and due process without substantial additional work.").

27. Mark S. Brodin, Bush v. Gore: *The Worst (or at least second-to-the-worst) Supreme Court Decision Ever*, 12 NEV. L.J. 563 (2012); Erwin Chemerinsky, Bush v. Gore *Was Not Justiciable*, 76 NOTRE DAME L. REV. 1093 (2001); Richard L. Hasen, Bush v. Gore *and the Future of Equal Protection Law in Elections*, 29 FLA. ST. U. L. REV. 377 (2001) (arguing that the Court's decision in *Bush v. Gore* cannot be taken seriously because, in part, the Court's analysis was insufficient).

28. VLADECK, *supra* note 1, at 134–61 (contrasting the historical limits on the presumption of constitutionality with the unprecedented number of applications for emergency relief from the Trump Administration).

29. *Id.*, *Preface*, at xi.

C. The Shadow Docket, the Trump Administration, and the Current Court

Administrations prior to and subsequent to the first Trump Administration have asked the Court to invoke its emergency power infrequently. For example, between 2001 and 2017, the Solicitor General asked the Court for emergency relief only eight times.[30] By comparison, during President Trump's first term, his Solicitor General sought emergency relief forty-one times.[31] Of course, that was the executive asking the Court to depart from settled practice, as was so often the case during the Trump Administration.[32] The Court's response is the subject of Vladeck's book and of this chapter.

Let me put the previous point in context. In the past, in cases involving lower court injunctions that prevented the government from implementing its policies, the Solicitor General argued that the United States was harmed by not being able to implement its policy, and the Court largely agreed.[33] The Trump Administration often put in place highly questionable policies that would likely not survive on the merits. The Administration would then ask for emergency relief so that the policy could survive for at least a little while.[34] Trump would then claim victory when the Court stayed the lower court action. As indicated, the use of the request for emergency relief became addictive, with Trump's Solicitor General asking for such relief far more often than any other administration. Consistent with Professor Vladeck's thesis, "after the June 2017 travel ban ruling, twenty-five of the remaining twenty-six grants of emergency relief to the Trump administration would come with no opinion from the court."[35]

Viewed in isolation, the Court's behavior might not raise questions. The Biden Administration also sought emergency relief, of course. But

---

30. *Id.* at 144.

31. *Id.*

32. David Montogomery, *The Definitive List of the 20 Presidential Norms Trump Broke—and How Joe Biden Can Restore Them*, WASH. POST (Nov. 10, 2020), https://www.washingtonpost.com/graphics/2020/lifestyle/magazine/trump-presidential-norm-breaking-list/ (discussing ways the Trump administration changed the presidency).

33. VLADECK, *supra* note 1, at 133.

34. *Id.* at 138.

35. *Id.* at 144.

here, according to Professor Vladeck, one can start to understand how the current Court has used the shadow docket to advance Justices' right-wing policy preferences in ways that are suspect.[36]

The Shadow Docket focuses on important areas of the law that reflect the right wing's policy preferences. Notably, the Court has used the shadow docket to allow states to execute prisoners in ways that the Court has not done in the past.[37] Further, it has used the shadow docket to favor religious organizations in ways that conflict with existing precedent.[38] While those areas of the law should cause us concern, this Chapter focuses on a third area that Professor Vladeck's work has brought to light: election law cases.

Professor Vladeck's chapter on election law cases begins with a discussion of early cases involving the limited role of federal courts in state elections, even for members of Congress. That changed in 1965 when President Johnson was able to get the Voting Rights Act through Congress. Perhaps President Johnson's greatest accomplishment, as described by Professor Vladeck,

> It required jurisdictions with a documented history of discrimination to have any changes to their election rules "precleared" by the federal Justice Department or by the DC federal district court, and abolished literacy tests as a prerequisite for voting. One of the most effective pieces of civil rights legislation in American history, the VRA [Voting Rights Act] also reconceived the role of the judiciary in election-related disputes; the statute's sweeping new protections were meant to be enforced not only by the Justice Department, but also by the federal courts.[39]

---

36. *Id.* at 156.

37. Stephen Vladeck, *The Machinery of Death: How Capital Punishment Gave Rise to the Modern Shadow Docket, in* The Shadow Docket 93, 96–104 (discussing the Court's use of the shadow docket to permit executions without first resolving legal challenges to them); *see also* Jenny-Brooke Condon, *The Capital Shadow Docket and the Death of Judicial Restraint*, 23 Nev. L.J. 809 (2023) (arguing the Court's use of the shadow docket allows the Court to carry out executions with less accountability than before).

38. Stephen Vladeck, *COVID and the Court: How the Court Abused the Shadow Docket to Expand Religious Liberty, in* The Shadow Docket 163, 170–80 (discussing the Court's broadening of First Amendment religious liberty through the shadow docket).

39. Vladeck, *supra* note 1, at 203.

Not surprisingly, the law led to much greater involvement of the federal courts in election disputes, even up to election day.[40]

As the Court began to swing to the right during the Reagan Administration and beyond, justices became skeptical about federal intervention in elections.[41] Although the constitutional question is beyond the scope of this book, students may want to study the Court's eventual rulings that have seriously undercut the Voting Rights Act, rulings that have raised significant questions about the Court's constitutional interpretation of the issue.[42]

Since the 1990s and early 2000s, the Court has continued to intervene in election disputes. According to Professor Vladeck, the problem with the Court's interventions is that it has failed to identify an objective standard. Instead, the justices use "the shadow docket to adopt, and then enforce, a profoundly and underexplained test. Under that approach, politics once again at least appear to have taken precedence over principle."[43]

Election law disputes come in a few varieties. Notably, litigants challenge rules relating to elections and to redistricting before elections. They also may challenge results after the election has taken place. The common denominator is that courts must decide the issues involved under a compressed timetable.[44]

As indicated, the Court hesitated to become involved in such cases over twenty years ago. In *Purcell v. Gonzalez,*[45] a case arising out of Arizona, the Court made a ruling as part of the shadow docket that, in Professor Vladeck's words, "has caused far more mischief than it has prevented."[46]

---

40. *Id.*

41. Stephen Vladeck, *The "Purcell Principle": How the Current Court Uses the Shadow Docket to Help Republicans, in* The Shadow Docket 197.

42. *See, e.g.*, Kristen Clarke, *Reflecting on the 10th Anniversary of* Shelby County v. Holder, U.S. Dep't of Just. (June 23, 2023), https://www.justice.gov/opa/blog/reflecting-10th-anniversary-shelby-county-v-holder.

43. Vladeck, *supra* note 1, at 203.

44. The circumstances leading up to the *Purcell* decision demonstrate the challenge of resolving legal issues timely before elections. There, the Ninth Circuit received an appeal from a district court's denial of a request to enjoin a new voter ID law in September of 2006 and decided to block the law in October. With the November election fast-approaching, the Supreme Court became involved. Vladeck, *supra* note 1, at 204–05.

45. 549 U.S. 1 (2006).

46. Vladeck, *supra* note 1, at 204.

Purcell involved an Arizona ballot initiative imposing a strict voter identification requirement. The George W. Bush Justice Department gave the law "preclearance." But various Arizona voters, including Native Americans, challenged the law in the federal district court. In early September, the federal district court denied the request for an injunction. Now faced with the reality that they lacked time to have the courts make a full determination of the issue before the November election, the litigants asked the Court of Appeals for the Ninth Circuit to prevent the initiative from applying for at least the upcoming election. The Ninth Circuit agreed.[47]

The state asked the Court to stay the Ninth Circuit's injunction to allow the state law to take effect for that election. Instead, the Court treated the request for the stay as a request for the writ of certiorari. It then issued an unsigned opinion that has garnered criticism from liberal and conservative legal scholars. Dubbed the "*Purcell* principle" by UCLA election law scholar Rick Hasen, the Court's holding amounted to the following rule: "to avoid confusion among voters and election administrators, courts should generally not change the rules governing elections as Election Day approaches, meaning that injunctions against even unlawful election rules are increasingly disfavored as Election Day draws near."[48]

Despite some justifications for such a rule, the Court's application of the rule has created serious doubts about the Court's neutrality. *Purcell's* "too close" to the election seems to be applied entirely subjectively. Officials had thirty-three days to address any confusion before the election in that case. How close, then, is too close?[49]

A second problem with *Purcell* is that it replaced traditional equitable principles that, among other things, balance competing harms (e.g., the harm of imposing the injunction vs. the harm caused by allowing the election to proceed with the questionable election procedures in place). Instead, the Court's new rule means that all late changes to the law are presumed to outweigh other considerations. So, what if the injunction might prevent clearly unlawful conduct by election officials? *Purcell* dictates that the lower courts stay out of the fray until after the election. In

47. *Id.* at 204–05.

48. *Id.* at 205.

49. *Id.* at 206.

effect, the illegal suppression, let's say, of voter participation stays in place for at least one voting cycle.[50]

The reality of the risk was evident in the 2022 midterm election and may have cost the Democrats a real chance to retake control of the House of Representatives. Vladeck describes Georgia governor Brian Kemp's delay in signing the legislature's redistricting map, almost certainly with an eye toward running out the *Purcell* clock. It worked. A federal district court refused to enjoin the use of the election redistricting map because the lawsuit came too close to the election. But the court concluded that the map violated the VRA.[51]

Although the *Purcell* Court wrote a short opinion, the case was a shadow docket case. That is, the Court decided the case without meaningful briefing and argument. Scholars are unkind in their descriptions of the opinion, as reflected by one scholar who described the reasoning as "vacuous, self-contradictory, [and] amorphous...."[52]

The use of the shadow docket might be less controversial than critics suggest if the Court applied its *procedural* rules consistently. Yes, the Court does not have to explain its reasoning for decisions like those denying the writ of certiorari. To require that the Court do so would be extremely time-consuming. Often, one can infer that the writ application did not present a sufficient conflict between lower court decisions.[53] But critics of the shadow docket like Professor Vladeck argue forcefully that the current Court has used the shadow docket in ways that have favored President Trump and, later, disfavored former President Biden.[54]

Here are a few examples. Keep in mind that, increasingly, the Court has not accompanied its grant or denial of emergency relief with a written opinion and has done so without extensive briefing and argument.

---

50. As stated by Professor Vladeck, "*Purcell* seemingly invites bad behavior by local and state election officials, who might themselves change the rules on the eve of an election because they know they can do so without worrying about the interference of the courts." VLADECK, *supra* note 1, at 207. While that was less likely before the Court invalidated much of the Voting Rights Act (VRA) in *Shelby County v. Holder*, 570 U.S. 529 (2013), the risk of serious misconduct by local election officials has increased in recent years, especially in light of election denialism. VLADECK, *supra* note 1, at 208.

51. VLADECK, *supra* note 1, at 208–09.

52. Wilfred U. Codrington III, Purcell *in Pandemic*, 96 N.Y.U. L. REV. 941, 945 (2021).

53. VLADECK, *supra* note 1, at 46.

54. One can find that theme throughout *The Shadow Docket*. Chapter 7 provides a concise discussion of that issue.

The Trump administration scored numerous victories during the COVID pandemic.

Because of COVID, states faced concerns about how to assure that voters could have their ballots counted. In Wisconsin, a federal district court ordered the state to extend the deadline for receiving mail-in ballots. The Republican National Committee asked the Court of Appeals to stay the court's ruling. The Seventh Circuit stayed part of the district court's injunction but left intact the extension of time allowed by the lower court. In a 5–4 ruling, the Supreme Court put the original mailing deadline back in place and quoted *Purcell* for the proposition that a court should not alter election rules on the eve of an election.[55] In an opinion joined by three other justices, Justice Ginsburg dissented and argued that the extension of the deadline did not create a risk of voter confusion because uninformed voters would return their ballots earlier, not relying on the district court's extension of time.[56] Further, the majority's order created confusion about when ballots were due. Under pre-*Purcell* practice, the Court would have considered countervailing considerations, including the extraordinary impact COVID had on the ability of voters to get their ballots into the mail in a timely fashion.[57]

Contrast the Wisconsin case with a case that arose in Florida, where the Florida voters had amended the state constitution to allow convicted felons to regain their right to vote. The Republican dominated legislature enacted a statute making it extremely difficult and expensive for former felons to regain their right to vote. Former felons could not do so unless they paid all outstanding fines, for example. When ex-felons challenged the state law, a federal district court held that the law likely violated due process and equal protection and, therefore, temporarily blocked enforcement of the state law. After an eight-day trial, the court entered a final judgment striking down the pay-to-vote requirements.[58]

In July 2020, the Eleventh Circuit stayed the lower court's injunction. In effect, that court changed the law that had been in effect since the summer of 2019 when the district court initially enjoined enforcement of the state law. Plaintiffs asked the Supreme Court to lift the Eleventh Circuit's stay and argued that under *Purcell*, the Eleventh Circuit changed

55. Vladeck, *supra* note 1, at 211.

56. *Id.*

57. *Id.*

58. *Id.* at 212.

the rules governing the election, in effect, on the eve of that election (only 19 days away). Without explanation, a majority of the Supreme Court denied relief to the plaintiffs. Given that the re-enfranchisement of ex-felons most likely would have benefitted Democrats, the Court's inconsistent rulings, especially without any hint of explaining the reasoning that may have supported its differing conclusions, leaves the distinct impression that the decision had more to do with raw politics than legal principles.[59]

Not long after the Court ruled on the Florida case, Justice Ginsburg died, and then-Senate Majority leader Mitchell McConnell rammed through Amy Coney Barrett's nomination even though the Presidential election was only 38 days away. After Justice Barrett joined the Court, the process described above (rulings favoring Republicans and disfavoring Democrats) became, if anything, more noticeable than in the past. As Professor Vladeck concluded,

> ... [the] partisan trend appeared to be the most consistent thread running through an otherwise inconsistent series of holdings in which the Court cited *Purcell.* A cynical observer could look at these rulings, all but one of which lacked a majority opinion, and see politics prevailing over principle. Given the internally contradictory nature of the Court's interventions and the lack of any attempt by the justices in the majority to reconcile them (at least publicly), it would be hard to prove that cynicism unfounded.[60]

As mentioned in passing above, the situation would become even more troubling in 2022 during the midterm elections.

Prior to that election, litigants in various states challenged redistricting maps. For example, in Alabama, Black voters challenged a redistricting map advanced by the state. After a seven-day hearing, the district court found for the Black voters and held that the state needed to redraw its map to create a second district that would contain a majority of minority voters. The state appealed to the Supreme Court, which held that the district court ruling would not apply to the election, which had been

---

59. *Id.* at 212, 216–17 (discussing Justice Sotomayor's dissent which points out the irony of the Court's use of *Purcell* differently in the Wisconsin case compared to the Florida case and explaining how the two cases benefit Republicans and hurt Democrats).

60. *Id.* at 217.

nine months before the election. The result was that during the 2022 midterm election, Alabama was allowed to use an election map that favored Republicans despite the fact that the map was almost certainly a violation of the VRA.[61] Elsewhere, the Court used its shadow docket to prevent redistricting that favored Democrats in Georgia and Louisiana, again despite strong evidence of VRA violations.[62]

Contrast those rulings with a decision to prevent Wisconsin from putting in place its proposed new districting map that would have added another majority-minority district. In Wisconsin, the state supreme court adopted a proposal offered by the governor to achieve greater racial balance in its various congressional districts. Republican legislators and voters asked the Supreme Court to stay the new legislative map or to grant the writ of certiorari and to rule on the merits that the governor's map violated the Constitution. On March 23, 2022, the Court summarily reversed the Wisconsin Supreme Court. It did so on the grounds that the state actor had to show the newly drawn district was required by the VRA, not merely consistent with that law.[63]

The problem with the Court's reversal in the Wisconsin case was that the state court had yet to consider the question whether the new district was required by the VRA or merely consistent with it. That determination would have come later in litigation brought in the lower courts. At worst, if the Wisconsin court was wrong in ordering the majority-minority district, the determination might have come close to the election and, therefore, as in the cases described above, the ruling might have caused confusion among voters. That would have meant that Wisconsin's putatively illegal voting map would have been in place for one election cycle.[64] That may explain why the Court was so eager to rule in the Wisconsin case.

What then was the net effect of the various cases described above? In the cases arising out of the South, the result seems to have been that the

---

61. *Id.* at 218–22 (discussing the Court's application of *Purcell* to shut down Alabamans' VRA challenge to the redrawn U.S. House districts, despite plenty of time to redraw and what Justice Kagan describes as "clear vote dilution").

62. *Id.* at 223 ("Ten days after the Supreme Court's Alabama ruling, for instance, a Georgia district court refused to enjoin Georgia's redistricting *despite* finding the exact same violation. . . .") (emphasis in original).

63. *Id.* at 223–24.

64. *Id.* at 225.

states were allowed to use illegally drawn districts that violated the VRA for one election cycle even though federal judges in those cases held extensive hearings on the merits and found those states in violation of the VRA. Almost certainly, had the district court judges' orders in the Southern cases been allowed to take effect during the 2022 midterm elections, Democratic candidates would have won seats in those predominately Black voting districts.[65] Deciding the case summarily in the Wisconsin case prevented a majority-minority district from being put in place. Had it been allowed, the lower federal courts might have found the district to be illegal, but that finding would not have taken effect for the 2022 election because under *Purcell*, the ruling would have come too close to the election.[66]

What was the net effect of the Court's several holdings? Notably, although election law scholars see the Court's various decisions as unprincipled, the use of the shadow docket leaves the Court's analysis unclear. As in many shadow docket cases, the Court does not submit formal opinions explaining how it reached its results. Further, given the fact that litigants are often asking the Court for the use of its emergency powers, litigants may not have the chance to brief the issues fully and the Court may be deciding the case with a limited factual record.[67]

Given that use of the shadow docket shrouds the Court's reasoning, as indicated above, critics are cynical about the Court's decision-making. Remember that Republicans maintained a narrow majority in the House during the 2022 midterm election. As observed by the Court's critics, its election law decisions helped secure that anti-democratic result.

---

65. Had the Court agreed with the special three-judge district court in the Alabama VRA challenge, for example, the court-ordered redistricting required a second majority-minority district which "would [have] almost certainly create[d] a second Democratic seat within Alabama's 6–1 Republican House delegation." VLADECK, *supra* note 1 at 219.

66. VLADECK, *supra* note 1, at 220 (highlighting Justice Kavanaugh's confusing *Purcell* analysis which seeks to prevent changing election laws "'in the period too close to an election'" by permitting states to "get one free election cycle using unlawful district maps every ten years").

67. *Id.* at 193; Koppelman, *supra* note 24 ("In these cases, there has been no trial and no opportunity to develop an evidentiary record."); Caroline Fredrickson, *Will American Democracy Last in Light of the Shadow Docket?*, 23 NEV. L.J. 727, 728 (2023) ("So without written lower court decisions, only fragmentary briefing or oral argument by parties, and a limited time span to consider the complex legal questions and contested facts, the Supreme Court nonetheless issues decisions that can have significant and long-lasting consequences, including making major changes to doctrine.").

D. Concluding Thoughts

On occasion, the Court uses the shadow docket in cases that advance liberal policy preferences. But, as developed in this chapter, the right wing of the Court has been the most aggressive in its use of such procedures.

Some conservative scholars and even Chief Justice Roberts, who at times has joined the right wing of the Court in using the shadow docket to advance right-wing policy preferences, have raised serious questions about the use of the shadow docket.

Donald Ayers, a former high-ranking Department of Justice official in the George H.W. Bush administration, wrote a *New York Times* op-ed in 2021. Despite agreeing with many of the eventual outcomes, Ayers stated, "what is new is the court's frequency and brashness in achieving these radical outcomes, and its willingness to do so without an honest explanation and acknowledgement of what is actually going on."[68] Professor Baude, who popularized the term and expressed doubts about its use, is a conservative scholar.[69]

Justices like Alito and Kavanaugh have tried to portray criticisms of the use of the shadow docket as simply a criticism from left-leaning scholars who disagree with the Court's results. As developed in this chapter, that misses the core problem with the shadow docket. In trying to defend the Court, Justice Barrett stated in a speech that critics should "read the opinion" of cases that the Court was about to decide on controversial issues, including affirmative action, abortion, and gun control. Her point was that fair-minded readers would see that the Justices are not primarily political actors intent upon imposing their political preferences on the nation. Instead, her position was that readers would see that, even if readers disagreed with the results, the Justice who wrote the opinion made "an honest effort and persuasive effort... to determine what the Constitution and precedent requires."[70]

Justice Barrett's point is well-taken but for the reality that she along with other justices, especially on the Court's right wing, are now routinely deciding major issues on the shadow docket. There is no opinion

68. Vladeck, *supra* note 1, at 247.

69. *Id.*

70. *Id.* at 245.

to read to see if the Court has compelling reasons based in the law to decide as it has.[71] That is in direct conflict with the rule of law, whereby our system relies on legal opinions that provide binding precedent for future litigants and lower courts.[72]

Imagine two cases: one in which the Court decides a case expanding or abandoning a substantive right. In doing so, the Court publishes a full opinion explaining its reasoning.[73] In the second case, imagine a case in which the Court uses a procedural vehicle not well understood by members of the public and perhaps not even by members of the bar. In doing so, the Court expands or impairs a substantive right without addressing that fact. Members of the public are almost certainly less likely to react with the same level of passion as they would in a case where the Court openly expanded or impaired a substantive right.[74] That is one of the effects of the use of the shadow docket. As developed in this book, increasingly, the right wing of the Court has used procedural decisions in ways that advance the right-wing Justices' substantive policy preferences. By doing so, they advance their agenda with far less public outcry than if they decided cases on substantive grounds. Along the way, you will see the unquestionable power of procedure.

---

71. *Id.*

72. As Justices O'Connor, Kennedy, and Souter stated in their joint opinion in *Planned Parenthood v. Casey,* "the Court's legitimacy depends on making legally principled decisions under circumstances in which their principled character is sufficiently plausible to be accepted by the Nation." 505 U.S. at 866.

73. *See supra* Chapter 1 (comparing public commentary on cases involving substantive rights to public commentary on cases involving procedural rights).

74. There is only one *Washington Post* article from 2007 that discusses *Purcell*, but it does not allow user comments. *See* Michael Waldman & Justin Levitt, *The Myth of Voter Fraud*, Washington Post (Mar. 28, 2007), https://www.washingtonpost.com/archive/opinions/2007/03/29/the-myth-of-voter-fraud/62ca7a2c-c1ca-45d3-89b4-982269763bd9/. Likewise, there are few N.Y. Times articles that discuss the Louisiana voting rights case, *Merrill v. Milligan*, 142 S. Ct. 879 (2022), and only one allows user comments. Even when discussed as one of "Three Huge Supreme Court Cases That Could Change America," there are only six user comments on the article discussing the Louisiana voting rights case. *See* Blake Hounshell, *Three Huge Supreme Court Cases That Could Change America*, N.Y. Times (Oct. 3, 2022), https://www.nytimes.com/2022/10/03/us/politics/supreme-court-conservative-politics.html.

THREE

Personal Jurisdiction[1]

A. Introduction

Imagine the following situation: J.M. McIntyre Machinery, Ltd., a British company, manufactures metal recycling machines in England. It works with its exclusive dealer in the United States to sell as many of its recycling machines throughout the United States. At least one machine ends up in New Jersey, the leading metal recycling state in the United States. The machine was purchased by a company that employs Robert Nicastro. While working with the machine, Nicastro is severely injured, resulting in the loss of his right hand. Where should the injured worker be able to file a lawsuit against the manufacturer?[2]

What are the strongest reasons to allow Nicastro to sue the manufacturer in New Jersey? Are there important reasons not to allow Nicastro to sue in New Jersey? Can McIntyre claim that New Jersey is not a convenient forum for the lawsuit?

---

1. This chapter relies on Michael Vitiello, *Limiting Access to U.S. Courts: The Supreme Court's New Personal Jurisdiction Case Law*, 21 U.C. DAVIS J. INT'L L. & POL'Y 210 (2015). *See also* Michael Vitiello, *Reflection on Hoffheimer's The Stealth Revolution in Personal Jurisdiction*, 70 FLA. L. REV. F. 31 (2018); Michael Vitiello, *The Supreme Court's Latest Attempt at "Clarifying" Personal Jurisdiction: More Questions Than Answers*, 57 TULSA L. REV. 395 (2022); Michael Vitiello & Daniel Croxall, *Mallory v. Norfolk Southern Railway Co., Due Process and Strange Bedfellows*, 89 MO. L. REV. 217 (2024).

2. J. McIntyre Mach., Ltd. v. Nicastro, 564 U.S. 873 (2011).

New Jersey, like most states in the United States, has tort laws that provide injured individuals significant protections, often more protective than laws in foreign countries. Typically, states within the United States permit more significant damages in tort cases than do other countries. In addition, unlike many other countries, jurisdictions within the United States allow attorneys who handle personal injury cases to take cases based on contingency fee agreements, whereby the plaintiff pays only if the plaintiff prevails at trial (or settles the claim against the defendant).[3]

Finally, focus on one other factor as you consider where the injured plaintiff ought to be able to sue. Today, should rules governing a plaintiff's ability to bring an out-of-state or foreign company to court be more or less restrictive than in the past?

A few minutes of reflection about the case described above should make you aware that a great deal is at stake for the injured worker. Establishing personal jurisdiction in a convenient forum will be far more important for the injured plaintiff than almost any other question in the lawsuit. And yet few students gush with enthusiasm when they study personal jurisdiction, despite the clear importance of establishing a court's jurisdiction in a convenient forum.

Personal jurisdiction is the first topic in many casebooks. And many of those books start the chapter with *Pennoyer v. Neff*,[4] a case written in nineteenth century prose that seems impenetrable to modern readers. Professors on the civil procedure listserv often debate whether we should teach the case at all. But even if professors skip *Pennoyer*, students find personal jurisdiction tough material to wade through. The Court's personal jurisdiction cases introduce students to the evolving meaning of due process. The Court's test is elusive at best and is open to considerable criticism as incoherent and misguided.[5] I believe that students can un-

3. *See What to Expect Regarding Fees and Billing*, The State Bar of California, https://www.calbar.ca.gov/Public/Free-Legal-Information/Working-with-an-Attorney/What-to-Expect-Regarding-Fees-and-Billing (last visited Jan. 9, 2025) (stating that contingency fee is often used in accident and personal injury cases).

4. Pennoyer v. Neff, 95 U.S. 714 (1877).

5. *See, e.g.*, Vitiello, *Limiting Access to U.S. Courts*, *supra* note 1, at 214–15 (referring to *Pennoyer*'s underlying theory as "analytically jarring" and its results as often "unfair"); Jack H. Friedenthal, Mary Kay Kane & Arthur R. Miller, Civil Procedure 100–01 (5th ed. 2015) (noting that the *Pennoyer* test proved to be "useless" and overly rigid, often allowing corporations to fortuitously evade liability when incorporated, and thus

derstand the topic more clearly if they understand what is at stake in personal jurisdiction cases. The Supreme Court's decisions allow a meaningful discussion about the values that may animate the Court's decisions. That is the subject of this chapter.

As demonstrated by some of the cases discussed in this chapter, the Court often decides personal jurisdiction cases without a clear majority opinion. From case to case, the majority of justices seem to repudiate the Court's earlier holdings, even if decided by the same Court. In part, that explains why commentators see the Court's case law as incoherent. It also suggests that a great deal is at stake in personal jurisdiction cases: they are not about arcane principles but about whether the Court favors plaintiffs or defendants' choice of a forum. Ultimately, at stake is whether a plaintiff may be able to recover at all.[6]

This chapter begins with a review of several historically important cases. Those decisions, including *Pennoyer v. Neff*, provide essential background for understanding the tensions within the Court's doctrine. The discussion explores the expansion of state courts' jurisdictional reach at the same time our nation's communication and transportation systems expanded. Those changes made interstate transactions more frequent and increased the need for injured plaintiffs to be able to sue out-of-state defendants in a plaintiff-convenient forum. The chapter then turns to a period of retrenchment, with a focus on some of the political implications of that retrenchment. Thereafter, it focuses on the Court's cases decided during the period from 2011 to 2017. Despite advances in modern communication and transportation making interstate and international business dealings easier, the Court's case law was extraordinarily begrudging to injured plaintiffs. Finally, the chapter examines the Court's two most recent cases, which finally uphold the plaintiffs' choice of forum. While that may suggest a shift in the Court's begrudging analysis, this chapter focuses on the possibility that the right wing of the Court will engage in further retrenchment.

---

legally present, in a different state). As developed below, that concern about the Court's case law is even truer today than at any time in the past.

6. *See, e.g.*, *Nicastro*, 564 U.S. 873.

B. *Pennoyer v. Neff*'s Dicta

In 1865, J. H. Mitchell sued Marcus Neff in Oregon state court. Seeking to recover damages for unpaid legal services, Mitchell began his suit *in personam* by filing the notice in a newspaper. When Neff did not appear in the suit, the court entered a default judgment in favor of Mitchell. Mitchell secured a writ of execution against land subsequently acquired by Neff in Oregon. Although the historical record differs slightly from the facts cited in the Supreme Court's opinion, Mitchell bought the land at auction and then transferred title to Sylvester Pennoyer. Several years later, Neff sued Pennoyer in federal court and sought to evict him from the property.[7]

The lower court found for Neff based on narrow technical grounds not relevant here. The Supreme Court also found for Neff, specifically holding that Pennoyer could not rely on the prior judgment, in effect, by analogy to the Full Faith and Credit Clause. The Court found that the original plaintiff, Mitchell, did not begin that suit by proper attachment of the property that would have given the state court *in rem* jurisdiction. The Court relied on an analogy borrowed from international law: a sovereign state has exclusive jurisdiction over persons and property within its borders; it followed that one state could not reach into another state to assert jurisdiction over persons or property within the other sovereign. In effect, a state's borders defined the jurisdictional reach of that state. Because Mitchell filed his original action *in personam* and did not serve Neff in-hand, in-state, the state court lacked personal jurisdiction over Neff.[8]

Had that been the end of its analysis, the Court might have spared generations of law students and lawyers the difficult task of deciphering a straightforward holding from an opinion written in nineteenth century prose. The holding seems simple enough: a court lacks *in personam* jurisdiction over a non-consenting, non-resident defendant unless that

---

7. *Pennoyer*, 95 U.S. at 719–20. For a fascinating historical account of *Pennoyer*, including a discussion of the larger-than-life characters involved in the case, see Wendy Collins Perdue, *Sin, Scandal, and Substantive Due Process: Personal Jurisdiction and* Pennoyer *Reconsidered*, 62 Wash. L. Rev. 479 (1987).

8. *Pennoyer*, 95 U.S. at 719–20.

defendant is served in-hand, in-state. The bedeviling aspect of the Court's decision was its discussion of due process.[9]

After discussing the application of principles of international law, the Court turned to the Fourteenth Amendment's Due Process Clause. The Court's discussion is dicta because the nation adopted the Fourteenth Amendment after Mitchell began his original suit. Nonetheless, the Court found that the Due Process Clause, in effect, contained the same principle as did international law: the Fourteenth Amendment limited states' powers. Thus, in *Pennoyer*, the Fourteenth Amendment somehow protected California's sovereignty by preventing Oregon from reaching into California to assert jurisdiction over a defendant in that state.

The decision's underlying theory is jarring at best: by any plausible historical understanding, the Fourteenth Amendment is a limitation on state power. To read the Fourteenth Amendment as grounded in the idea that the provision protects a state from overreaching another state's sovereign power makes little sense.[10]

C. Abandoning *Pennoyer*'s Constraints

While the Court has since overruled or eroded much of *Pennoyer*, the decision's reliance on state power as part of the Due Process Clause continues to cause mischief in the law of personal jurisdiction, as developed more fully below. Decided at the very beginning of the industrial revolution in the United States, *Pennoyer* initially did not pose significant problems for plaintiffs. In an agrarian society, most litigation did not involve parties from far-and-wide.

As the United States developed its road and rail systems, *Pennoyer*'s restrictive rule began to produce unfair results. Consistent with *Pennoyer*, an in-state resident could not sue an out-of-state motorist for harm caused by the out-of-state motorist unless the injured party found and served the out-of-state party in-state. That forced the injured party to litigate in the out-of-state motorist's home state, adding inconve-

---

9. U.S. Const. amend. XIV § 1; *Pennoyer*, 95 U.S. at 733–34.

10. Vitiello, *Limiting Access to U.S. Courts*, *supra* note 1, at 214 ("[t]reating the Fourteenth Amendment as protecting states' rights is to ignore a central message of the Civil War").

nience and expense for the plaintiff. The out-of-state motorist had, after all, come to the forum where he caused the injury. Presumably, he did so to seek benefits in the state where the injury occurred.

Flirting briefly with the untenable theory that a defendant impliedly consented to the court's jurisdiction,[11] the Court eventually began overruling aspects of *Pennoyer.* The Court's decision in *International Shoe*[12] marked the beginning of the modern era of personal jurisdiction. *International Shoe* presented the Court with an opportunity to clarify how courts should assess due process claims when the defendant was a corporation. This issue presented analytical problems from the inception, but also gave the Court the chance to modernize the framework of analysis.

International Shoe, located in Missouri, had a workforce in Washington State. Its salesmen solicited orders from customers there. Almost certainly by design to avoid jurisdiction in-state, International Shoe did not allow its sales force to enter into contracts with sellers in Washington. Instead, employees at the Missouri headquarters decided whether to fill orders. (At the time, the Supreme Court case law distinguished between entering contracts within a state or merely soliciting orders in-state. In the latter case, the Court had held that the defendant had not done business in-state.[13]) The corporation failed to pay funds into Washington's unemployment compensation fund. Sued by the state for those funds, the corporation contended that the court lacked personal jurisdiction over it. In light of the way in which it set up its business, the defendant argued before the Court that it did not do business in-state.[14]

11. Hess v. Pawloski, 274 U.S. 352 (1927); *see also* Olberding v. Ill. Cent. Co., 346 U.S. 338, 341 (Justice Frankfurter, writing the majority opinion, described the consent theory as "some fictive talk" and stated that "[i]n point of fact... jurisdiction in these cases does not rest on consent at all. The defendant may protest to high heaven his unwillingness to be sued and it avails him not."). Many states still have implied consent statutes on the books, but since *Hess*, the Court has not relied on implied consent in its personal jurisdiction case law.

12. Int'l Shoe Co. v. Washington, 326 U.S. 310 (1945).

13. Philip B. Kurland, *The Supreme Court, the Due Process Clause and the In Personam Jurisdiction of State Courts*, 25 U. Chi. L. Rev. 569, 589 (1958) ("'[m]ere solicitation' was inadequate to sustain personal jurisdiction over a foreign corporation... and 'solicitation plus' provided a sufficient base.") (first quoting Green v. Chicago, Burlington, and Quincy Ry. Co., 205 U.S. 530, 530 (1907); then quoting Int'l Harvester Co. v. Kentucky, 234 U.S. 579, 587 (1914)).

14. *Int'l Shoe*, 326 U.S. at 313–16.

The Court's opinion swept broadly. It abandoned the idea that, when determining whether a corporation was subject to personal jurisdiction, the trial court had to determine if the defendant was doing business in-state. Instead, it focused on the nature and quality of the defendant's contacts with the state. While not using contemporary language, the Court described cases that fell within a court's specific or general jurisdiction. It also suggested a theory explaining the basis of its holding, uncoupled from state sovereignty: the Court expanded on the *quid pro quo* theory that it had adopted in cases involving jurisdiction based on state residency. When a defendant sought the benefits and protections of the laws of the forum state—at least when the claim arose out of or related to the underlying contacts—the defendant had a reciprocal obligation to respond to suit in that forum. The opinion also made clear that the implied consent theory was a fiction and that the minimum contacts analysis applied not only to corporations but also to individuals.[15]

The Court's analysis had come a long way since *Pennoyer.* Consider how a court applying *International Shoe* would analyze whether an Oregon state court had personal jurisdiction over Neff in the original *Mitchell v. Neff* litigation. As long as Oregon had a long-arm statute authorizing service of process on a non-resident, Neff's objection to that court's jurisdiction would almost certainly fail. He entered into a contract with Mitchell to provide legal services, apparently in Oregon, and he failed to pay for those services. He had sufficient contacts with the state and the plaintiff's claim arose out of those contacts.[16]

D. Getting It Right: A Coherent Theory

International Shoe provided an invitation to state legislatures and courts to expand their states' jurisdictional reach. Not long after the decision, states began adopting long-arm statutes designed to conform the reach of their courts to the *International Shoe* due process analysis. Those efforts demonstrated that states were far more interested in pro-

15. *Id.* at 318–20.

16. *See* McGee v. Int'l Life Ins. Co., 355 U.S. 220 (1957), for a case in which the Court upheld jurisdiction based on a single contract between an in-state plaintiff and out-of-state defendant.

tecting their residents from harm caused by out-of-state actors than they were with preventing other states from reaching into their states to require their citizens to respond to suits elsewhere.[17]

Expanded long-arm statutes invited constitutional challenges, but the Supreme Court kept pace with the states' expansion of their jurisdictional reach. From my perspective, the Court's decision in *McGee v. International Life*[18] was the high-water mark.

Lowell Franklin purchased a life insurance policy from Empire Life Insurance. Later, International Life assumed Empire's insurance obligations and subsequently sent Franklin a certificate of renewal of his insurance policy. When Franklin died, probably by suicide, the insurance company refused to pay Lulu McGee, Franklin's mother and beneficiary under the policy. McGee sued in California state court. International Life did not appear. After McGee obtained a default judgment, she filed a collection action in Texas, where the defendant had its principal place of business. The Texas courts refused to give the California judgment full faith and credit on the ground that the California court lacked personal jurisdiction over the defendant.[19]

A unanimous Supreme Court reversed. Nothing in the opinion suggested that jurisdiction turned on the fact that International Life sent the certificate of insurance to Franklin. The Court decided the case on what almost certainly was an incomplete record; it observed that "so far as the record before us shows, respondent has *never solicited or done any insurance business* in California apart from the policy involved here."[20]

As presented to the Court, the case involved a single contract between the defendant and a person in the forum state. Writing for the Court, Justice Black reviewed the history of personal jurisdiction and noted the

---

17. Vitiello, *Limiting Access*, *supra* note 1, at 216; for an example of a state adopting such a long-arm statute after *Int'l Shoe*, see Cal. Civ. Code § 410.10 (2014) ("A court of this state may exercise jurisdiction on any basis not inconsistent with the Constitution of this state or of the United States."); *see also* John A. Gorfinkel & Richard A. Lavine, *Long-Arm Jurisdiction in California Under New Section 410.10 of the Code of Civil Procedure*, 21 Hastings L.J. 1163, 1165–67 (1970) (noting that the statute was adopted a few months prior to the article's publication in 1970 and anticipating that "California will not find itself in the position of other states whose statutes prevent their courts from taking advantage of the full sweep of the minimum contacts doctrine.").

18. *McGee*, 355 U.S. 220.

19. *Id.* at 221.

20. *Id.* at 222 (emphasis added).

clear trend towards "expanding the permissible scope of state jurisdiction over foreign corporations."[21] In effect, the Court recognized the need to expand jurisdiction in light of modern realities. Commerce had become nationalized, the mails allowed commercial transactions across the continent, and the Court found that any burden on the defendant was minimal in light of modern transportation and communication.[22]

In light of post-*McGee* developments, I provide my students with a hypothetical before moving on to more modern cases. Would the results of the case come out differently if, after International Life bought out Empire, Franklin wrote to International Life to update his policy? My reading of the case suggests not. The Court was unanimous in its ruling. As emphasized in the quotation above, the Court stated that the insurance company had never done any insurance business in California apart from Franklin's contract of insurance. It did not suggest that the result turned on who solicited whom. The focus of the analysis was on modern transportation and communication. In light of those realities, at least a large corporate defendant could not claim that it lacked an opportunity to be heard. Indeed, Justice Black seemed to equate due process with adequate notice and the opportunity to be heard.[23]

Insofar as a state's interest was relevant, it was California that had an interest in protecting its citizens. Further relevant to the analysis was the plaintiff's interest in a convenient forum, here her home state.[24]

McGee's reading of due process is far more consonant with ideas of procedural fairness than was Justice Field's reading of the clause in *Pennoyer*. *McGee*'s analysis focused on the burden on the defendant. Can it claim that it lacked notice? Is the forum so burdensome that it lacked a reasonable opportunity to be heard? By comparison, the Supreme Court would later characterize *Pennoyer*'s states' rights approach as "the shibboleth" of personal jurisdiction.[25]

I do not pretend that, were *McGee* the Court's last word on the meaning of due process, the case would always lead to clear results. Assessing a plaintiff's need for a forum and the extent of the burden on a defendant

21. *Id.*
22. *Id.* at 222–23.
23. *Id.* at 224.
24. *Id.* at 221–23.
25. World-Wide Volkswagen Corp. v. Woodson, 444 U.S. 286, 293 (1980).

would often require imprecise balancing of interests. Of course, the law often requires such imprecision. Determinations of "reasonableness" in areas like tort law or in Fourth Amendment analysis are notoriously imprecise, as are rules governing when punitive damages are excessive.[26] If the underlying rules otherwise make doctrinal sense, one should accept line-drawing as inherent in the law.

Apart from doctrinal coherence, *McGee's* holding was consonant with the trend towards longer jurisdictional reach for state courts. But for a blip on the radar, that trend continued for over twenty years. That blip is the subject of the next section.

E. Really Hard Cases Make Really Bad Law

No one roots for King Lear's venal daughters Goneril and Regan. Dissatisfied with the gift of their share of their father's kingdom, they conspired against him and then against one another to take over his entire realm. Had Cordelia accepted her third of her father's kingdom and her sisters sought to have that grant overturned so that they could own her share, a court would be hard-pressed to find for Goneril and Regan.[27] But that is what happened in *Hanson v. Denckla.*[28]

---

26. *See, e.g.*, Lent v. New York Cent. and Hudson River R.R. Co., 24 N.E. 653, 655 (N.Y. 1890) (the court explained that when it comes to reasonableness in tort law, "[s]ome allowance may be made for the influences which ordinarily govern human action, and what would under some circumstances be a want of reasonable care might not be such under others."); United States v. Place, 462 U.S. 696, 703 (1983) (explaining that, to determine reasonableness in the context of the Fourth Amendment, a court must "balance the nature and quality of the intrusion on the individual's Fourth Amendment interests against the importance of the governmental interests alleged to justify the intrusion"); BMW of North America v. Gore, 517 U.S. 559, 574–75 (1996) (providing three "guideposts" by which to establish the reasonableness of an award of punitive damages: "the degree of reprehensibility of the nondisclosure; the disparity between the harm or potential harm suffered by [the plaintiff] and his punitive damages award; and the difference between this remedy and the civil penalties authorized or imposed in comparable cases").

27. William Shakespeare, King Lear (Barbara Mowat and Paul Werstine, eds., Simon & Schuster 2010) (1606), http://www.folgerdigitaltexts.org/?chapter=5&play=Lr&loc=p7.

28. Hanson v. Denckla, 357 U.S. 235 (1958).

Mrs. Donner, a wealthy widow living in Pennsylvania, paid a Delaware trust company to serve as a trustee. Subsequently, she moved to Florida. The trust remained in effect until her death. During the eight years when she lived in Florida, the trust company maintained its business relationship with her, including managing the trust and sending income checks to her home in Florida.[29]

After moving to Florida, Mrs. Donner created a will in which she left the bulk of her estate to two of her three daughters, Katherine Denckla and Dorothy Stewart. Upon their mother's death, they would inherit about $500,000 each under the will. Mrs. Donner named her third daughter, Elizabeth Hanson, as her executor. Around the same time, she exercised her power of appointment under the trust, whereby she made Hanson's two sons the beneficiaries of the trust principal. Under the trust, each son would receive about $200,000. Given tax laws at the time (whereby estate tax rates were higher than gift tax rates) and the possibility that Hanson would be entitled to an executor's fee, Mrs. Donner's intent to divide her estate into thirds seems obvious.[30]

Despite that, Denckla and Stewart sought to frustrate their mother's estate plan. They challenged the validity of the trust in a Florida proceeding to settle their mother's estate. As the residual legatees of Mrs. Donner's will, they would receive the $400,000 trust principal. They sought to name the Delaware trust company as a defendant in the suit in Florida. Before the court resolved the Florida action, Hanson sued in Delaware to have the trust declared valid. The Florida court found for Denckla and Stewart; the Delaware court found for Hanson.[31]

The Supreme Court could have decided the case on other grounds—for example, whether the Delaware trust company was a "necessary and indispensable" party in the Florida action. Instead, the Court found that the Florida court lacked personal jurisdiction over the Delaware trust company.[32]

---

29. *Id.* at 238–40.

30. *Id.* at 239–40; Vitiello, *Limiting Access to U.S. Courts*, *supra* note 1, at 216; Darien B. Jacobson, Brian G. Raub & Barry W. Johnson, *The Estate Tax: Ninety Years and Counting*, IRS, https://www.irs.gov/pub/irs-soi/ninetyestate.pdf (last visited Jan. 9, 2025) (explaining that before the Tax Reform Act of 1976, which unified estate and gift tax, the gift tax rate was "substantially" lower than the estate tax rate).

31. *Hanson*, 357 U.S. at 238.

32. *Id.* at 254–55.

The Court decided the case six months after *McGee.*[33] It divided 5–4. I challenge my students to apply *McGee* to the facts of *Hanson*, in effect, to apply a case holding to a new set of facts. If one ignores the effects of upholding the Florida judgment, a strong case for the Florida court's jurisdiction exists. Mrs. Donner had maintained an 8-year business relationship with the trust company; many of her other assets were in Florida; some of the parties lived there; Florida had an interest in providing those parties with a convenient forum; and any inconvenience to a Delaware corporation was minimal. If the modern travel and communications reduced the burden on a Texas corporation when a California plaintiff sued it in a California court, one would be hard-pressed to assert that the burden on the Delaware trust company was greater. Even the distance between the states involved in the two cases was comparable, if not closer in *Hanson* than in *McGee.*[34]

Chief Justice Warren's majority opinion only thinly veiled its result-orientation. The Chief Justice's statement—"Residuary legatees Denckla and Stewart, *already the recipients of over $500,000 each,* urge that . . . the $400,000 appointed to sister Elizabeth's children . . . should . . . pass to them"[35]—suggests as much.

Although the Chief Justice suggested that the plaintiffs' claim did not arise out of the Delaware company's contacts with the forum state (surely something open to debate), the important part of the opinion, when one has the advantage of hindsight, is what the Court said about the nature of those contacts. The trust company did not purposefully avail itself of the benefits of doing business with its customer in Florida. As Justice Black emphasized in dissent, the trust company had an eight-year business relationship with Mrs. Donner after she moved to Florida.[36] But those contacts were insufficient; they came about through the "unilateral activity" of a third party.[37]

What about *McGee*? Weren't International Life's contacts with California similar or even more limited than were the Delaware trust com-

33. *McGee*, 355 U.S. 220 (decided December 16, 1957); *Hanson*, 357 U.S. 235 (decided June 23, 1958).

34. *Hanson*, 357 U.S. at 242, 259.

35. *Id.* at 240 (emphasis added).

36. *Id.* at 257 (Black, J., dissenting) ("Mrs. Donner was domiciled in Florida from 1944 until her death in 1952. The controversial appointment was made there in 1949.").

37. *Id.* at 253 (majority opinion).

pany's contacts with Florida? The record in *McGee* revealed only one insurance contract with a California resident, one involving a small insurance claim as well. Surely, the Delaware trust company made far more money from its 8-year relationship with Ms. Donner than did International Life from its premiums from Mr. Franklin. However, the contacts were of a different nature entirely: International Life "solicited a reinsurance agreement in"[38] California. The case thus turned on a difference between knowledge and purpose. Although, as argued above, *McGee* did not in itself seem to hint at such a distinction, the Chief Justice now recast *McGee* as turning on it.

Many courts ignored *Hanson* for about twenty years. Taken seriously, it presented a serious challenge to courts interested in expanding the reach of state court jurisdiction over out-of-state corporations that caused harm in-state. Many civil procedure casebooks include a classic stream of commerce case, *Gray v. American Radiator & Standard Sanitary Corp.*,[39] to illustrate the point. In *Gray*, Ms. Gray's hot water heater exploded and caused her extensive injuries. She sued in Illinois, her home state. She joined as co-defendants American Radiator, the manufacturer of the hot water heater, and Titan Valve, the manufacturer of the pressure valve that may have caused the explosion. Titan manufactured the valve in Ohio and shipped it to American Radiator in Pennsylvania, where it incorporated the valve into the completed product.[40]

The Illinois Supreme Court's opinion demonstrates how eager courts were to extend the jurisdictional reach of their state courts to protect in-state plaintiffs. The court's opinion gave a "creative" reading to its long-arm statute. Unlike states like California, where the long-arm allows the assertion of jurisdiction over an out-of-state defendant as long as the assertion of jurisdiction is constitutional, Illinois's statute allowed the assertion of jurisdiction only if the facts of the case came within a specified sub-category. In *Gray*, the applicable provision stated that an out-of-state defendant was subject to the court's jurisdiction if it committed a tortious act within the state. Despite the natural reading of the statute—the tortious act was the improper manufacture of the valve in

38. *McGee*, 355 U.S. at 221.

39. Gray v. Am. Radiator & Standard Sanitary Corp., 22 Ill. 2d 432 (1961).

40. *Id.* at 434, 438.

Ohio—the court read "tortious act" to mean "tort." And a tort is complete only where the injury occurs, here, in Illinois.[41]

The court also had to find that the assertion of jurisdiction complied with due process. Had the court applied *Hanson*, Titan would have had a strong argument that jurisdiction was improper, even on the court's assumption that many of Titan's products ended up in the forum—a fact that did not appear in the record. While its employees may have been aware that Titan's products arrived in Illinois, the record did not show any purposeful activity directed towards the forum. The record showed merely that Titan shipped its valves to American Radiator in Pennsylvania.[42]

No doubt, *Gray* and *McGee* are consistent. A large manufacturer in Ohio cannot make a serious argument that the burden of responding to a suit in Illinois denies it of an opportunity to be heard. Illinois and Ms. Gray had an interest in having the case heard in Illinois. Illinois had an interest in protecting its citizens from harm caused by out-of-state manufacturers; Ms. Gray had an interest in bringing suit near home for her convenience and for the easy access to evidence relating to her injuries. Courts that ignored *Hanson* during the 1960s and 70s must have considered it a sport in the law because it was so obviously result-oriented.[43]

F. Retrenchment

The expansion of state courts' jurisdictional reach was not the only factor during the post-war era that led to greater use of the courts in the United States. Courts and legislatures in many states and in the federal system expanded individual rights as well. Courts developed new tort theories of recovery, including torts that allowed suits against manufacturers based on strict liability. Changes in the law now created rights of action against many groups that had largely been immune from suit in the past. For many years, the Supreme Court made the lower federal

41. *Id.* at 435–36.

42. *Id.* at 434, 438.

43. Vitiello, *Limiting Access to U.S. Courts*, *supra* note 1, at 221.

courts plaintiff-friendly venues for civil rights plaintiffs and many other right holders.[44]

Other writers have focused on the retrenchment in substantive rights beginning in the 1970s and beyond. The Burger Court got out of the business of implying private rights of action when Congress created a right without providing for a private remedy. Manufacturers, doctors, and others pushed for a variety of tort reforms, including caps on damages. Various organizations began targeting punitive damages by claiming that the Constitution limited the amount of such damages that a jury could award. Almost certainly not coincidentally, by the end of the 1970s, the Court began to narrow the jurisdictional reach of state courts as well.[45]

The Court decided a number of cases that stopped the expansion of state court jurisdiction that had accelerated after *International Shoe*. By comparison to more recent case law, the results seemed incremental and appeared to balance out.

In retrospect, *Shaffer v. Heitner*[46] began the process of retrenchment. There, the Court narrowed *in rem* jurisdiction before it began narrowing *in personam* jurisdiction. Prior to *Shaffer*, a plaintiff could begin suit by attaching property in lieu of serving the owner in-hand, in-state. The property did not have to have any connection to the suit, and courts found notice by publication sufficient. According to the formalistic nineteenth century mind, an action *in rem* was against the property, not the person, justifying the different rules. As the Court expanded *in personam* jurisdiction and moved away from nineteenth century formalism, scholars and organizations like the American Law Institute urged that the Court rethink its *in rem* jurisprudence. It did so in *Shaffer*.[47]

---

44. *Id.* at 222, 224–26.

45. *Id.* at 227–28.

46. Shaffer v. Heitner, 433 U.S. 186 (1977).

47. *Id.* at 205 ("The overwhelming majority of commentators have... rejected *Pennoyer's* premise that a proceeding 'against' property is not a proceeding against the owners of that property. Accordingly, they urge that the 'traditional notions of fair play and substantial justice' that govern a State's power to adjudicate in personam should also govern its power to adjudicate personal rights to property located in the State."); *see, e.g.*, Arthur T. von Mehren & Donald T. Trautman, *Jurisdiction to Adjudicate: A Suggested Analysis*, 79 Harv. L. Rev. 1121, 1139 (1966) ("To base any form of general jurisdiction on indirectly affiliating circumstances is problematical, particularly in light of the emergence in recent years of a variety of bases for specific jurisdiction. In American practice,

There, a plaintiff brought a shareholder derivative action in Delaware. He began suit by attaching shares of stock owned by officers of the corporation whose stock they had harmed by engaging in an antitrust conspiracy on the west coast. The Court found that the assertion of jurisdiction—even if characterized as *in rem*—violated the principles of *International Shoe.* In a sweeping dictum, Justice Marshall stated that all assertions of jurisdiction had to satisfy the *International Shoe* standard. At the core of the holding was the modern recognition that an action nominally against property was an action that was going to determine a person's right to that property.[48]

Relatively few observers found the Court's decision in *Shaffer v. Heitner* to be a cause for concern about access to the courts. Modern long-arm statutes and liberal court decisions upholding jurisdiction over out-of-state defendants reduced the importance of *in rem* actions.[49] By the end of the 1980s, court-watchers had more reason for concern.

In 1976, the Robinsons bought an Audi from a dealer in New York. During their move to Arizona, while in Oklahoma, Kay Robinson and her two children were in the Audi when a drunk driver smashed into the rear of the car. The collision jammed the doors shut and ruptured the gas tank. Unable to exit the vehicle, they were severely burned. The Robinsons sued in state court in Oklahoma against Audi (the manufacturer), Volkswagen of America (the importer), World-Wide Volkswagen (the regional distributor), and Seaway Volkswagen (the dealership).[50]

At issue was whether the Oklahoma state court had personal jurisdiction over World-Wide and Seaway. By the time the case was before the Supreme Court, Audi and Volkswagen of America had conceded personal jurisdiction. Not readily visible to most readers of the case is why Audi and Volkswagen of America sought to get the claims against the two New York defendants, World-Wide and Seaway, dismissed. The Robinsons' lawyers filed their action in state court because juries in the county where the accident occurred were plaintiff friendly. Because the Robinsons had yet to resettle in Arizona, they retained their New York

---

however, the 'location' of the defendant's property within the jurisdiction remains a basis for limited general jurisdiction.").

48. *Shaffer*, 433 U.S. at 207.

49. Vitiello, *Limiting Access to U.S. Courts*, *supra* note 1, at 228.

50. *World-Wide Volkswagen*, 444 U.S. at 288.

state citizenship. If the court dismissed World-Wide and Seaway, the remaining defendants could remove the action to federal district court, where the juries were more defendant friendly. That ended up being a winning strategy.[51]

The state court dismissed the defendants' motion to dismiss on jurisdictional grounds. It and the Oklahoma Supreme Court's decisions reflect the trend described above, expanding the jurisdictional reach of state courts. For example, those courts gave an extremely broad reading to Oklahoma's long-arm statute. Like the Illinois Supreme Court in *Gray*, the Oklahoma Supreme Court read a limited long-arm statute as applicable to the facts before the court. It disagreed with *Gray*'s holding that the tortious act occurred in Oklahoma. But it read expansively a separate provision allowing the assertion of jurisdiction if the defendant committed the tortious act elsewhere but gained substantial revenue from goods used in the forum state. The court found that the defendants could foresee that the cars they sold were mobile and were driven in Oklahoma. Given the retail cost of a vehicle and the fact that the goods sold by the defendants were used in-state, the court upheld the trial court's conclusion that the defendants derived substantial revenue from use in Oklahoma.[52]

The Oklahoma Supreme Court did not address whether the assertion of jurisdiction violated due process.[53] But one can imagine how the court could have analyzed the question. Defendants World-Wide and Seaway had a contact with the forum state (a car they sold was involved in an accident there); the claim arose directly out of that contact; Oklahoma had a significant interest in providing a forum for parties injured on their highways by potentially dangerous vehicles; the plaintiffs had a strong need for that forum; much of the evidence of the accident remained there; and the burden on the defendants in a modern era of transportation was minor by comparison to those other considerations. Indeed, Oklahoma was the center of gravity in this dispute. Although the plaintiffs did not sue the judgment-proof driver who caused the ac-

---

51. *Id.* at 298. For a detailed treatment of the background to this case, see Charles W. Adams, *World-Wide Volkswagen v. Woodson—The Rest of the Story*, 72 NEB. L. REV. 1122 (1993).

52. World-Wide Volkswagen Corp. v. Woodson, 585 P.2d 351, 353–55 (Okla. 1978).

53. *Id.* at 354–55.

cident, had they done so, their argument for an Oklahoma forum would have been even stronger: Oklahoma would have been the only state where the plaintiffs could bring their action against all the defendants in one suit (on the assumption that the other driver was not subject to suit in New York, for example.) Much of this analysis should sound familiar: a lot of it is right out of *McGee.*[54]

In finding that the assertion of jurisdiction violated due process, Justice White implicitly recognized that, were the Court to assess the question in light of the multiple factors relied on in cases like *McGee*, jurisdiction would have been proper. But instead of balancing the various burdens, Justice White found that, as a threshold matter, the defendants' contacts with the forum state were insufficient. There was no evidence that the defendants purposefully availed themselves of the benefits of Oklahoma. The Court relied on *Hanson* for that conclusion—the first significant citation to the case since the Court decided it in 1958.[55]

Justice White attempted to explain why a defendant's purposeful contact with the state, rather than the burden on the defendant, was the touchstone for jurisdiction. As I discussed in connection with *McGee*, there, the Court seemed to hold that a state complied with due process if a defendant had adequate notice and an opportunity to be heard. True, *Pennoyer* had treated state borders as the limits of a state's jurisdictional reach and found that the Due Process Clause somehow protected one state from overreaching by a sister state. But *Pennoyer* was (to quote Miracle Max from Princess Bride) if not all dead, mostly dead. Justice White acknowledged "the shibboleth"[56] that each state is limited by its territorial borders. Nonetheless, the Court, according to Justice White, has "never accepted the proposition that state lines are irrelevant for jurisdictional purposes."[57] In search for a reason why that is so, Justice

54. *World-Wide Volkswagen*, 444 U.S. 286; *McGee*, 355 U.S. 220.

55. *World-Wide Volkswagen*, 444 U.S. at 294–98 (taking its logic from *Hanson*, the Court reasoned that, even if litigation in the forum state would satisfy the *International Shoe* minimum contacts test, "the Due Process Clause, acting as an instrument of interstate federalism, may sometimes act to divest the State of its power to render a valid judgment").

56. *Id.* at 293–94.

57. *Id.* at 293.

White stated that "the Due Process Clause act[s] as an instrument of interstate federalism."[58]

That notion—that the Due Process Clause protects states—was unsustainable for many reasons and was as jarring as Justice Field's discussion of due process in *Pennoyer*. It took Justice White only two years to confess error. In *Insurance Corp. of Ireland v. Compagnie des Bauxites de Guinee*,[59] Justice White admitted his error in relying on federalism as part of due process. There, he explained that the personal jurisdiction requirement "protects an individual liberty interest. It represents a restriction on judicial power not as a matter of sovereignty."[60]

Justice White, however, failed to articulate why state borders matter if *Pennoyer*'s reasoning was "shibboleth" and due process does not serve as "an instrument of interstate federalism."[61] As developed below, the Court has yet to give a credible account to explain why state borders matter. Without some plausible account for why state borders matter, *McGee*'s emphasis on the opportunity to be heard increases its explanatory power even more. The difference between the two approaches is apparent when one considers a hypothetical like one used in civil procedure casebooks. Why should a Yreka, California defendant with no contacts with Oregon be able to avoid suit in a convenient forum a short drive from his home, but not be able to raise a due process argument if the plaintiff sues him instead in San Diego, over 750 miles away?

World-Wide signaled battle lines within the Court. Always favoring expanded jurisdiction, Justice Brennan dissented in *World-Wide*. In *Burger King Corp. v. Rudzewicz*[62] Justice Brennan would concede that, at the very least, the Constitution requires some minimum contacts. His *World-Wide* dissent stated in passing that the defendants had contacts with the forum, but most of his dissent focused on modern commerce and the minimal burden on the defendants. For him, a court had to balance all the various factors identified in *McGee*.[63]

58. *Id.* at 294.

59. Ins. Corp. of Ireland v. Compagnie des Bauxites de Guinee, 456 U.S. 694 (1982).

60. *Id.* at 702.

61. *World-Wide Volkswagen*, 444 U.S. at 293–94.

62. Burger King Corp. v. Rudzewicz, 471 U.S. 462 (1985).

63. *World-Wide Volkswagen*, 444 U.S. at 304, 308–10 (Brennan, J., dissenting).

The Court did not always adhere to the majority's insistence that contacts had to come about through the defendant's activity purposefully directed at the forum, as insisted upon in Justice White's majority opinion in *World-Wide*. For example, in an opinion that at best can be described as opaque, *Calder v. Jones*[64] stated in broad terms that a writer and an editor for the *National Enquirer* were subject to jurisdiction in California because they knew that their conduct would have an effect in the forum state. Other parts of the opinion insisted that the defendants targeted the forum state. Without explanation, the unanimous opinion cited *World-Wide* as support for its discussion of the "effects" felt in the forum state.[65]

World-Wide signaled a narrower view of personal jurisdiction than the view of many lower courts. Even without an explanation for the necessity of contacts with the forum, *World-Wide* was in place. A court could not merely ask whether the assertion of jurisdiction was too burdensome to deprive a defendant of an opportunity to defend; it had to find some threshold of contacts with the forum state. And as discussed above, taking the requirement of purposeful activity directed at the forum as the necessary minimum could significantly limit the jurisdictional reach of state courts.

Not surprisingly, *World-Wide* created uncertainty for lower courts. In a passing reference to *Gray*, Justice White seemingly approved its result. The facts before the Court were distinguishable because the stream of commerce ended in New York when the Robinsons, the ultimate consumers, purchased the vehicle. But applied literally, the Court's test suggested that in a case like *Gray*, a component-parts manufacturer like Titan Valve was not subject to jurisdiction because it did not ship its product to or direct other purposeful activity at the forum state.[66]

---

64. Calder v. Jones, 465 U.S. 783 (1984).

65. *Id.* at 789 ("In sum, California is the focal point both of the story and of the harm suffered. Jurisdiction over petitioners is therefore proper in California based on the 'effects' of their Florida conduct in California.") (citing *World-Wide Volkswagen*, 444 U.S. at 297–98).

66. Asahi Metal Indus. Co. v. Super. Ct. of Cal., 480 U.S. 102, 109–11 (O'Connor, J., concurring) (describing how, after *World-Wide Volkswagen*, lower courts disagreed as to whether a defendant's awareness that the stream of commerce would bring its product into the forum state was sufficient to satisfy the Due Process Clause); *World-Wide Volkswagen*, 444 U.S. at 297–98.

As a result of the division among lower courts, the Court granted certiorari to resolve that issue in *Asahi Metal Industry Co., Ltd. v. Superior Court of California.*[67] There, the plaintiff and his wife were involved in an accident when the tire on his motorcycle deflated. The plaintiff was injured, and his wife died. He sued the Taiwanese company that manufactured the tire. The Taiwanese company filed a third-party complaint against Asahi, thought to be the manufacturer of the valve stem. The original plaintiff settled his case. The jurisdictional issue arose between the original defendant and the third-party defendant.[68]

The Court was unanimous in finding that California could not assert jurisdiction over Asahi. Eight Justices agreed that the assertion of jurisdiction was unreasonable. They focused on the lack of any interest that California had in the litigation, the lack of any special need that the original defendant had in having the dispute resolved in California, and on the significant burden on Asahi in defending the case in California.[69] However, eight Justices believed that the threshold question was the sufficiency of contacts with the forum. Justice Stevens concurred in the result and believed that the case should be resolved by reference only to the reasonableness analysis.[70]

Because the remaining eight Justices were equally divided on the sufficiency of the contacts, Justice Stevens, no doubt pressured by his fellow Justices, addressed the sufficiency of the contacts.[71] Justice O'Connor, writing for four Justices, stated that contacts that come about through operation of the stream of commerce without more are insufficient to satisfy the contacts part of the Court's test.[72] Awareness that the product would end up in the forum was not enough. Here was *Hanson* coming back to roost. Justice Brennan, also writing for four Justices, found the contacts sufficient and would so hold if the product arrived in the forum state through the stream of commerce.[73]

Justice Stevens would have found that the contacts in the case before the Court were sufficient. While more tentative than Justice Brennan, he

---

67. *Asahi*, 480 U.S. at 108 (majority opinion).

68. *Id.* at 105–06.

69. *Id.* at 114–16.

70. *Id.* at 121–22 (Stevens, J., concurring).

71. *Id.* at 122.

72. *Id.* at 112 (O'Connor, J., concurring).

73. *Id.* at 121 (Brennan, J., concurring).

stated that in the case before the Court, the contacts were sufficient in light of the volume, value, and hazard of the product placed in the stream of commerce.[74]

Asahi seemed to resolve little. Although some lower courts relied on Justice O'Connor's opinion,[75] ignoring the fact that her contacts analysis had only four votes, one could hardly state with much confidence what the law was. Five Justices endorsed the view that on the facts of the case before the Court, the contacts would have been sufficient. But line drawing based on Justice Stevens' opinion was speculative at best.

As bad as the Court's division in *Asahi* was, it got worse in the Court's last foray into personal jurisdiction between 1990 and 2010. *Burnham v. Superior Court of California*[76] was, according to all nine Justices, an extremely easy case. Dennis Burnham's family moved to California, leaving him residing in New Jersey. After a three-day visit to California, as he returned one of his children to his wife's home, Burnham was served in hand with a court summons and divorce petition. At issue was the continued vitality of what remained of *Pennoyer*: was in-hand, in-state service of process sufficient to satisfy due process? Speaking for four justices, Justice Scalia said "yes." He did so based on tradition; in fact, his opinion used the term "tradition" or "traditional" thirty-two times.[77] Despite the agreement that the result was easy, Justice Scalia spent considerable time attacking the soundness of Justice Brennan's reasoning in his concurring opinion.[78]

Also writing for four Justices, Justice Brennan, relying upon dicta from *Shaffer*, insisted that all assertions of jurisdiction must satisfy due process. He found that the defendant's contacts were sufficient to make the assertion of jurisdiction reasonable. He left open whether one's con-

---

74. *Id.* at 122 (Stevens, J., concurring).

75. Levi McAllister, Comment, *Paddling the Stream of Commerce: The Supreme Court's Need to Cautiously Re-Examine One Aspect of Personal Jurisdiction, and the Judicial and Financial Consequences Resulting from Current Approaches*, 3 High Ct. Q. Rev. 53, 57–58 (2007) (citing cases from the First, Sixth, and Fourth Circuits utilizing O'Connor's test).

76. Burnham v. Super. Ct. of Cal., 495 U.S. 604 (1990).

77. *Id.*

78. *Id.* at 622–28.

tact with the forum may be too transient to support jurisdiction even if the defendant is served in hand.[79]

Justice Stevens' concurring opinion in *Asahi* offered some limited guidance to lower courts. His brief concurring opinion in *Burnham* offered none at all.[80]

Asahi and *Burnham* demonstrated the deep divisions within the Court. In both cases, the Court squandered the opportunity to offer much guidance to lower courts because of the split among the Justices. Some have speculated with good reason that the Court intentionally did not grant certiorari in another personal jurisdiction case until Justice Stevens retired.[81]

---

79. *Id.* at 628–39 (Brennan, J., concurring).

80. *Id.* at 640 (Stevens, J., concurring). Cases that would force a court to resolve differences between the different opinions in Burnham are unlikely to arise outside of law school classrooms. For example, one can envision a case where a defendant's presence in-state is so transient that Justice Brennan would have found that the assertion of jurisdiction violated due process. Sources like case books cite one over-flight case where a defendant was served when he was flying over the forum-state. Grace v. MacArthur, 170 F. Supp. 442 (E.D. Ark. 1959). Such a case might have forced Justice White to decide whether a defendant not intentionally in the forum state was subject to jurisdiction based only on transient presence. *Burnham*, 495 U.S. at 640 (Stevens, J., concurring). But a look at cases citing *Burnham* suggests that most cases of transient presence raised a different issue; was the defendant voluntarily in the state when he was served? *See, e.g.*, Rutherford v. Rutherford, 193 Ariz. 173 (Ariz. Ct. App. 1998) (finding a father was voluntarily in the state when visiting his son); Santa Escolastica, Inc. v. Pavlovsky, 736 F. Supp. 2d 1077 (E.D. Ky. 2010) (holding that an Argentine citizen was properly served and subject to personal jurisdiction in Kentucky because he was voluntarily in the state on business). Most law school hypotheticals in which a defendant is in state briefly but voluntarily are unrealistic because a plaintiff is highly unlikely to be able to anticipate the defendant's brief stay in state without inducing the defendant to come into the state (and thereby implicating the voluntariness question).

81. Rodger D. Citron, *The Last Common Law Justice: The Personal Jurisdiction Jurisprudence of Justice John Paul Stevens*, 88 U. Det. Mercy L. Rev. 433, 469 (2011) ("[d]espite—or more likely because of—his refusal to provide a fifth vote to any opinion in *Asahi* or *Burnham*, the Supreme Court did not revisit the doctrinal disputes at issue in those cases until after Stevens retired.").

G. General Jurisdiction

The Court also took a begrudging view of general jurisdiction during the 1980s. The plaintiffs in *Helicopteros Nacionales de Colombia, S.A. v. Hall*[82] were the representatives and survivors of four Americans who died in a helicopter crash in Peru. They were employed by a Peruvian alter ego of an American company based in Texas. The employer contracted with Helicopteros, a Colombian corporation, to provide transportation to the Peruvian worksite where the crash occurred. Helicopteros' contacts with Texas, where the plaintiffs sued, were limited but meaningful. The chief executive officer of the company negotiated the contract in Texas. The company accepted payments drawn on a Texas bank. More substantially, it sent personnel to Texas for training and, over a period spanning several years, made substantial purchases of equipment there.[83]

The Court found that the contacts were not continuous and systematic. The defendant did not maintain an office in Texas and did not apply for a license to do business there. In reliance on pre-*International Shoe* precedent, the Court observed that purchases and related trips to the forum do not constitute sufficient contacts with the forum.[84]

The opinion provided little guidance about where the line existed between the kinds of contacts in *Perkins v. Benguet Consol. Mining Co.*,[85] where the Court upheld jurisdiction, and those in *Helicopteros*, where it did not. But the Court did not limit general jurisdiction only to a corporation's principal place of business or state of incorporation. It denied jurisdiction on facts where many lower courts would have granted jurisdiction. Undoubtedly, many lower courts would have been influenced by the plaintiffs' need for a Texas forum because it was the only plausible venue within the United States. The alternative was to file the action in a foreign country, which almost certainly would provide less

---

82. Helicopteros Nacionales de Colombia, S.A. v. Hall, 466 U.S. 408 (1984).

83. *Id.* at 410–11.

84. *Id.* at 417 ("The Court's opinion in *Rosenberg Bros. & Co. v. Curtis Brown Co.*, 260 U.S. 516 (1923) . . . makes clear that purchases and related trips, standing alone, are not a sufficient basis for a State's assertion of jurisdiction.").

85. Perkins v. Benguet Consol. Mining Co., 342 U.S. 437 (1952).

favorable law and where factfinders might not have been sympathetic to foreign nationals.[86]

One problem with the Court's general jurisdiction case law was the lack of an explanation of the underlying theory that explained why general jurisdiction was appropriate. As in *Perkins*, the Court was silent on the underlying theory justifying general jurisdiction. The Court might have explained *Perkins* as a case of jurisdiction by necessity; if suit were not proper in Ohio, the plaintiff would have had no practical venue in which to bring suit. But in neither *Perkins* nor *Helicopteros* did the Court attempt to explain *Perkins* on such a narrow ground. As such, general jurisdiction would be a limited safety valve for plaintiffs. Although the Court has had opportunities to limit *Perkins* to its facts, it has never done so. In addition, the Court did not discuss the relative convenience or burdens faced by the parties. In both cases, the Court focused on the continuous and systematic nature of the defendants' contacts with the forum; in *Perkins* they were substantial, in *Helicopteros* they were not. Left open was whether contacts alone—or contacts plus the additional fairness factors that developed in specific jurisdiction cases—applied to general jurisdiction analysis.[87]

Scholars have debated various rationales for general jurisdiction. But even among scholars, no theory has emerged as a coherent explanation. For example, Professor Mary Twitchell identified the origins of general jurisdiction in history when jurisdiction was based on sovereign power, consent, or allegiance. At that time, courts did not consider the relationship of the suit to the defendant's conduct in the forum. Thus, in the pre-*International Shoe* era, general jurisdiction may have been an important doctrine to ensure a plaintiff a forum against a corporation in a jurisdiction other than its state of incorporation. But with the expansion

---

86. Louise Weinberg, *The Helicopter Case and the Jurisprudence of Jurisdiction*, 58 S. Cal. L. Rev. 913, 916 (1985) ("[a]mong the facts that should have had bearing was that the alternative forum for the *Helicopteros* plaintiffs would not have been some other state. Helicol was amenable to suit in no state if not in Texas; the alternative would have been a foreign country.").

87. Daimler AG v. Bauman, 134 S. Ct. 746, 764–65 (2014) (Sotomayor, J., concurring) ("[a]ll of the cases in which we have applied the reasonableness prong have involved specific as opposed to general jurisdiction. Whether the reasonableness prong should apply in the general jurisdiction context is therefore a question we have never decided, and it is one on which I can appreciate the arguments on both sides."); *Helicopteros*, 466 U.S. at 408, 418–19; Perkins v. Benguet Consol. Mining Co., 342 U.S. 437, 437, 447 (1952).

of specific jurisdiction in the modern era, according to Professor Twitchell, the need for general jurisdiction diminished. She argued that it should be reserved for "its most essential function: providing one forum where a defendant may always be sued."[88] Twitchell argued in favor of retention of general jurisdiction even with the modern expansion of specific jurisdiction. But she urged a much narrower view of its availability, basically to where the defendant has its principal place of business or state of incorporation. Her test would provide predictability.[89]

Professor Lea Brilmayer identified four justifications for general jurisdiction. The first was convenience for the defendant. The rationale parallels the Court's holding that a natural person's state of residence is a proper forum. A second justification is convenience for the plaintiff. Third, on the basis of power, a state must be able to "compel the appearance of defendants"[90] to adjudicate the rights of a party. This essentially equates to the state border concept of *Pennoyer*. Critical of the first three justifications, Professor Brilmayer found the "most satisfactory basis"[91] for general jurisdiction to be the quid pro quo theory between a state and its domiciliaries. Having sufficient contacts with the forum state gives the defendant a stake in the political process. "The basic inquiry must be whether the defendant's level of activity rises to the level of activity of an insider, so that relegating the defendant to the political processes is fair."[92] Although she wrote about general jurisdiction long before recent Court cases extending the right of corporations to give political contributions, her theory would seemingly have increased relevance today. That would be so even though a corporation cannot vote. In addition to a corporation's power to influence politics through monetary contributions, the numerous employees living in the forum state vote and, presumably, represent the interests of their employer.[93]

---

88. Mary Twitchell, *The Myth of General Jurisdiction*, 101 Harv. L. Rev. 610, 667 (1988).

89. *Id.* at 668–71.

90. Lea Brilmayer et al., *A General Look at General Jurisdiction*, 66 Tex. L. Rev. 721, 730 (1988).

91. *Id.* at 733.

92. *Id.* at 742.

93. Citizens United v. Fed. Election Comm'n, 558 U.S. 310 (2010); McCutcheon v. Fed. Election Comm'n, 572 U.S. 185 (2014); *see* Brendan Fischer, *On NFIB Conference Call, Romney Urges Employers to Tell Employees How to Vote, Just Like the Kochs*, Common Dreams (Oct. 18, 2012) (Presidential candidate Mitt Romney encouraged business

Professor Brilmayer's approach would be more consonant with more liberal theories of general jurisdiction. For example, the presence of many Walmart stores in a state would provide Wal-Mart Stores, Inc. with political clout and should therefore justify the assertion of jurisdiction even in cases unrelated to the forum contacts.[94] Limiting general jurisdiction to the state of incorporation and principal place of business creates greater certainty but ignores the fact that a corporation may gain extraordinary benefits from the forum state even if that is not its principal place of business.[95]

Many lower courts adopted broad interpretations of general jurisdiction. They often did so to provide the plaintiff, often a state resident, with a convenient place to sue. Some courts, for example, held that general jurisdiction was proper only upon a showing of systematic and continuous contacts with the forum, allowing suit, for example, against large corporations in almost any state in the United States. That view often allowed creative forum-shopping to ensure favorable law applies to the plaintiff's suit. While courts may be influenced by their views of forum-shopping in how broadly they read general jurisdiction precedent, little in the theoretical underpinnings of general jurisdiction explained why a

---

owners to tell their employees how to vote: "I hope you make it very clear to your employees what you believe is in the best interest of your enterprise and therefore their job and their future in the upcoming elections. And . . . whatever your political view, I hope—I hope you pass those along to your employees. Nothing illegal about you talking to your employees about what you believe is best for the business, because I think that will figure into their election decision, their voting decision and of course doing that with your family and your kids as well.").

94. In the 2013 fiscal year, Walmart U.S. net sales reached $274.5 billion. *Walmart 2013 Annual Report* 5, https://s201.q4cdn.com/262069030/files/doc_financials/2013/ar/2013-annual-report-for-walmart-stores-inc_130221024708579502.pdf (last visited Jan. 9, 2025). Wal-Mart Stores, Inc. operated 4005 Walmart stores in the United States in fiscal 2013, with 217 of those stores in California. *Id.* at 59. The estimated average net sales per store was $70 million and the net sales in California alone is estimated at $15,190,000. *Id.* at 5, 59.

95. Roy L. Brooks, *The Essential Purpose and Analytical Structure of Personal Jurisdiction Law*, 27 IND. L. REV. 361, 375 (1993). For a more liberal application of the doctrine, see Lea Brilmayer, *Related Contacts and Personal Jurisdiction*, 101 HARV. L. REV. 1444 (1988) (positing that general jurisdiction exists for companies and corporations that have a large presence in a state); Brilmayer et al., *supra* note 90, at 742 (indicating that the systematic activity of a defendant within a forum, "such as domicile, incorporation, or doing business, suggests that the person or corporate entity is enough of an 'insider' that it may safely be relegated to the State's political process.").

plaintiff's successful forum-shopping is relevant to the breadth of general jurisdiction.[96]

H. Summary of the 1980s

The 1980s did more than demonstrate deep divisions within the Court. In some instances, like *Calder v. Jones*, the Court upheld jurisdiction.[97] But some troubling themes emerged.

Despite upholding jurisdiction in *Burnham*, the conservatives on the Court demonstrated a desire to limit jurisdiction in other cases. The notion that jurisdiction turned on convenience was at risk. Instead, in reliance on *Hanson*, the conservative wing of the Court was trying to develop a narrow theory of jurisdiction.[98]

Entering the 1980s, one could have argued that *McGee*'s due process analysis was the dominant theme. At that time, procedural due process meant that a defendant could be haled into court as long as the forum provided the defendant with adequate notice and an opportunity to be heard. Consistent with *McGee*, a court needed to determine the extent of the burden on the defendant in light of other competing needs, including those of the plaintiff. The ease of travel and communications made state borders less important in a modern society. As argued above, that is a coherent theory of the relevance of due process to the jurisdictional analysis.

But *Pennoyer*'s questionable theory of federalism still lurked in the Supreme Court at the end of the 1980s. That is, state borders still mattered—even though the Court failed to offer a compelling explanation for why that was so. Further, *Hanson*'s flawed analysis was now front and center. A result-oriented decision, motivated by an understandable desire to avoid a gross injustice, now reemerged as important precedent.

96. Charles W. "Rocky" Rhodes, *Clarifying General Jurisdiction*, 34 Seton Hall L. Rev. 807, 830–55 (2004) (detailing some of the many approaches lower courts have taken to general jurisdiction including the Ipse Dixit approach, precedential comparisons, factor analysis, central business activities, and quid pro quo).

97. Calder v. Jones, 465 U.S. 783 (1984).

98. *World-Wide Volkswagen*, 444 U.S. at 292–94 (finding that the minimum contacts test of the due process analysis was related to interstate federalism); *see* Vitiello, *Limiting Access to U.S. Courts*, *supra* note 1, at 214–15.

Lost in its reemergence were the facts that it was not only result-oriented but was also decided by a slim majority. Further, the Court now cited its approach to the contacts part of the due process test as a threshold question to the assessment of reasonableness, even though *Hanson* did not engage in such a two-step analysis. The Court ignored ways in which *Hanson* could have been narrowed.[99]

Although it occurred in the 1970s and not the 1980s, the Court's new *in rem* jurisprudence—conflating *in rem* and *in personam* due process analysis—would have unexpected ramifications in the future. At the time, *Helicopteros*' implications may not have been obvious. On its face, the decision indicated that purchases, even if substantial, did not amount to continuous and systematic contacts that could justify an assertion of general jurisdiction. But as Professors Judy Cornett and Michael Hoffheimer have argued, narrowing *in rem* jurisdiction made more important the use of general jurisdiction. Thus, prior to *Shaffer*, plaintiffs could have commenced suit by attaching property even if it had no relationship to the underlying dispute. After *Shaffer*, plaintiffs gained little by attaching property—without satisfying *International Shoe*, the assertion of *in rem* jurisdiction violated due process. In such cases, plaintiffs might need to rely on general jurisdiction; but retrenchment in general jurisdiction meant that those plaintiffs would no longer be able to file suit in a plaintiff-friendly venue. As Cornett and Hoffheimer have pointed out, as *Shaffer*'s author, Justice Marshall would no doubt be surprised at the effect of the Court's decision. But the full effects of *Shaffer* are coming into focus only now.[100] That is part of the rest of the story.

---

99. *World-Wide Volkswagen*, 444 U.S. 286 (1980) (apparently endorsing a broad reading of *Hanson*, the court omitted discussion of any flaws in *Hanson* or of limiting its application to its facts); *see* Vitiello, *Limiting Access to U.S. Courts*, *supra* note 1, at 219–22, 231.

100. Judy M. Cornett & Michael H. Hoffheimer, *Good-Bye Significant Contacts: General Personal Jurisdiction After* Daimler AG v. Bauman, 76 Ohio St. L.J. 101 (2015).

I. The Modern Era

The world changed dramatically between 1990 and 2010. International trade agreements and the development of the Internet increased cross-border transactions within and without the United States. Cases like *Calder* demonstrated hard issues that could arise when a defendant caused harm in-state but did not purposefully do any act within the forum. Imagine the greater complexity when the defendant published information on the Internet from a remote part of the world. Also imagine the uncertainty that *Asahi* caused for lower courts that had before them suits brought by their citizens, injured by products manufactured abroad from parts manufactured far-and-wide. How would the Court's unsettled case law apply to these myriad situations?

Many courts have addressed, with differing results, the way in which contacts analysis works in Internet cases. Lower courts faced cases where defendants caused harm by circulating false information over the Internet, engaging in deceptive business practices, or violating the intellectual property rights of in-state citizens from remote locations. In response, many courts extended their state's jurisdictional reach. Often, they ignored decisions like *World-Wide* and *Hanson* that required a demonstration of purposeful activity directed at the forum. Instead, they relied on *Calder*, which required knowledge that the harm would take place in the forum.[101]

After *Asahi*, courts continued to struggle with the analysis when a product was swept into the forum via the stream of commerce. But many courts relied on the stream of commerce theory to extend jurisdiction. They did so by applying some mix of Justice Brennan's liberal test and Justice Stevens' narrower test in *Asahi*, or by relying on dicta from *World-Wide* in which Justice White cited *Gray* with approval.[102] Again, that seemed consonant with the two themes developed above: modern com-

101. *See* Patrick J. Borchers, *J. McIntyre Machinery, Goodyear, and the Incoherence of the Minimum Contacts Test*, 44 Creighton L. Rev. 1245 (2011). Professor Borchers describes how "lower courts have wrestled with specific jurisdiction based on Internet contacts for several years now and have divided sharply. . . ." *Id.* at 1267.

102. *Nicastro*, 564 U.S. at 874 ("[t]he rules and standards for determining state jurisdiction over an absent party have been unclear because of decades-old questions left open in *Asahi*."); *World-Wide Volkswagen*, 444 U.S. at 297–98 (citing *Gray*, Justice White explained that "[t]he forum State does not exceed its powers under the Due Process Clause if it asserts personal jurisdiction over a corporation that delivers its products into the

merce has increased instances in which out-of-state companies may create in-state harm, and a court can uphold jurisdiction as long as the defendant has a reasonable opportunity to be heard. That is, due process is not offended if the burden on the defendant is not overwhelming.

General jurisdiction remained an available option as well, and many courts took a liberal view of it. For example, the Ninth Circuit found that jurisdiction over L.L. Bean was proper, despite the absence of any of the company's physical assets in the forum state.[103] Again, while not all courts joined the trend, many continued to extend their jurisdictional reach.[104] But as with the trend towards liberalization culminating in the 1970s, the Court seems to be in the process of a second retrenchment.

With Justice Stevens' retirement, the Court granted certiorari in several personal jurisdiction cases. Until 2021, the Court found in favor of defendants in every one of those cases. Finally, in 2021 and again in 2023, the Court upheld the assertion of personal jurisdiction over corporate defendants. The next section explores the lead cases decided between 2010 and 2017. A subsequent section explores the two most recent cases, including whether they presage a more liberal view towards upholding plaintiff's choice of convenient forums.

(1) The Court Narrows General Jurisdiction

Prior to 2010, lower courts divided on how to interpret the Court's general jurisdiction case law. Some lower courts interpreted the doctrine broadly, requiring only continuous and systematic contacts with the forum state even when the claim was unrelated to any forum contact. Others went further and, in addition to focusing on the contacts, also assessed the Court's fairness factors. Some courts construed the test more narrowly, upholding general jurisdiction only in a state where the corporation was incorporated or had its principal place of business. The first two tests offered injured plaintiffs significant forum-shopping op-

---

stream of commerce with the expectation that they will be purchased by consumers in the forum State.").

103. Gator.Com Corp. v. L.L. Bean, Inc., 341 F.3d 1072 (9th Cir. 2003), *vacated en banc*, 366 F.3d 789 (9th Cir. 2004).

104. *See* Richard D. Freer & Wendy C. Perdue, Civil Procedure: Cases, Materials, and Questions 102 (6th ed. 2012) (discussing cases in which courts exercised general jurisdiction based on limited contacts with the forum state).

tions when the defendants were wide-flung national or international corporations. The Court was about to cut back dramatically on plaintiffs' ability to sue defendants based on a general jurisdiction theory.

In one of the Court's first grants of certiorari after Justice Stevens' retirement, the Court signaled that general jurisdiction would be curtailed. In *Goodyear Dunlop Tires Operations, S.A. v. Brown*, the Court considered a case arising in North Carolina.[105] There, the parents of two boys who died in a bus accident near Paris sued Goodyear USA and three foreign subsidiaries in state court in North Carolina. Goodyear USA, which had plants in North Carolina, did not contest the court's jurisdiction, but the three foreign companies did.[106]

A unanimous Supreme Court reversed the North Carolina appellate court's determination that jurisdiction was proper based on a stream of commerce theory. Most importantly for the discussion here was the Court's discussion of general jurisdiction.

Writing for the unanimous Court, Justice Ginsburg recognized that the Court had seldom addressed general jurisdiction, suggesting that its parameters would be uncertain. After discussing the defendants' contacts with the forum and comparing them to the Court's holdings in *Perkins* and in *Helicopteros*, she found that, as in *Helicopteros*, the contacts were not continuous and systematic.[107]

In dicta that signaled how the Court would rule in the near future, Justice Ginsburg went further. She quoted Professor Brilmayer's view that general jurisdiction over a corporation is akin to finding domicile for an individual, a place where the corporation is "fairly regarded as at home."[108] In a parenthetical, she indicated that the "paradigm" where a corporation would be at home is in the state of incorporation or where it has its principal place of business. She concluded that the foreign subsidiaries "are in no sense at home in North Carolina."[109]

The insertion of "at home" into the opinion divided commentators. Some saw the opinion as limiting general jurisdiction to those two venues. Others pointed out that, had the Court intended to limit general

105. Goodyear Dunlop Tires Operations, S.A. v. Brown, 564 U.S. 915 (2011).

106. *Id.* at 918.

107. *Id.* at 920.

108. *Id.* at 924.

109. *Id.* at 929.

jurisdiction in that manner, it could have stated such a rule unequivocally. Those two venues were "paradigms," not exclusive places where general jurisdiction would be permitted.[110]

Justice Ginsburg made no effort to explain the theoretical underpinnings of general jurisdiction. Her analogy to domicile is intriguing, but not particularly helpful. *Pennoyer* recognized domicile as a basis of the assertion of jurisdiction. At that time, the explanation would have been that a person within the state's borders is within the court's exclusive jurisdiction, just as was property. Once the Court moved away from formalism, it explained that a person's domicile is an appropriate place for suit against the defendant because he or she derives benefits from residing in the state. In *Burnham*, when the Court returned to the rule that a non-resident is subject to jurisdiction in a state when the defendant was served in-hand, in-state, Justice Scalia relied on tradition as a sufficient justification for adherence to the rule. Even Justice Brennan's concurring opinion indicated that, in an expanded *International Shoe* analysis, the historic rule upholding in-hand service put a defendant on notice that he was subject to a court's jurisdiction.[111]

As a matter of tradition, state of incorporation was a proper place to sue a corporation by analogy to domicile. The Court needed some place where suit was proper and the state of incorporation was a fixed place, like one's domicile. Later, when the Court shifted its focus to its benefits-burden analysis, one could argue that a corporation willingly affiliates with a state in which it chooses to incorporate. Its board of directors makes a conscious choice, certainly with an eye towards tax and liability issues.[112]

"Principal place of business" has a shorter history. In some pre-*International Shoe* cases, courts found personal jurisdiction proper in states where the corporation had its principal place of business. But the

---

110. *Id.* at 924; *Daimler*, 134 S. Ct. at 760; Michael H. Hoffheimer, *General Personal Jurisdiction After Goodyear Dunlop Tires Operations, S.A. v. Brown*, 60 U. Kan. L. Rev. 549, 551–52, 590–92 (2012).

111. *Burnham*, 495 U.S. at 619, 636; *Pennoyer*, 95 U.S. at 722–23 (1878); Hoffheimer, *supra* note 110, at 551.

112. *Pennoyer*, 95 U.S. at 735–36; *see* Cornett & Hoffheimer, *supra* note 100, at 153.

case law did not equate general jurisdiction with the principal place of business.[113]

As indicated, an individual is subject to suit wherever she is domiciled because she has accepted benefits and protections of the law of that state. She cannot complain that the suit did not arise out of any conduct in the forum. By analogy, a corporation that does a substantial amount of business in a particular state is certainly accepting benefits and protections of the state where a suit might be filed. Further, given a host of decisions supporting jurisdiction based only on contacts, a corporation cannot claim surprise when it is haled into court for activity unrelated to forum conduct.[114]

Many lower courts did not notice a change in the rules governing general jurisdiction if the Court intended to make such a change. As two scholars found, courts were back to business as usual after *Goodyear*. The reasons may be obvious; many courts favor a long jurisdictional reach to protect injured plaintiffs. But the Court was about to narrow general jurisdiction further.[115]

The Court was about to resolve the uncertainty that lower courts had about general jurisdiction. In 2004, twenty-three citizens of South American countries sued Daimler AG in a federal district court in California. The complaint alleged that Daimler collaborated with the military dictatorship in Argentina between 1976 and 1983 during the "Dirty War." Specifically, the complaint alleged that the defendant was responsible for killing, torturing, and kidnapping the plaintiffs and members of their families.[116]

The defendant filed a motion to dismiss for lack of personal jurisdiction. The plaintiffs argued that the defendant's contacts with California were sufficient because of its subsidiary's extensive contacts with the state. The subsidiary, Mercedes-Benz USA (MBUSA), is incorporated in Delaware with its principal place of business in New Jersey. MBUSA

---

113. *Int'l Shoe Co.*, 320 U.S. at 317–319 (citing Hutchinson v. Chase & Gilbert, 45 F.2d 139, 141 (2d Cir. 1930)).

114. *Id.* at 319; *see* Brilmayer et al., *supra* note 90, at 732, 741; Rhodes, *supra* note 96.

115. Camilla Cohen, Comment, *Goodyear Dunlop's Failed Attempt to Refine the Scope of General Jurisdiction*, 65 FLA. L. REV. 1405, 1414–15 (2013); Cornett & Hoffheimer, *supra* note 100, at 104 n.12.

116. *Daimler*, 134 S. Ct. at 750–51.

distributes the defendant's vehicles to independent dealerships throughout the United States.[117]

The district court granted the defendant's motion to dismiss for lack of personal jurisdiction. After initially affirming the district court, the Ninth Circuit reconsidered its decision and reversed. It concluded that MBUSA was the defendant's agent and attributed its forum contacts to the defendant. The Ninth Circuit did not address *Goodyear*.[118]

The Supreme Court reversed. The Court had at its disposal narrow approaches that it could have used to decide the case before it. Apart from forum non-conveniens analysis, the Court could have found simply that MBUSA's contacts were not attributable to the defendant and that the remaining contacts were insufficient. The Court could also have concluded that, even if the contacts were continuous and systematic, the assertion of jurisdiction was otherwise unreasonable. Instead, the Court went further.[119]

Justice Ginsburg made several observations, suggesting other possible arguments that may surface in the future. For example, she noted that the defendant "failed to object to plaintiffs' assertion that the California courts could exercise all-purpose jurisdiction over MBUSA."[120] She also found that the Court did not have to decide on the standard to be used when a plaintiff seeks to impute contacts of a subsidiary to its parent corporation. Thus, the Court did not reach the defendant's argument that the subsidiary's contacts were to be imputed to the parent company "only when the former is so dominated by the latter as to be its alter ego."[121] Instead, the Court rejected the Ninth Circuit's view because "[t]he Ninth Circuit's agency finding rested primarily on its observation that MBUSA's services were 'important' to [the defendant], as gauged by

---

117. *Id.* at 751–52.

118. *Id.* at 752–53, 758–59.

119. *Id.* at 763; *see id.* at 764 (Sotomayor, J., dissenting) ("[t]he Court can and should decide this case on the far simpler ground that, no matter how extensive Daimler's contacts with California, that State's exercise of jurisdiction would be unreasonable given that the case involves foreign plaintiffs suing a foreign defendant based on foreign conduct. . . .").

120. *Id.* at 758 (majority opinion).

121. *Id.* at 759.

[the defendant's] hypothetical readiness to perform those services itself if MBUSA did not exist."[122] That proved too much.

The Court assumed that MBUSA was "at home" in California and that its contacts were "imputable to Daimler."[123] Even on the assumption that MBUSA's contacts were imputable to the defendant, "Daimler's slim contacts with the State hardly render it at home [in California]."[124] The analysis focused on *Goodyear*'s discussion of general jurisdiction.

While "*Goodyear* did not hold that a corporation may be subject to general jurisdiction *only* in a forum where it is incorporated or has its principal place of business,"[125] Justice Ginsburg found that the plaintiffs' alternative reading of general jurisdiction swept too broadly. According to her, the plaintiffs' position would make a corporation subject to jurisdiction "in every State in which [it] 'engages in a substantial, continuous, and systematic course of business.'"[126] Such a formulation—despite the view of many lower courts to the contrary—"is unacceptably grasping."[127]

Justice Ginsburg then discussed an issue only hinted at in *Goodyear*. Recognizing that a corporation could have such extensive contacts with the forum to make it "at home" even if that state were not its state of incorporation or principal place of business, Justice Ginsburg found that was not plausible with regard to the defendant. That was so because even if a corporation had substantial connections with the forum, "the same global reach would presumably be available in every other State in which MBUSA's sales are sizeable."[128] The explanation of that statement was placed in a footnote where she dropped a bombshell: the general jurisdiction inquiry does not "focu[s] solely on the magnitude of the defendant's in-state contacts."[129] Instead, a court must appraise a corporation's activities in their entirety. Even if a corporation conducts billions of dol-

---

122. *Id.* at 759–60 ("[t]he Ninth Circuit's agency theory thus appears to subject foreign corporations to general jurisdiction whenever they have an in-state subsidiary or affiliate, an outcome that would sweep even beyond the 'sprawling view of general jurisdiction' we rejected in *Goodyear*.").

123. *Id.* at 760.

124. *Id.*

125. *Id.* at 760–61 (emphasis in original).

126. *Id.*

127. *Id.* at 761.

128. *Id.*

129. *Id.* at 762 n.20. Commentators have criticized Justice Ginsburg's opinion for being too zealous in protecting corporations from the "perceived evils of forum shop-

lars' worth of business in the forum, that does not necessarily render the corporation "at home" in that state.

Justice Ginsburg, citing comity as a partial justification for the Court's holding, wrote, "[o]ther nations do not share the uninhibited approach to personal jurisdiction advanced by the Court of Appeals in this case."[130] The Court observed that in the European Union, a corporate defendant generally may be sued only where it is domiciled—unless the claim arises out of the corporation's conduct in another location. The clear suggestion in *Daimler* is that the Court is bringing U.S. law into conformity with the prevailing European view.[131]

But Justice Ginsburg's suggestion that *Daimler* was bringing United States law in line with European law tells only part of the story. Regulations promulgated under the European Union Convention on Jurisdiction and the Enforcement of Judgments in Civil and Commercial Matters[132] provide that an EU member state may normally exercise general jurisdiction over a European corporation only in a forum in which the corporation is domiciled. Thus, one might argue that Justice Ginsburg is recognizing "best practices" within the EU. But the convention and regulations do not govern when a plaintiff seeks to assert jurisdiction over a corporation that is domiciled outside of Europe.[133]

Some European countries take a narrow view when a plaintiff seeks to assert jurisdiction over a non-European corporation on a claim that does not arise out of forum contacts. But other member states take a much more expansive approach. For example, German law allows the

---

ping," to the detriment of injured individuals who will now have more difficulty bringing lawsuits. *See, e.g.*, Cornett & Hoffheimer, *supra* note 100, at 107.

130. *Daimler*, 134 S. Ct. at 763.

131. *Id.*

132. Convention on Jurisdiction and the Enforcement of Judgments in Civil and Commercial Matters, Sept. 27, 1968, 1972 O.J. (L 299) 32. This Convention, also known as the Brussels Convention, was largely superseded in 2001 by the Brussels Regulation with few changes. Council Regulation 44/2001, 2001 O.J. (L 12) 1 (EC) [hereinafter Brussels I].

133. Even if following the Brussels I regulation on general jurisdiction adheres to EU best practices, the Court may be putting plaintiffs suing in the United States at a disadvantage because the Supreme Court, or at least a substantial wing of the Court, is not committed to following the EU's liberal approach to specific jurisdiction. *See also* Brussels I, art. 5(3) (permitting a defendant to be sued "where the harmful event occurred or may occur," regardless of domicile); Cornett & Hoffheimer, *supra* note 100 (predicting that the Court will continue to reject any attempts by plaintiffs to expand specific jurisdiction).

exercise of jurisdiction over a defendant who owns property in Germany even if the property is unrelated to the claim.[134]

France, Greece, Luxembourg, and the Netherlands have adopted jurisdictional rules that allow their citizens to sue any non-European defendant without regard to the defendant's contacts with the forum. Obviously, plaintiffs securing judgments in such cases experience difficulty when seeking enforcement outside the forum nation. But as long as the defendant has assets in the forum, plaintiffs can enforce their judgments.[135]

In light of the different approaches to jurisdiction among European and other trading partners, the Court's adoption of a restrictive interpretation of the Due Process Clause does not seem to be the most efficacious approach to international comity. Surely, comity would be advanced by an international compact regulating enforcement of judgments.

(2) General Implications for General Jurisdiction

The Court's new general jurisdiction rules are significant both for foreign corporations seeking to avoid suit in the United States and for domestic corporations. This section first reviews the lessons for corporate counsel advising foreign corporations. It then turns to implications for domestic corporations.

(A) SUING FOREIGN CORPORATIONS

No one likes to be sued. But foreigners may like it even less than American citizens. Our system is alien to them in many ways. The United States is unique in allowing lawyers to make contingency fee arrangements with clients. Substantive law is often far more plaintiff-friendly than is foreign law, including the availability of punitive damages. Federal discovery rules are a shock to foreign litigants. Most notably, litigants in federal court have a right to damning information from

---

134. *See* Thomas O. Main, Global Issues in Civil Procedure, 83 (Franklin A. Gevurtz, ed., 2006); Freer & Perdue, *supra* note 104, at 137.

135. Main, *supra* note 134, at 85; Freer & Perdue, *supra* note 104, at 137; 3 Linda Silberman, Laws of International Trade § 97:6, Procedure for Enforcement of a Foreign Judgment.

their opponents. Other systems that allow discovery limit it to information that the party from whom discovery is sought will use to make that party's case.[136]

A debate about whether those unique features of the United States system are good is beyond the scope of this chapter. But proponents—and I am one who supports those rules—argue that these unique aspects of our system advance justice. They allow access to courts and help produce fair results. And liberal access to court is part of the rule of law. Elaborate personal rights are meaningless if a litigant cannot find a convenient court in which to pursue their enforcement.[137]

The Court's new personal jurisdiction analysis impairs access to court in meaningful ways. That is clearly the case with regard to foreign corporations. Think back to *World-Wide Volkswagen*. There, the plaintiffs sued Audi and other defendants in Oklahoma state court. By the time the case went to the Supreme Court, Audi did not challenge the court's jurisdiction in Oklahoma. Under most lower courts' interpretations of general jurisdiction, Audi's contacts with the forum were so substantial that challenging jurisdiction made little sense. That was so even if a court looked to the fairness factors to determine whether the assertion of jurisdiction was reasonable.[138] As discussed above, many of those factors weighed into the plaintiffs' choice of Oklahoma as a convenient forum.

Goodyear and *Daimler* leave little room for an American injured by a foreign corporation to sue that corporation in the United States based on an accident occurring abroad. Unlike the plaintiffs in *Daimler*, the plaintiffs in *Goodyear* were United States citizens. But for the fact that Goodyear USA, the parent corporation, was subject to suit somewhere in the United States, the plaintiffs' only recourse would have been to sue abroad in France, Luxembourg, or Turkey. Few foreign corporations, if any, are likely to satisfy Justice Ginsburg's "at home" test in any state within the United States. Even if they conduct a massive amount of business in a particular state, that alone is not enough. Her test focuses not only on the amount of business in state, but it also requires that the

136. *See, e.g.*, Weinberg, *supra* note 86, 933–34 (listing some of the difficulties the American plaintiffs would have faced if litigating the dispute in Colombia or Peru).

137. Vitiello, *Limiting Access to U.S. Courts*, *supra* note 1.

138. *World-Wide Volkswagen*, 444 U.S. at 292; Vitiello, *Limiting Access to U.S. Courts*, *supra* note 1, at 272–73; *see also* Adams, *supra* note 51, at 1133.

amount of business in that state predominates; systematic and continuous contacts are not sufficient. That standard is a major departure from precedent and far more rigorous than the previous standard. Predicting how the test applies may be difficult, but the test seems to require a showing of more than substantial contacts with the forum; "[g]eneral jurisdiction . . . calls for an appraisal of a corporation's activities in their entirety, nationwide and worldwide. A corporation that operates in many places can scarcely be deemed at home in all of them."[139]

Surprisingly, only Justice Sotomayor recognized the significant change in the law that the Court made in the *Daimler* decision. Instead of focusing on in-state contacts, the Court also now requires an inquiry into contacts elsewhere. As she quipped, some corporations are "too big for general jurisdiction."[140]

One can debate whether United States courts should hear a case like the one involved in *Daimler*. Certainly, opening our courts to resolve conflicts with little connection to the United States raises serious questions. What interest does a state have in providing a courtroom for a dispute with little connection to that state? Why are litigants who have little to do with the United States seeking access to our courts? Other questions abound.[141]

Cases like *Daimler*, however, could easily be resolved based on other doctrines, notably forum non-conveniens.[142] That doctrine has the advantage of greater flexibility than the Court's new general jurisdiction rules. An American plaintiff might be able to prevail in opposition to a motion to dismiss on forum non-conveniens grounds where she will lose on a motion to dismiss for lack of personal jurisdiction, given the Court's restrictive rules. That is unfortunate. Although foreign companies with liberal access to markets in the United States secure significant benefits, injured American plaintiffs may not have meaningful access to justice. As discussed in more detail below, a plaintiff like Nicastro, whose injury resulted from use of a foreign manufacturer's product, did not sue the defendant abroad after he lost in the Supreme Court. Suit abroad

---

139. *Daimler*, 134 S. Ct. at 762 n.20.

140. *Id.* at 764 (Sotomayor, J., concurring).

141. *See id.* at 762–63 (majority opinion); *see also* Vitiello, *Limiting Access to U.S. Courts*, *supra* note 1, at 257.

142. Cornett & Hoffheimer, *supra* note 100, at 160.

posed too many costs for an injured plaintiff to bear and offered limited chances of significant recovery that would have been available under domestic law.

Goodyear and *Daimler* invite numerous questions. Why would the Court narrow general jurisdiction so significantly when doing so potentially impairs the rights of United States citizens? What values underlie the decision? But before turning to those questions, I turn to a different inquiry. How broad are those decisions? More specifically, what are their implications for assertions of general jurisdiction over domestic corporations? That is the topic in the next subsection.

(B) SUING DOMESTIC CORPORATIONS

Not only are the implications of the new general jurisdiction cases significant for a plaintiff seeking to sue a foreign corporation in the United States; the implications may be significant even for a plaintiff suing a domestic corporation and seeking a convenient forum in the United States.

When demonstrating to my students why procedure matters, I borrow the facts from a case involving one of the federal transfer of venue statutes, 28 U.S.C. § 1404. But the case demonstrates dramatically the importance of forum selection. In *Ferens v. John Deere*, Ferens, a farmer in Pennsylvania, injured his hand when he was working on a John Deere combine. He did not consult a lawyer until his tort claim was time barred. After his lawyer filed a breach of warranty claim in federal court in Pennsylvania, counsel also filed a tort action in federal court in Mississippi. Because the Supreme Court requires federal courts to apply the choice of law rules of the state where the federal court sits in diversity actions, the district court applied Mississippi's choice of law, which in turn required application of Mississippi's longer statute of limitations. Not only was the tort claim now revived, but the plaintiff then made a motion to transfer the case to the federal court in Pennsylvania. The court did so. Back in Pennsylvania, the federal court was required to apply Mississippi's choice of law because the action was properly filed in Mississippi. As a result, the tort claim was not time-barred in Pennsylvania.[143]

143. Ferens v. John Deere Co., 494 U.S. 516 (1990).

Interestingly, John Deere did not challenge personal jurisdiction in the Mississippi federal court. Counsel for the defendant may have assumed that jurisdiction would have been upheld because the defendant's contacts with the forum state were so extensive. Alternatively, jurisdiction might have been based on consent; that is, in many states, domestic corporations must appoint an agent for service of process in order to conduct business within the state.[144]

Domestically, as long as legislatures keep in place such consent statutes and the Court upholds that kind of consent,[145] plaintiffs may not lose their forum-shopping ability based on *Goodyear* and *Daimler*. That could change if industry groups pressure legislatures to narrow their consent statutes. In fact, some states already limit the scope of the appointment of an agent for receiving service of process to cases arising out of business conducted within the state. Thus, those states allow consent only in specific jurisdiction cases. In states with narrower statutes, *Goodyear* and *Daimler* will have a significant impact.[146]

Consider the John Deere example. If Mississippi lacked a broad consent statute and the plaintiff relied on a general jurisdiction theory, the plaintiff would have to prove that John Deere was "at home" in Mississippi. Prior to *Goodyear* and *Daimler*, the plaintiff would have had to prove that John Deere had continuous and systematic contacts with the forum state (and perhaps that the assertion of jurisdiction was otherwise reasonable). John Deere's substantial business activity in the state, including a large number of dealerships, would almost guarantee the finding of jurisdiction. Today, that is no longer true.[147]

The plaintiff would have to prove something more than John Deere's Mississippi contacts. As Justice Ginsburg stated in *Daimler*, John Deere would not necessarily be "at home" there. The court would have to examine John Deere's nationwide and worldwide contacts. With little guidance in the majority opinion, a plaintiff would have to show that the forum state was the state in which an overwhelming majority of the

---

144. Kurland, *supra* note 13, at 578; Brilmayer et al., *supra* note 90, at 757–58.

145. As discussed below, in 2023, a deeply divided Court upheld such a consent statute in *Mallory*. *See* Mallory v. Norfolk S. Ry. Co., 600 U.S. 122 (2023).

146. Vitiello, *Limiting Access to U.S. Courts*, *supra* note 1, at 226.

147. *See* Goodyear Dunlop Tires Operations, S.A. v. Brown, 564 U.S. 915, 919 (2011); Rhodes, *supra* note 96, at 893–99.

defendant's activity took place in the forum state, even if that state was somehow not its principal place of business.[148]

This approach is a dramatic departure from a significant body of case law. Until *Goodyear*, the Court did not suggest such a narrow view of general jurisdiction. And the overwhelming body of lower court case law was to the contrary.[149]

Justice Ginsberg's opinion implies that the goal for the new test is twofold. First, it avoids unfair forum shopping. As she explained, without the narrowing of general jurisdiction, a Polish driver injured in Poland could sue Daimler in the United States. Second, despite the imprecision of her test, Justice Ginsburg believed that it offers greater clarity than does, for example, Justice Sotomayor's more traditional test which considers contacts and fairness factors.[150]

Her analysis invites a question discussed above. What is the underlying justification for general jurisdiction? Neither *Goodyear* nor *Daimler* offers very compelling answers.[151] By comparison, if due process protects a defendant's right to fair notice and an opportunity to be heard, rejecting general jurisdiction in a venue where a corporation may conduct extensive day-to-day activity makes little sense. Perhaps limiting general jurisdiction does not matter. After all, the scholars who proposed limiting general jurisdiction did so with the expectation that specific jurisdiction would be readily available. But as developed in the next section, some members of the Court are ready to narrow specific jurisdiction as well.

(3) Specific Jurisdiction: Up in the Air

In *Daimler*, Justice Ginsburg stated that, in effect, specific jurisdiction has expanded dramatically since it was "cut loose from *Pennoyer*'s sway," while general jurisdiction has "followed [a] markedly different trajector[y]."[152] In effect, she could vote to narrow general jurisdiction because in the modern setting, courts were expanding specific jurisdiction. Her statement concerning specific jurisdiction may be premature.

---

148. *Daimler*, 134 S. Ct. at 762 n.20; *see* Cornett & Hoffheimer, *supra* note 100, at 104.

149. *See Daimler*, 134 S. Ct. at 773 (Sotomayor, J., concurring); Hoffheimer, *supra* note 110, at 549.

150. *Daimler*, 134 S. Ct. 746; Cornett & Hoffheimer, *supra* note 100, at 107.

151. Vitiello, *Limiting Access to U.S. Courts*, *supra* note 1, at 246–54.

152. *Daimler*, 134 S. Ct. at 757–58.

As indicated above, by 1990, the Court was deeply divided over the appropriate rules governing jurisdiction. This is most evident in *Asahi*, where the Court could not agree on the relevance of contacts that came about through the stream of commerce. At the root of the division was a disagreement dating back to the 1950s when the Court decided *McGee* and *Hanson*: must contacts come about through purposeful activity on the part of a defendant? Since 2010, the Court has revisited specific jurisdiction several times. This section discusses cases that raise concerns about how some members of the Court might narrow specific jurisdiction at the same time as they voted to limit general jurisdiction. In *J. McIntyre Machinery, Ltd. v. Nicastro*,[153] the Court remained deeply divided over the same issues that divided the Court in *Asahi*.

(A) *J. McINTYRE MACHINERY, LTD. V. NICASTRO*[154]

After Justice Stevens retired, commentators expected the Court to clarify the test for determining the sufficiency of the stream of commerce when it granted certiorari in *Nicastro*. That did not happen.[155]

The plaintiff, Robert Nicastro, seriously injured his hand when he was operating a machine manufactured by J. McIntyre, Ltd., a British corporation. The plaintiff sued in New Jersey where he worked and was injured. Perhaps because the plaintiff's lawyer engaged in limited discovery, the record demonstrated little contact between the defendant and the forum state. As observed by Justice Kennedy in his plurality opinion, "The question here is whether the New Jersey courts have jurisdiction over J. McIntyre, notwithstanding the fact that the company at no time either marketed goods in the State or shipped them there."[156] The quantity and quality of the defendant's contacts with New Jersey were a mat-

153. *Nicastro*, 564 U.S. 873.

154. *Nicastro*, 564 U.S. 873.

155. *See, e.g.*, Jonathan A. Berkelhammer, *Supreme Court to Readdress Stream of Commerce Theory of Personal Jurisdiction*, 78 Def. Couns. J. 350, 351 (2011); *see also* Elisabeth A. Beal, Note, *J. McIntyre Machinery, Ltd. v. Nicastro: The Stream-of-Commerce Theory of Personal Jurisdiction in a Globalized Economy*, 66 U. Miami L. Rev. 233, 241–42 (2011).

156. *Nicastro*, 564 U.S. at 878.

ter of dispute within the Court, with each of the three opinions offering a different view of the facts.[157]

The defendant created a subsidiary, J. McIntyre America, to market its products in the United States. By the time of trial, the subsidiary was bankrupt. In addition, as hinted at by Justice Breyer in his concurring opinion, the plaintiff's lawyer did not try to show the degree of control exercised by the defendant over its American distributor. As a result, the record was sparse. According to Justice Breyer, the record included evidence of the sale of only one machine in New Jersey, that the defendant hoped to sell its machines to anyone in the United States, and that its employees attended trade shows in the United States, but not in New Jersey. Justice Kennedy's plurality opinion also observed that the plaintiff did not allege that J. McIntyre America was under the defendant's control. He observed that the New Jersey Supreme Court relied in part on the fact that J. McIntyre America "structured [its] advertising and sales efforts in accordance with [the defendant's] direction and guidance whenever possible."[158]

Justice Ginsburg's dissent, joined by Justices Sotomayor and Kagan, focused on efforts by the defendant to market its products in the United States. The defendant "engaged McIntyre America to attract customers 'from anywhere in the United States.'"[159] It sought to "reach and profit from the United States market as a whole." Justice Ginsburg found that the defendant must have intended to sell its product in the "largest scrap metal market" in the United States when it targeted the national market.[160]

Six Justices disagreed with her approach. Using *Hanson* as the starting point for his analysis, Justice Kennedy and three other Justices agreed that "[a]s a general rule, the exercise of judicial power is not lawful unless the defendant 'purposefully avails itself of the privilege of

---

157. *See id.* at 886 ("[u]p to four machines ended up in New Jersey ..."); *id.* at 888 (Breyer, J., concurring) ("[t]he American Distributor on one occasion sold and shipped one machine to a New Jersey customer ..."); *id.* at 908 n.15 (Ginsburg, J., dissenting) ("[t]he plurality notes the low volume of sales in New Jersey.... A $24,900 shearing machine, however, is unlikely to sell in bulk worldwide, much less in any given state. By dollar value, the price of a single machine represents a significant sale.").

158. *Id.* at 878; *id.* at 887–92 (Breyer, J., concurring); *id.* at 896–97 & n.2 (Ginsburg, J., dissenting).

159. *Id.* at 897–98 (Ginsburg, J., dissenting).

160. *Id.* at 905.

conducting activities within the forum State, thus invoking the benefits and protections of its laws.'"[161] The plurality rejected the idea that due process involved a general notion of fair process on the grounds that "[f]reeform notions of fundamental fairness divorced from traditional practice cannot transform a judgment rendered in the absence of authority into law."[162] Citing *Hanson* again, Justice Kennedy emphasized the fact that a defendant must act with purpose towards the forum. According to the plurality, a defendant must submit to the state's authority and may do so in a number of ways, including through explicit consent, presence within the state, citizenship or domicile, incorporation in the state or establishment of a principal place of business in the state. These examples demonstrate circumstances or a course of conduct from which to infer "an intention to submit to the laws of the forum State."[163] For out-of-state defendants, acting with purpose towards the state provides similar evidence that the defendant submits to the state's authority with regard to suits arising out of the forum contact.[164] As developed below, the plurality staked out a radical position, harking back to the rejected theory of consent.

For Justices Breyer and Alito, the case before the Court did not raise many of the yet unresolved challenges facing courts around the country. Recognizing that many changes in commerce and communications may require rethinking the Court's precedent, Justice Breyer found that *Nicastro* did not present those questions. He underscored that the plaintiff failed to meet his burden of demonstrating sufficient contacts with the forum state. McIntyre America was "an independent distributor."[165] The distributor had only made one sale in New Jersey, even though the defendant was willing to sell machines to anyone interested in buying them anywhere in the United States. Justice Breyer rejected the idea that

---

161. *Id.* at 877 (plurality opinion).

162. *Id.* at 880.

163. *Id.* at 881.

164. *Id.* at 880–81. Justice Kennedy indicated that if Congress wanted to allow a suit against a foreign manufacturer, it could authorize world-wide service of process. As the Court indicated in *Fuld v. PLO*, 606 U.S. ___, 145 S. Ct. 2090 (2025), in such a case, a court would analyze the jurisdictional question under the Fifth Amendment Due Process Clause. Further, it indicated the Fourteenth Amendment analysis, focusing on contacts with the forum state, is not the method of analysis under the Fifth Amendment.

165. *Id.* at 888 (Breyer, J., concurring).

the Court's precedent allowed the assertion of jurisdiction based on a single sale "accompanied by the kind of sales effort indicated here."[166] The concurring opinion suggested that the two Justices might be open to a stream of commerce argument but found that the record showed no regular flow of goods into the forum.[167]

The concurring opinion rejected the idea that the mere arrival of the product in the forum state should lead to jurisdiction. The opinion left open several questions and suggested participation by the Solicitor General, presumably to provide a better insight into broad concerns about modern commercial circumstances.[168]

Discussed in more detail below, the current state of affairs after *Nicastro* is troubling. Justice Kennedy was one vote short of significantly narrowing specific jurisdiction. The dissent and others have commented on the theory implicit in the plurality opinion, which is the idea that one has to consent to jurisdiction. In *Nicastro*, Justice Ginsburg argued that the theory was rejected long ago and found no support in the Court's modern case law.

Justice Kennedy's opinion is a reminder of the point raised above that hard cases make bad law. *Hanson*, a decision that was out of line with the Court's then current view of due process evidenced in *McGee*, was grounded in overt result orientation. It has become the centerpiece of the conservative Justices' due process jurisprudence. Unlike Justice White's opinion in *World-Wide*, where he linked the contacts part of the Court's test to sovereignty, Justice Kennedy did not fall into that morass. Instead, he gave predominant importance to a defendant's choice to make itself amenable to suit in the forum. Hence, a defendant who can point to no great inconvenience or lack of opportunity to be heard may avoid suit in a forum despite benefiting indirectly from the sales of its product in the forum state.[169]

---

166. *Id.*

167. *Id.* at 888–89.

168. *Id.* at 888, 892.

169. *Id.* at 879 (plurality opinion); *World-Wide Volkswagen*, 444 U.S. at 291–92; *see* Vitiello, *Limiting Access to U.S. Courts*, *supra* note 1, at 219–21.

(B) *BRISTOL-MYERS SQUIBB CO. V. SUPERIOR COURT*:[170] MORE DOOR CLOSING

As developed below, *Bristol-Myers Squibb Co. v. Superior Court* (*BMS*) reflected such a departure from traditional personal jurisdictional analysis that it invited arguments that would have been frivolous a decade earlier. Perhaps a positive effect of *BMS*'s (especially in conjunction with the Court's general jurisdiction case law) departure from those principles is that in two recent cases, the Court has upheld personal jurisdiction for the first time in years.

In the 2000s, Bristol-Myers Squibb (BMS) began to receive complaints about Plavix, one of its most successful drugs. During that time, questions began to surface concerning bad side effects of the drug.

In 2012, a large group of plaintiffs joined together to file a lawsuit against BMS in California state court. To avoid removal to federal court, they did not file a plaintiffs' class action.[171] Many of the plaintiffs were California citizens, but the group of plaintiffs included individuals from thirty-three other states as well. BMS challenged the assertion of jurisdiction of the state court over the claims brought by out-of-state plaintiffs.

In *Due Process and the Myth of Sovereignty*, I summarized BMS's connection with California:

> Bristol-Myers Squibb (BMS) is one of the largest pharmaceutical companies in the world with thousands of employees and about $20 billion in revenue annually. While over half of its work force is in New York and New Jersey, the company has a large footprint in California. BMS has five laboratories in California where about 160 employees work. It has a sales force of about 250 people in the state and a state-government advocacy office in Sacramento.

170. Bristol-Myers Squibb Co. v. Super. Ct. of Cal., 582 U.S. 255 (2017).

171. Michael Vitiello, *Due Process and the Myth of Sovereignty*, 50 U. Pac. L. Rev. 513, 533 (2019) (explaining that "[b]y filing separately, rather than by seeking class certification, the plaintiffs avoided removal under the Class Action Fairness Act, which allows removal even absent complete diversity and even if a defendant is an in-state defendant." (citing Andrew D. Bradt & D. Theodore Rave, *Aggregation on Defendants' Terms: Bristol-Myers Squibb and the Federalization of Mass-Tort Litigation*, 59 B.C. L. Rev. 1251, 1275 (2018)).

> BMS produces and sells Plavix, a blood thinner. In the early 2000's, Plavix was BMS's best-selling product. Indeed, in 2009, U.S. sales of Plavix exceeded $9 billion. The manufacturing, labeling, and work on gaining regulatory approval of Plavix did not take place in California. Between 2006 and 2016, BMS sold about 187 million Plavix pills in California, taking in more than *$900 million* from those sales over that period of time. Beyond doubt, BMS sold many other drugs in California as well.[172]

At the time of filing, the plaintiffs' lawyers believed, as did the state trial court, that the court had jurisdiction based on a general jurisdiction theory: BMS's contacts were so continuous and systematic that the assertion of jurisdiction comported with due process.

At the time of filing, the plaintiffs' lawyers believed, as did the state trial court, that the court had jurisdiction theory.[173] In *Goodyear Dunlop Tires Operations, S.A. v. Brown,* the Court signaled that it was reconsidering the broad rule for general jurisdiction. There, Justice Ginsburg anticipated the Court's ruling in *Daimler AG v. Bauman*, which held in all but the most unusual circumstances that all-purpose jurisdiction would be proper only in a corporation's state of incorporation or in the state where it had its principal place of business. But general jurisdiction was widely recognized as a proper theory of asserting jurisdiction dating back to the *Pennoyer* era. In addition, *Goodyear* involved foreign manufacturers with far fewer contacts with the forum state than BMS had with California.[174]

Consistent with the previous point, the California trial court found that jurisdiction was proper based on a general jurisdiction theory. In the interim, the Supreme Court announced its *Daimler* decision. The

---

172. *Id.* at 515–16.

173. *Id.* at 516 (explaining that the plaintiffs in *BMS* filed their actions in 2012, after the Supreme Court's decision in *Goodyear Dunlop Tires Operations, S.A. v. Brown*, where the Court indicated that it was about to narrow general jurisdiction).

174. *Bristol-Myers Squibb Co.*, 582 U.S. at 258–59 (suggesting that five of the company's research and laboratory facilities, which employed a total of around 160 employees, were located in California; about 250 sales representatives were employed in the state; a small state-government advocacy office was maintained in Sacramento; and between 2006 and 2012, BMS sold almost 187 million Plavix pills in California, earning more than $900 million).

California appellate court and state Supreme Court upheld jurisdiction on a specific jurisdiction theory, consistent with California precedent from years earlier that developed a sliding scale theory of jurisdiction. The United State Supreme Court disagreed.[175]

To understand the Court's decision, one should be clear that the state trial court had jurisdiction over claims by California plaintiffs, who received prescriptions for the drug and used the drug in California. But the Court's analysis of why the out-of-state plaintiffs could not invoke the court's jurisdiction has produced considerable criticism from Civil Procedure scholars.[176]

Start with the contacts that BMS had with California. Those contacts were massive. To use the language of *International Shoe*, the contacts were systematic and continuous and have been for years. Further, those contacts came about through BMS's purposeful activity. Although read narrowly, the out-of-state claims may not have arisen from BMS's forum contacts, read broadly, they related to those contacts.[177]

Dating back to *International Shoe*, the Court had used an alternative formulation of the test: arising out of or relating to forum contacts. Lower courts divided over how to read that test. Some courts, including the California Supreme Court, had developed a "sliding scale" concept: if a plaintiff's claim did not arise out of proven forum contacts, but came about from one of a defendant's products in the forum state (not one that the plaintiff proved that the defendant shipped to the state), the court found that the assertion of jurisdiction did not violate due process if the forum contacts were significant.[178] Only once did the issue arise in the United States Supreme Court, only in Justice Brennan's dissent in *Helicopteros Nacionales de Colombia, S.A. v. Hall*, where the Court found that the plaintiffs waived the specific jurisdiction issue and that the contacts were insufficient to establish general jurisdiction.[179] Justice Alito's

175. *Bristol-Myers Squibb Co.*, 582 U.S. at 258.

176. *See* Vitiello, *Due Process and the Myth of Sovereignty, supra* note 171; Bradt & Rave, *Aggregation on Defendants' Terms, supra* note 171; Michael H. Hoffheimer, *The Stealth Revolution in Personal Jurisdiction*, 70 Fla. L. Rev. 499 (2018).

177. *Bristol-Myers Squibb Co.*, 582 U.S. at 274 (Sotomayor, J., dissenting) (stating that "[a]ll of the plaintiffs—residents and nonresidents alike—allege[d] that they were injured by the same essential acts. Our cases require no connection more direct than that.").

178. *Bristol-Myers Squibb Co.*, 582 U.S. at 260 (majority opinion).

179. *Helicopteros*, 466 U.S. at 419–28 (Brennan, J., dissenting).

majority opinion in *BMS* rejected the sliding scale theory of specific jurisdiction. According to Justice Alito, the sliding scale theory amounts to general jurisdiction dressed up in specific jurisdiction terminology.[180]

In many recent decisions, the Court failed to explain the interplay of contacts' analysis and the fairness/reasonableness factors. Justice Alito did not do so either.[181] But he did address those factors. Dating back to *McGee*, the Court examined several factors, including the forum state's interest in the litigation, the plaintiff's interest in the litigation, witness convenience, and the burden on the defendant, among other factors. Now, Justice Alito stated that the key component is the burden on the defendant in defending the lawsuit within the forum.[182]

Stop for a moment and consider the last point. How great a burden did BMS face in defending the lawsuits in California? Apart from the massive amount of business activity in the state, including laboratories and a large work force in California, BMS maintains a lobbying office in Sacramento, allowing it to attempt to influence state legislation in-state. Further, BMS retains local counsel. When asked, BMS's counsel acknowledged that the burden on BMS to defend in California was not burdensome.[183] To have answered to the contrary would almost certainly have been frivolous.

How then did Justice Alito deal with that concession to reach the conclusion that the assertion of jurisdiction over non-resident plaintiffs' claims violated due process? In part, his analysis suggested that the claims did not arise out of the forum contacts.[184] The plaintiffs attempted to argue that nonetheless, their claims related to the forum. Dating back to much earlier precedent, the Court routinely described specific jurisdiction as requiring a plaintiff to show that the plaintiff's claim arose out of forum contacts or was related to those contacts. Justice Alito's opinion suggested that the two formulations were not distinct.[185]

---

180. *Bristol-Myers Squibb Co.*, 582 U.S. at 256.

181. *See* Vitiello, *The Supreme Court's Latest Attempt at "Clarifying" Personal Jurisdiction*, *supra* note 1 at 415; Richard D. Freer, *Justice Black Was Right About International Shoe, But for the Wrong Reason*, 50 U. Pac. L. Rev. 587, 603 (2019).

182. *Bristol-Myers Squibb Co.*, 582 U.S. at 263.

183. Bradt & Rave, *Aggregation on Defendants' Terms*, *supra* note 171 at 1279.

184. *Bristol-Myers Squibb Co.*, 582 U.S. at 265.

185. Although the Court seemed to narrow the test to "arising out of" the forum contacts and to suggest that "related to" the forum contacts amounted to the same thing,

But more importantly, in explaining away BMS's concession that defending the suit in California was not burdensome, he argued, to some of us, somewhat opaquely, as follows:

> Assessing this burden obviously requires a court to consider the practical problems resulting from litigating in the forum, but it also encompasses the more abstract matter of submitting to the coercive power of a State that may have little legitimate interest in the claims in question. As we have put it, restrictions on personal jurisdiction "are more than a guarantee of immunity from inconvenient or distant litigation. They are a consequence of territorial limitations on the power of the respective States".... [T]he States retain many essential attributes of sovereignty, including, in particular, the sovereign power to try causes in their courts.[186]

Rephrased, Justice Alito seems to be saying, like Justice White stated in *World-Wide Volkswagen,* that the reasonableness analysis relates to due process, but that the contacts part of the analysis relates to sovereignty.[187]

Scholars have met Justice Alito's assertion that the Court was applying established rules of law with great skepticism. For example, Professor Hoffheimer has argued that *BMS* is yet another example of the Roberts Court's attempt to portray its radical new due process analysis as flowing naturally from controlling precedent.[188] Here is one example of what seems like a clear misstatement of the Court's precedent: while Justice White did argue in *World-Wide Volkswagen* that somehow the minimum contacts part of the Court's due process analysis protected sovereign interests, he disavowed that idea a mere two years later. Without acknowledging that fact, Justice Alito seems to have made the same argument in *BMS.*[189] As indicated earlier in this chapter, arguing that the Fourteenth Amendment protects sovereignty is bad history and bad policy. At a minimum, in light of the Civil War, the Fourteenth Amendment

---

Justice Kagan argued to the contrary six years later in her *Ford* majority opinion.

186. *Bristol-Myers Squibb Co.*, 582 U.S. at 263.

187. Vitiello, *Due Process and the Myth of Sovereignty, supra* note 171 at 526–27.

188. Hoffheimer, *The Stealth Revolution in Personal Jurisdiction, supra* note 176 at 505.

189. Vitiello, *Due Process and the Myth of Sovereignty, supra* note 171 at 527.

was part of the post-Civil War amendments limiting sovereign power, not protecting it.

Reliance on sovereignty is not only historically questionable, but it tends to have the effect of protecting corporate defendants from having to defend lawsuits in venues chosen by injured plaintiffs. As discussed elsewhere in this chapter, the problem may be that the Court disfavors some kinds of forum shopping, but the Court has failed to explain why some forum shopping is not good.

Cases like *BMS* demonstrate the Court's willingness to abandon settled precedent in ways that disfavor injured plaintiffs. Consider the law right before the plaintiffs' attorneys filed their action against BMS. BMS would have been subject to jurisdiction based on a general jurisdiction theory and, plausibly, on a specific jurisdiction theory. The Court has foreclosed both theories in *Daimler* and *BMS*.

Further, rapid changes in the law prevented the plaintiffs' lawyers from developing different theories to uphold jurisdiction. Focus closely on the facts in *BMS*. BMS contracted with McKesson Corporation, a huge pharmaceutical distributor, to market its product. Justice Alito observed that the record did not indicate that BMS directed McKesson's marketing strategy.[190] The plaintiffs' attorneys may have recognized the need to develop a fuller record demonstrating that BMS directed McKesson's marketing efforts from California. Had the plaintiffs been able to allege that they used Plavix because of BMS's agent's forum activity, jurisdiction might have been proper. One can only guess whether that would have been sufficient. Be clear, however, especially when read in conjunction with *Daimler*, *BMS* reflects a radical narrowing of personal jurisdiction.[191]

As developed in the next section, the Court's caselaw amounted to such a departure from the rules governing jurisdiction until 2010 and beyond that counsel for Ford Motor Company attempted an argument that would have been frivolous but for the Court's recent caselaw.

---

190. *Bristol-Myers Squibb Co.*, 582 U.S. at 259.

191. Hoffheimer, *The Stealth Revolution in Personal Jurisdiction*, *supra* note 176.

(C) *FORD MOTOR CO. V. MONT. EIGHTH JUD. DIST. CT.*:[192] ENOUGH IS ENOUGH

A Montana resident was driving her Ford Explorer in her home state when the rear tire separated. Her vehicle went out of control, causing her death. An accident took place in Minnesota involving a different Ford vehicle. The Montana resident's estate representative and the injured Minnesota resident sued Ford in their respective states. Quite surprisingly, Ford moved to dismiss, claiming that the assertion of jurisdiction violated due process.[193]

Prior to *Daimler* and *BMS*, Ford's attorneys' arguments would have been frivolous. Beyond any serious question, Ford's contacts with Montana and Minnesota were so substantial that jurisdiction would have been proper under the theory of general jurisdiction. Post-*Daimler*, that theory is no longer available because neither Ford's state of incorporation nor principal place of business was in the forum states.[194]

Prior to *BMS*, the argument against specific jurisdiction seemed to be a stretch. I have described that argument elsewhere,

> The Court routinely stated its specific jurisdiction test requiring that a claim arose out of forum contacts or was related to the forum contacts. Ford obviously purposefully availed itself of doing business in Montana and Minnesota. The possible missing link was that the vehicles involved in the suits were purchased elsewhere and brought to the forum state. While strictly speaking, the claim did not arise out of the *defendant's* activity in the forum, instead the Court might have easily found that the claim was related to forum activity: forum ac-

---

192. Ford Motor Co. v. Mont. Eighth Jud. Dist. Ct., 592 U.S. 351 (2021).

193. *Ford*, 592 U.S. at 351.

194. As observed by Charles W. "Rocky" Rhodes, between 1945 when the Court decided *International Shoe* and the two lower court cases in this litigation, Ford had never contested jurisdiction. *See* Charles W. "Rocky" Rhodes, *The Roberts Court's Jurisdictional Revolution Within Ford's Frame*, 51 Stetson L. Rev. 157, 159 (2022). In some instances, no doubt, the plaintiffs could rely on the fact that the claim arose out of the forum contacts. But even if not, then a plaintiff could rely on a general jurisdiction theory. Prior to 1978, were neither of those options available, a plaintiff could have attached Ford's in-state property and begun an action *in rem*.

> tivity involved marketing, selling, and servicing the same vehicles as involved in the two lawsuits.[195]

But then, the Court decided *BMS*.

Complicating the plaintiffs' specific jurisdiction theory was that in both of the state cases, the owner of the vehicle bought the car in a different state. Here, focus closely on at least one way that one might read the Court's holding in *BMS*. As I summarized elsewhere,

> First, the nonresident plaintiffs did not obtain the drug from California. Second, BMS did not manufacture or distribute the drug in California. Third, BMS did not work on regulatory compliance material from California. Finally, although Justice Alito recognized that BMS hired McKesson, headquartered in California, to develop its marketing strategy, the nonresident plaintiffs did not allege that BMS directed its marketing strategy from California.[196]

Ford's attorneys attempted a broad reading of that language. Thus, the Montana and Minnesota Ford vehicle owners could not claim that they bought their vehicles in-state. Ford did not manufacture the vehicles in those states. Nor could they show any regulatory compliance in those states. Finally, the record was devoid of any indication that the owners of the Ford vehicles had somehow purchased their vehicles because of in-state activity.[197]

Almost any observer would argue that the plaintiffs should be able to sue a multinational corporation with massive contacts with those states. Apart from any hyper technical contacts' analysis, the basic due process concept of adequate notice and an opportunity to be heard was more than met. Ford could not point to any burden of defending in those states. Those states had considerable interest in protecting injured residents, and those residents had a strong interest in being able to sue in their home states. Evidence would likely be located in those states. And

---

195. Vitiello, *The Supreme Court's Latest Attempt at "Clarifying" Personal Jurisdiction*, *supra* note 1 at 418–19.

196. Vitiello, *Due Process and the Myth of Sovereignty*, *supra* note 171 at 517–18.

197. *Ford*, 592 U.S. at 356.

yet, through a series of decisions that closed the courthouse door, the Supreme Court suddenly seemed to have painted itself into a corner.[198]

For a brief period of time, many Court observers thought that the Court might take Ford's argument seriously. The Montana and Minnesota courts had rejected Ford's argument, leading court observers to wonder why the Court granted the writ of certiorari. No doubt, one could almost hear a collective sigh of relief when a unanimous Court ruled against Ford.[199]

By contrast, anyone reading the Court's decision in *Ford* may have some unease in figuring out what the Court's holding means. About all that one can say with certainty is that when a company has such overwhelming contacts with the forum state and one of its products causes harm to a resident of that state, that state's courts may exercise jurisdiction over the company without violating due process.[200]

Some aspects of Justice Kagan's analysis are uncontroversial. This is not a case where contacts with the forum are created by the stream of commerce. Ford's purposeful activity within the forum was beyond dispute. Although not a clearly addressed issue in the case, the traditional fairness/reasonableness factors were also beyond dispute.

Despite the contrary discussion in *BMS*, Justice Kagan indicated that specific jurisdiction may be established if a claim arose out of forum contacts *or* was related to those contacts. As she stated, "there must be 'an affiliation between the forum and the underlying controversy, principally, [an] activity or occurrence that takes place in the forum State

---

198. *Id.* at 361 (suggesting that, according to Ford, Montana's and Minnesota's courts were prevented from deciding these two suits because specific jurisdiction attached "only if the defendant's forum conduct gave rise to the plaintiff's claims," which could happen only in states where the vehicle was purchased or manufactured).

199. Vitiello, *The Supreme Court's Latest Attempt at "Clarifying" Personal Jurisdiction*, *supra* note 1 at 396 (citing Richard D. Freer, *SCOTUS Analysis: Ford Motor Co. and Personal Jurisdiction*, Emory L. News Ctr. (Apr. 19, 2021), https://law.emory.edu/news-and-events/releases/2021/04/scouts-analysis-ford-motor-company-v.-montana-eighth-judicial-district-court.html (recognizing that *Ford* "holds promise for an expansion of specific jurisdiction"); Erwin Chemerinksy, *Chemerinsky: Despite SCOTUS Ruling, Questions of Personal Jurisdiction Remain Unsettled*, ABA Journal (May 3, 2021), https://www.abajournal.com/columns/article/chemerinsky-despite-scotus-ruling-questions-of-personal-jurisdiction-remain-unsettled)).

200. Vitiello, *The Supreme Court's Latest Attempt at "Clarifying" Personal Jurisdiction*, *supra* note 1 at 420. *See also* Freer, *supra* note 199.

and is therefore subject to the State's regulation.'"[201] She contrasted *BMS* and *Ford* as follows: in *BMS*, the forum and state and defendant's activities were unconnected to the out-of-state plaintiffs' claims. They were merely forum-shopping. The facts in *Ford* were different: yes, the sales of the vehicles were out-of-state, but the plaintiffs were in-state residents; they used the products in-state and suffered injuries in-state.[202]

But what of the facts that the in-state residents created the injury-causing contacts with the forum state? Elsewhere, the Court has found that contacts that exist between the forum and the litigation must come about through the defendant's, not the plaintiff's, conduct.[203]

I have explained how one might try to summarize the meaning of *Ford*: "a plaintiff can create forum-contacts by bringing the injury-causing product into a state if the defendant is otherwise involved in a substantial amount of similar business within the state."[204] Of course, that statement suggests hard questions for lower courts, including how much business is substantial enough to subject the defendant to jurisdiction.

Here is another example of uncertainty created by Justice Kagan's opinion: what if the facts were as they were in *Ford*, but for the fact that the injured party was driving through the state? In describing the factors that supported the assertion of jurisdiction in *Ford*, Justice Kagan emphasized more than once that the plaintiffs were in-state residents. And yet, she also stated that, in *World-Wide Volkswagen*, the Oklahoma court would have had jurisdiction over Audi and Volkswagen of America based on her analysis in *Ford*.[205] But weren't the Robinsons engaged in some form of forum shopping in that case?[206]

---

201. *Ford*, 592 U.S. at 359.

202. Vitiello, *The Supreme Court's Latest Attempt at "Clarifying" Personal Jurisdiction*, *supra* note 1 at 421.

203. *See, e.g.*, Walden v. Fiore, 571 U.S. 277, 284 (2024) (stating that for a state to exercise jurisdiction consistent with due process, a substantial connection must exist between the forum state and the suit-related conduct of the defendant himself).

204. Vitiello, *The Supreme Court's Latest Attempt at "Clarifying" Personal Jurisdiction*, *supra* note 1 at 421.

205. *Ford*, 592 U.S. at 363. Many commentators assumed that the basis of jurisdiction over Audi and Volkswagen of America would have been general jurisdiction. *See* Vitiello, *The Supreme Court's Latest Attempt at "Clarifying" Personal Jurisdiction*, *supra* note 1 at 422.

206. Vitiello, *The Supreme Court's Latest Attempt at "Clarifying" Personal Jurisdiction*, *supra* note 1 at 422 (explaining that the Robinsons "were clearly engaged in intra-

Consistent with earlier precedent, one might also have argued that Justice Kagan's opinion was based on a sliding scale theory. One might read Justice Kagan's opinion as relying on such a theory.[207] But of course, the Court explicitly rejected that theory in *BMS*. Alternatively, consistent with a case like *McGee*, the Court might have found that the state venues were reasonable, and that Ford had ample notice and more than an ample opportunity to be heard. But Justice Kagan reiterated the importance of federalism and sovereignty in the Court's caselaw. Indeed, she suggested that Washington State and North Dakota, the states where the Ford vehicle owners purchased their vehicles, would not have a sufficient interest to justify those states from hearing the suits brought by the injured plaintiffs. Ford's attorneys urged that those were the only suitable venues in which suit would be proper.[208] From one perspective, those venues seem to fit within the classic definition of specific jurisdiction: the plaintiffs' claims, the purchase of defective vehicles, related to the defendant's contact with those states, and, indeed, arose out of them.

Where does this leave litigants in a modern world where interstate and international transactions occur in dizzying frequency? Think back to Professor Mullenix's suggestion that I am a procedural Cassandra, who sees all of the Court's procedural decisions in a downward arc. Perhaps, *Ford* proves her point. But as developed in this section, *Ford* demonstrates how far the Court had gone so that Ford's attorneys could advance a position that would have been rejected as frivolous not all that long ago.

But there is more. In his concurring opinion in *Ford*, Justice Gorsuch suggested that the Court should consider returning to the pre-*International Shoe* rule, in effect, suggesting that the Court, or some members of the Court, were interested in developing an originalist approach to personal jurisdiction.[209] As developed in the next section, in the Supreme Court's most recent personal jurisdiction case, questions during oral argument seemed to suggest that the Court might return due process personal jurisdiction analysis to Nineteenth Century prec-

---

jurisdictional forum shopping (adding two New York defendants to avoid removal to federal court) and chose Oklahoma over New York where they purchased their vehicle for their convenience").

207. *Id.* at 427.

208. *Ford*, 592 U.S. at 368.

209. *Id.* at 383 (Gorsuch, J., concurring); Vitiello & Croxall, *supra* note 1 at 222.

edent. How the Court avoided that and how the Court seemingly has given plaintiffs a renewed option for forum selection is the subject of the next section.

(D) *MALLORY V. NORFOLK SOUTHERN RAILWAY CO.*:[210] CURIOUS DEVELOPMENTS

In 2022, the Supreme Court granted the writ of certiorari in a case involving Robert Mallory, a former railway worker for the defendant, Norfolk Southern Railway. During his employment, he worked as a freight mechanic in Ohio and later in Virginia. After he retired, he moved to Pennsylvania, where he was diagnosed with cancer. He filed an action in a Pennsylvania state court. His complaint alleged a violation of the Federal Employee Liability Act based on his claim that exposure to carcinogenic chemicals during his employment caused his illness. By the time he filed suit, he had moved back to Virginia. The defendant is incorporated in Virginia where it also has its principal place of bustiness. Mallory's complaint did not allege that he was exposed to the chemical in Pennsylvania.[211]

The defendant objected to the court's assertion of personal jurisdiction over it. Mallory contended that jurisdiction was proper in reliance on a state law requiring out-of-state businesses to register to conduct business in state. In effect, according to Mallory, the statute gave the state courts the equivalent of general jurisdiction over suits involving such out-of-state businesses. The trial court granted defendant's motion to dismiss. The Pennsylvania Supreme Court affirmed the judgment of dismissal, largely in reliance on the Supreme Court's *Goodyear* and *Daimler* decisions.[212]

During oral argument before the Supreme Court, some of the justices asked questions suggesting that they were interested in taking Justice Gorsuch's suggestion seriously in *Ford* to rethink *International Shoe* and its progeny.[213] Over the rest of the term, Civil Procedure scholars speculated about what such a new "originalist" regime might look like. At least

---

210. Mallory v. Norfolk S. Ry. Co., 600 U.S. 122 (2023).

211. *Id.* at 126–28.

212. *Id.* at 127.

213. Vitiello & Croxall, *supra* note 1 at 221–22.

some of us questioned the wisdom of going back to Nineteenth Century rules better suited to the days of horses and buggies, not to a modern world of instant communication. Indeed, we questioned undoing a body of caselaw that repeatedly recognized that due process has evolved to reflect changes in communication and transportation.[214]

Interestingly, Mallory's attorney, not counsel for Norfolk Southern, argued in favor of a return to the original public meaning of the Fourteenth Amendment.[215] Nonetheless, many of us waited with bated breath until the Court announced its decision near the end of the 2022 term. For those of us interested in keeping the courthouse door open to injured plaintiffs, the decision provided a pleasant surprise: a closely divided Court reversed the Pennsylvania courts and remanded the case.[216] Also, many of us celebrated the fact that the Court did not announce a new paradigm. *International Shoe* remains in place. But the case presented some surprises and, at least Justice Alito's concurring opinion, has raised some concerns about possible new restrictions that plaintiffs may face. Worth noting also is the fact that, as in other important personal jurisdiction cases, the Court was deeply divided, leaving Justice Gorsuch without a majority for some sections of his lead opinion.[217]

In the pre-*International Shoe* era, the Court upheld statutes like the one involved in *Mallory*.[218] But after the Court's minimum contacts anal-

214. *Id.* at 225.

215. Brief for Petitioner at 10–11, Mallory v. Norfolk S. Ry. Co., 600 U.S. 122 (2023) (No. 21-1168) ("The sole question presented is whether the Due Process Clause of the Fourteenth Amendment prevents courts from treating that consent as voluntary and constitutionally valid because it was required as a condition of doing business in the State. The original public meaning of the Fourteenth Amendment supplies a clear answer: Pennsylvania's consent-by-registration requirement produces constitutionally valid consent. This Court's longstanding precedents reach the same conclusion, and nothing in more recent decisions undermines—or even speaks to—the validity of traditional forms of jurisdiction, including consent.").

216. *Mallory*, 600 U.S. 146.

217. *Id.* at 124 (suggesting that Justice Gorsuch delivered the opinion of the Court with respect to Parts I and III-B, and an opinion with respect to Parts II, III-A, and IV, in which Justices Thomas, Sotomayor, and Jackson joined).

218. *Mallory*, 600 U.S. at 133 (explaining that "Pennsylvania Fire could be sued in Missouri by an out-of-state plaintiff on an out-of-state contract because it had agreed to accept service of process in Missouri on any suit as a condition of doing business there." (citing Pa. Fire Ins. Co. of Phila. v. Gold Issue Mining & Milling Co., 243 U.S. 93, 95 (1917))).

ysis was in place, reliance on such statutes seldom featured in the caselaw. Only after the Court's decisions in cases like *Goodyear* and *Daimler* did plaintiffs need to rely on such statutes if they sought a venue where specific jurisdiction was not available. As a result, one could only guess whether the Court would uphold such statutes or whether, if the Court did, it would do so only if the statute provided for specific jurisdiction.[219]

Writing for five justices, Justice Gorsuch relied on the Court's 1917 unanimous decision in *Pennsylvania Fire Ins. Co. of Philadelphia v. Gold Issue Mining & Milling Co.*[220] As with the law involved in that case, he found that the Pennsylvania law applied even in a case involving jurisdiction akin to general jurisdiction.[221]

Other aspects of the case are not so settled. Justice Gorsuch secured only three votes in addition to his for sections II, III-A, and IV. Much of the discussion in Section II and III-A analogized consent statutes to tag jurisdiction for individuals. Section IV made clear Justice Gorsuch's view that consent is a separate path to the assertion of jurisdiction, not requiring a showing that the assertion comports with traditional notions of fair play and substantial justice.[222]

As my colleague Daniel Croxall and I observed in *Mallory v. Norfolk Southern Railway Co., Due Process and Strange Bedfellows,* Justice Barrett, joined by the Chief Justice, and Justices Kagan and Kavanaugh, dissented:

> They took issue with the plurality on two main points. First, as a policy matter, the dissenting Justices took a time and place approach and argued that the plurality opinion was not "in the spirit of our age." Ultimately, they felt it unreasonable for Pennsylvania to place conditions on foreign corporations in exchange for access to its markets because it would allow states to relabel their long-arm statutes to manufacture consent.[223]

Given that Justices Barrett and Kavanaugh were not on the Court when the Court decided most of the courthouse-door-closing cases in the past

219. Vitiello & Croxall, *supra* note 1 at 239.

220. *Mallory*, 600 U.S. at 134 (stating that "*Pennsylvania Fire* controls this case" (citing *Pa. Fire*, 243 U.S. 93)).

221. *Id.*

222. *Id.* at 136–46.

223. Vitiello & Croxall, *supra* note 1 at 242–43.

fifteen years, assessing how they might have voted on some of those cases is difficult. Would they agree with the door-closing analysis in Justice Kennedy's plurality opinion in *Nicastro*? Or with Justice Ginsburg's opinion in *Daimler*? Those questions remain open.

Justice Alito's concurring opinion is more troubling from my perspective. While he agreed with the result in *Mallory*, Justice Alito raised a new theory that, if adopted, would have the effect of limiting plaintiffs' ability to bring a suit against an out-of-state corporation. Recall that Justice Alito invoked the sometimes-discredited theory that personal jurisdiction somehow protects state sovereignty.[224] In his *Mallory* opinion, he observed that the defendant raised a dormant Commerce Clause argument below, but that the state supreme court did not address the issue. As a result, he stated that the defendant should do so on remand.[225] He also laid out the argument in his opinion.

Initially, he agreed that the assertion of jurisdiction over the defendant did not violate due process. But then he raised the dormant Commerce Clause argument. Here is an excerpt:

> The federalism concerns that this case presents fall more naturally within the scope of the Commerce Clause.... [T]his Court has long held that the Clause includes a negative component, the so-called dormant Commerce Clause, that "prohibits state laws that unduly restrict interstate commerce."...[T]he concept is "deeply rooted in our case law,"...and vindicates a fundamental aim in the Constitution: fostering the creation of national economy and avoiding the every-State-for-itself practices that weakened the country under the Articles of Confederation.[226]

He offered his view that a general jurisdiction statute like Pennsylvania's violated the dormant Commerce Clause in two ways. First, it discrimi-

224. *Bristol-Myers Squibb Co.*, 582 U.S. at 263 ("As we have put it, restrictions on personal jurisdiction 'are more than a guarantee of immunity from inconvenient or distant litigation. They are a consequence of territorial limitations on the power of the respective States.'... '[T]he States retain many essential attributes of sovereignty, including, in particular, the sovereign power to try causes in their courts. The sovereignty of each State...implie[s] a limitation on the sovereignty of all its sister States.'").

225. *Mallory*, 600 U.S. at 150 (Alito, J., concurring).

226. *Id.* at 157.

nates against interstate commerce; second, it places an undue burden on interstate commerce.[227]

Justice Alito's opinion has limited historical support, based on cases decided in the *Pennoyer*-era of territorial limits on jurisdiction. But the Court has been silent on the relevance of the dormant Commerce Clause since the onset of the *International Shoe* method of analysis.[228] One might ask what is at stake if the Court revives the relevance of the dormant Commerce Clause to cases involving the assertion of personal jurisdiction.

In *Mallory v. Norfolk Southern Railway Co., Due Process and Strange Bedfellows,* Professor Croxall and I raised several challenges to Justice Alito's views. Here is the gist of some of those concerns: Justice Alito is not alone in his interest in the dormant Commerce Clause. Some commentators with strong pro-business or libertarian leanings have advanced the concept. Given the sophistication of modern business and the ease of doing business in interstate commerce, we see advancing a new constitutional rule to limit plaintiffs from selecting convenient fora as policy driven: the policy is to favor corporations over injured individuals.[229]

For years, until *Daimler*, corporations were subject to suit where they engaged in sufficient in-state business activity. While Justice Ginsburg led the Court in narrowing general jurisdiction, she would also have expanded specific jurisdiction. Justice Alito joined her *Daimler* opinion, but he has not shown a similar willingness to expand specific jurisdiction.[230]

One advantage of *Daimler* was that it brought a level of certainty to general jurisdiction. But Justice Alito's dormant Commerce Clause test would require courts to engage in a case-by-case determination of the extent to which a state unduly burdened commerce.[231]

Professor Croxall and I also argued that if a plaintiff has unduly burdened a defendant by engaging in excessive forum-shopping, the doctrine of forum non conveniens allows a court to dismiss a case when the forum is too inconvenient. If suit is filed in federal court, the defendant

227. *Id.* at 160.

228. Vitiello & Croxall, *supra* note 1 at 257–65.

229. *Id.*

230. *Bristol-Myers Squibb*, 582 U.S. at 255.

231. Vitiello & Croxall, *supra* note 1 at 261.

can also invoke § 1404, requesting that the court transfer the suit to a more convenient venue.[232]

Beyond that, insofar as a plaintiff may have chosen an inconvenient forum because of the hope of having favorable law applied to the case, modern choice of law rules provide a litigant another argument to prevent unfairness. As we stated in our article, under most modern choice of law rules, in cases involving litigants from different states, the court engages in a balance of various interests, including the states from which the litigants come or where some of the events have occurred. Choice of law, in effect, protects a litigant who might otherwise contend that it has been sued in a forum to put it at disadvantage by imposing unfavorable law to the suit.[233]

Factually as well, one is hard pressed to understand how Norfolk Southern Railway could claim that it was unduly burdened by being compelled to respond to litigation in Pennsylvania or how it was discriminated against by having to defend the lawsuit there. As we observed,

> Justice Gorsuch's plurality recounts Norfolk's conduct in Pennsylvania as follows: "Norfolk Southern manages over 2,000 miles of track, operates 11 railyards, and runs 3 locomotive repair shops in Pennsylvania." Further, the plurality states that "Norfolk Southern has registered to do business in Pennsylvania in light of its 'regular, systematic, [and] extensive' operations there."[234]

The burden on Norfolk seems to have been that the company had to file papers with a state agency in which it appointed an agent for receiving service of process. That seems at best like a minor administrative burden.[235] Compare then how the law applies to in-state companies: under the Supreme Court's precedent, they are subject to suit in-state on claims that arise elsewhere. Under Justice Alito's analysis, somehow Norfolk is at a disadvantage because it too may have to respond to similar suits in-state. And yet, it has conducted a massive amount of business in-state.[236]

---

232. *Id.* at 263.
233. *Id.* at 267–68.
234. *Id.* at 263–64.
235. *Id.*
236. *Id.*

One can raise other questions about adding a new dimension to personal jurisdiction analysis that may close courthouse doors to plaintiffs. Suffice it to say that if Justice Alito's position gains traction, one senses that the winners will be large corporations.

As developed below, due process analysis remains uncertain, even more so than in 1990, when the Court got out of the business of reviewing personal jurisdiction cases because of its inability to resolve hard cases. One needs to ask whether *Ford* and *Mallory* signal a new, more plaintiff friendly direction, or whether they will have limited effects on reopening the courthouse door for injured plaintiffs.[237]

J. Closing the Courthouse Door

The first edition of this book focused on ways in which the Court had narrowed plaintiffs' access to justice in its personal jurisdiction case law. The process began in the late 1970s and into the 1980s. That took place despite increased ease of communication and transportation. The process continued in the 2000s, again as the world shrank with the development of the internet that allows instantaneous commercial activity to take place. The trend continued after publication of the first edition, only to slow with the Court's two most recent decisions.

This section reviews some of the concerns that I raised in the first edition of the book and then explores questions about how to interpret the Court's most recent cases. To circle back to Professor Mullenix's challenge, do those cases prove that I am "a procedural Cassandra" or does the right wing of the Court continue to demonstrate a pro-corporate bias that threatens access to justice?

---

237. In a case that raises an additional issue that is largely beyond the scope of this chapter (dealing with the appropriate analysis when a case involves world-wide or nationwide service of process under the Fifth Amendment Due Process Clause), the Court again upheld personal jurisdiction based on consent to be sued. *See* Fuld v. PLO, 606 U.S. 1 (2025)).

(1) The Liberal Wing of the Court

During part of the Court's retrenchment, liberal members of the Court joined their right-wing colleagues in several instances. That might suggest that the Court is applying neutral principles to interpret due process. This section suggests that is not the case.

Unquestionably, Justice Ginsburg's general jurisdiction opinions shut the courthouse door for many litigants who before could bring a claim unrelated to defendants' forum activity as long as the defendant had, for example, brick-and-mortar stores in the forum. After *Daimler*, plaintiffs will not be able to invoke general jurisdiction when the defendant corporation is a foreign corporation because that corporation will not be "at home" in any state within the United States. While plaintiffs may still be able to invoke general jurisdiction over domestic corporations, the Court's new case law limits the number of states in which general jurisdiction may be proper.[238]

Unlike her right-wing colleagues, Justice Ginsburg would have justified those decisions with two arguments. As reflected in her *Nicastro* dissent, she would have expanded specific jurisdiction. Further, she would have argued that specific jurisdiction produces the most sensible forum.[239] As was the case in *World-Wide Volkswagen*, Oklahoma was the most convenient forum, the place where the accident occurred.[240]

While that argument may explain how her expanded view of specific jurisdiction would have ameliorated the decision to narrow general jurisdiction, it does not explain what is wrong with general jurisdiction. Justice Ginsburg and the Justices who share her view of jurisdiction seem uncomfortable with forum shopping. As she wrote in *Daimler*,

---

238. *See* Nicholas D'Angelo, *Emerging from Daimler's Shadow: Registration Statutes as a Means to General Jurisdiction Over Foreign Corporations*, 91 St. John's L. Rev. 211, 236 (2017); Robert Ellis Stengel, *Boeing, Boeing, Gone: General Jurisdiction Over Corporations, Principal Place of Business, and a Second Look at the Total Activities Test*, 88 Brook. L. Rev. 275, 303 (2022).

239. *Daimler*, 134 S. Ct. at 132–33 (stating that "[a]s is evident from *Perkins, Helicopteros*, and *Goodyear*, general and specific jurisdiction have followed markedly different trajectories post-*International Shoe*. Specific jurisdiction has been cut loose from *Pennoyer*'s sway, but we have declined to stretch general jurisdiction beyond limits traditionally recognized.").

240. *Nicastro*, 564 U.S. at 893–914 (Ginsburg, J., dissenting); *World-Wide Volkswagen*, 444 U.S. 286.

general jurisdiction would allow a Polish driver who was driving a Mercedes in Poland to sue Mercedes in the United States.[241]

That hypothetical might make one uncomfortable with forum-shopping possibilities. But on closer inspection, the example is unrealistic from two perspectives. Such suits by foreigners in American courts based on claims unrelated to activity within the United States are quite rare. At a minimum, a lawyer would hesitate to bring an action in light of the probably successful motion to dismiss on forum non-conveniens grounds. A more realistic example would be one in which an American citizen brought such a suit. Under prevailing forum non-conveniens case law, a motion to dismiss might be unsuccessful, because the test for determining such a motion looks to multiple factors. One key factor present in the second case is that an American citizen can make a more compelling case for the need for a forum in the United States.[242]

But should an American injured abroad be able to sue Mercedes in the United States? Or should a farmer injured in Pennsylvania be able to sue John Deere in Mississippi? Often, as in *Ferens*, the plaintiff has engaged in some creative forum shopping, perhaps finding a court whose choice of law rules will result in a long statute of limitations being applied or in some other favorable law applying to the suit.[243] Answering the question whether an American should be able to sue Mercedes in the United States for injuries caused abroad or whether a farmer injured in Pennsylvania should be able to sue John Deere in Mississippi requires an exploration of two other questions. The first is why general jurisdiction is ever available. The second is whether forum shopping is illegitimate.

As discussed above, the Court has never given a particularly good account for why general jurisdiction should exist at all. If *Perkins* was a case of jurisdiction by necessity, then it should be used only in extreme cases. But elsewhere, for example, in *International Shoe*, the Court suggested that the courts had already recognized such a theory of jurisdiction. And that would be consonant with history. Historically, prior to

---

241. *Daimler*, 134 S. Ct. at 751.

242. *Id.* at 771 (Sotomayor, J., dissenting); *see* Piper Aircraft Co. v. Reyno, 454 U.S. 235, 247–49 (1981).

243. *See, e.g.*, Keeton v. Hustler Mag., 465 U.S. 770 (1984).

Shaffer, a plaintiff could have commenced a suit in a state where a defendant owned property by bringing an *in rem* action.[244]

Does the assertion of jurisdiction based on general jurisdiction comport with due process? That depends on how one reads notions of fundamental fairness and substantial justice. One advantage of the straightforward approach of *McGee* is that we know what question to ask and why. Due process is synonymous with fair notice and the opportunity to be heard. In many instances, a large corporation with substantial business activity in a given forum cannot claim that a suit in-state denies it a fair opportunity to be heard. That is especially true in the modern setting where transportation and communication are so efficient. When a plaintiff like Ferens sues a defendant like John Deere in Mississippi, the defendant no doubt has counsel on retainer in Mississippi. Access to information out-of-state no longer provides a significant problem. Attorneys can take depositions out-of-state without traveling by using modern communication channels.[245]

That invites the second question: Is forum-shopping illegitimate? When I teach *Ferens*, I confess to having conflicting emotions about what the plaintiff's lawyer accomplished. The result was to move the case back to the most convenient forum, where the action was otherwise time-barred. The result may be hard to explain to non-lawyers; it looks like a lawyer's trick. What about truth and justice, one might ask?

Forum shopping is inherent in an interstate and federal system with independent judiciaries in each sovereign. Further, both sides of any suit forum-shop to full advantage. In *World-Wide Volkswagen*, the defendants, including Audi and Volkswagen of America (which subsidized the trip to the Supreme Court), put the plaintiffs to extensive delay and expense to counter the plaintiffs' selection of an appropriate county court, but one that was pro-plaintiff. The case bounced around in the system for years before the plaintiffs eventually lost their suit. Were the defendants' forum-shopping efforts illegitimate? Probably not, at least absent violations of Federal Rule of Civil Procedure 11 or similar state

244. *Shaffer*, 433 U.S. 186; *Int'l Shoe Co.*, 326 U.S. 310; *Pennoyer*, 95 U.S. 714.

245. *McGee*, 355 U.S. 220; *see, e.g.*, Mullane v. Cent. Hanover Bank & Trust Co., 339 U.S. 306, 314 (1950). Although counsel for BMS succeeded in arguing that the California courts lacked jurisdiction over claims by out-of-state plaintiffs, counsel's concession that defending the suits in California was not burdensome was certainly an honest one.

sanctions laws. But one could make the same argument about the plaintiffs' forum-shopping efforts.[246]

Even though they must have recognized that forum shopping inheres in our system, Justice Ginsburg and Justices who joined her general jurisdiction opinions found the forum-shopping opportunities provided by general jurisdiction to be too much of a good thing. But other than the passing reference to the unrealistic example of the Polish driver suing in the United States, Justice Ginsburg made no effort to explain whether the fear with general jurisdiction was that it offered plaintiffs too much forum-shopping ability, nor did she make any effort to explain what is illegitimate about forum shopping.[247]

(2) The Right Wing of the Court

Even after Justice Scalia's death, at least three members of the Court's right wing viewed due process in ways that would greatly narrow access to court. Not only did they subscribe to the new narrow view of general jurisdiction, but they also took an extremely narrow view of specific jurisdiction. Read together, their views threatened access to justice for many plaintiffs.

Above, I explored how the Court's new general jurisdiction case law narrows access to courts, especially in cases involving foreign defendants. At the same time, former Justice Kennedy wrote for three other Justices in *Nicastro*. Of the Justices on the right, only Justice Alito did not join his opinion. Justice Kennedy's view of specific jurisdiction, if adopted by a majority of the Court, would have a profound effect on access to our courts for any number of plaintiffs.[248]

Imagine two plaintiffs. Like Nicastro, imagine a plaintiff seriously injured in the United States as the result of a product manufactured abroad. Assume that the manufacturer of the end product or a manufacturer of a component part incorporated into the product caused the plaintiff's injuries. Given the revelations about the danger posed by airbags manufactured by Takata Corporation, such cases are hardly hypo-

---

246. *World-Wide Volkswagen*, 444 U.S. 286.

247. *Daimler*, 134 S. Ct. 746.

248. *Nicastro*, 564 U.S. 873.

thetical.[249] Imagine further that the plaintiff hopes to join both manufacturers in a single action in the United States. Alternatively, imagine the same plaintiff whose injuries resulted from a product manufactured in the United States. But as in the first hypothetical, the plaintiff wants to join both defendants in a single action. How might those cases have been resolved historically and consistent with the various views of members of the right wing of the Court?

Prior to 1977, a plaintiff injured by a foreign manufacturer or a domestic manufacturer could begin suit by attaching the defendant's property within the state. *In rem* proceedings were proper without regard to the connection between the property and the underlying dispute. Hence, the hypothetical plaintiffs could have sued anywhere in the United States where the defendants had property, including a bank account. In its earliest discussions of due process, the Court seemed to acknowledge that such an assertion of jurisdiction comported with due process.[250]

After *Shaffer v. Heitner*, the defendants in those examples could successfully challenge the property attachment if, under the Court's modern jurisdictional case law, an *in personam* action would violate due process. As developed earlier, given the rapid expansion of the due process test, plaintiffs would not have been deprived of an otherwise convenient forum. That is so for two reasons. As long as the defendant had significant contacts with the forum state, the plaintiff could invoke general jurisdiction. Remember that Audi did not contest the Oklahoma State Court's jurisdiction over it in *World-Wide*. No doubt, Audi's counsel recognized that its contacts were so substantial that the challenge would have been frivolous. In addition, prior to *World-Wide Volkswagen*, many courts found that the state could exercise jurisdiction over component parts manufacturers. That was so even absent a showing that they pur-

---

249. Even though the problem arose with airbags from earlier in the 2000s, some manufacturers were still issuing recalls in 2024. *See Takata Airbag Recall: Everything You Need to Know*, CONSUMER REPORTS (Aug. 13, 2024), https://www.consumerreports.org/cars/car-recalls-defects/takata-airbag-recall-everything-you-need-to-know-a1060713669/#:~:text=Models%20flagged%20as%20being%20at,vehicles%20and%20seek%20immediate%20repairs.

250. *See, e.g.*, *Pennoyer*, 95 U.S. 714.

posefully directed activity to the forum state. Placing a product in the stream of commerce sufficed.[251]

Today, unless the Court rethinks *Shaffer*, a plaintiff cannot rely on *in rem* jurisdiction without satisfying *International Shoe*'s due process analysis. Despite his adherence to tradition, demonstrated in his plurality opinion in *Burnham*, Justice Scalia did not show willingness to reinstitute *Pennoyer*'s *in rem* approach.[252] Nor has any other Justice suggested returning to pre-1977 law. Further, as developed above, all of the Justices then on the right wing of the Court signed onto Justice Ginsburg's restrictive view of general jurisdiction. Finally, Justice Kennedy's view, joined by three other conservative Justices, would have denied jurisdiction over the component parts manufacturers. Even more troubling, depending on how they set up their business, even the foreign manufacturers may be able to avoid jurisdiction in the United States, as did J. McIntyre. Setting up a distributor as a sufficiently separate entity—even one that may be poorly capitalized—might immunize foreigner manufacturers from suit in the United States.[253]

Also as developed above, a plaintiff has fewer forums available even against a domestic corporation. The new general jurisdiction rules limit a plaintiff to the defendant's state of incorporation or principal place of business, absent a third forum where that corporation is "at home." And if Justice Kennedy's restrictive view of specific jurisdiction were to prevail, the plaintiff would not be able to join the component parts manufacturer in a convenient forum, for example, in the state where the plaintiff bought the product and was injured. Placing the product in the stream of commerce, without much more, fails under his restrictive view of the stream of commerce.[254]

These results seem odd at a time when trade is global, communication is immediate, and travel allows easy access throughout the country and world. As observed by former Justice Breyer in his concurring opinion in *Nicastro*, commerce and communications may require rethinking the Court's traditional approach to personal jurisdiction. The

---

251. *World-Wide Volkswagen*, 444 U.S. 286; *see, e.g.*, Gray v. Am. Radiator & Standard Sanitary Corp., 22 Ill. 2d 432 (1961).

252. *Burnham*, 495 U.S. 604.

253. *Daimler*, 134 S. Ct. 746; *Nicastro*, 564 U.S. 873; *Burnham*, 495 U.S. 605; *Shaffer*, 433 U.S. 186.

254. *Nicastro*, 564 U.S. at 882.

trend towards sweeping international trade agreements and the access to information via the Internet multiply the instances in which United States plaintiffs may seek to force an injury-causing foreign defendant to respond to suit in the United States, rather than in a foreign country. One would have thought that a court intent on protecting its citizens would expand the jurisdictional reach of its courts. And the answer is not that the Court's jurisprudence prevented expansion of jurisdiction. To the contrary, the Court's case law is new and more restrictive, narrowing its approach and rejecting the approach taken by many lower courts.[255] Why?

A good place to start is the right wing of the Court's pro-corporate bias. Cases like *Citizens United v. Federal Election Commission*[256] support such a conclusion. The right wing of the Court might also be accused of an anti-plaintiff bias—willing to narrow the courthouse door in cases involving the historically liberal pleading rules.[257]

As mentioned above, *Daimler* suggested that the Court was intent on bringing United States law in line with European law. Elsewhere, right-wing justices on the Court have railed against reliance on international norms in interpreting domestic law. They were, however, silent on Justice Ginsburg's reliance on European law.[258]

The decisions preceding *Ford* and *Mallory* were unsettling. While Justice Alito joined Justice Breyer's concurring opinion in *Nicastro*, his usual alliance with the right wing of the Court is not reassuring. Since *Nicastro*, the Court has not returned to the question whether a defendant must act with purpose in affiliating with the forum to comport with due process. If the Court does adhere to Justice Kennedy's *Nicastro* approach, plaintiffs will have increasing difficulty in finding convenient forums in which to bring suits against defendants in various kinds of cases, like ones involving manufacturers and their component parts manufacturers.

---

255. *Id.* at 887 (Breyer, J., concurring). *See also* Hoffheimer, *The Stealth Revolution in Personal Jurisdiction*, *supra* note 176 at 504 (exploring a "striking paradox of the Roberts Court's personal jurisdiction jurisprudence" which "in explaining decisions that alter[ed] the fundamental power of courts," repeatedly denied that it was altering existing law).

256. Citizens United v. Fed. Election Comm'n, 558 U.S. 310 (2010).

257. *See generally* Ashcroft v. Iqbal, 556 U.S. 662 (2009) (dismissing a case because it failed to plead sufficient facts to state a claim despite liberal pleading rules).

258. *See, e.g.*, Roper v. Simmons, 543 U.S. 551, 607–30 (2005) (Scalia, J., dissenting).

One might ask whether *Ford* and *Mallory* suggest a new and more pro-plaintiff majority emerging on the Court.[259] Perhaps. But Justice Alito's *BMS* opinion's suggestion that federalism is at play in personal jurisdiction cases was jarring. Even more so was his suggestion in his concurring opinion in *Mallory* that the assertion of jurisdiction in that case might violate the dormant Commerce Clause. He is suggesting a new attack on access to justice.

Insofar as *Mallory* was a victory for a plaintiff seeking access to a convenient forum, plaintiffs cannot count on always being able to rely on such open-ended statutes. Many states have narrower consent statutes, allowing, in effect, a litigant to pursue a defendant consistent with principles applicable to specific jurisdiction.[260] Also, no doubt business organizations will attempt to narrow such statutes.[261] I would not bet against their ability to prevail in many conservative states.

In his concurring opinion in *Ford*, Justice Gorsuch suggested that the Court might need to rethink its approach to personal jurisdiction, in effect, inviting litigants to ask the Court to abandon the *International Shoe* framework. Mallory's attorney attempted to make such an argument before the Supreme Court in the suit against Norfolk Southern Railway. The Court did not take that route in reaching its result.[262] But what if?

---

259. As noted above, *Fuld v. PLO*, 606 U.S. 1 (2025) , seems to continue that trend.

260. *See* Eric B. Wolff & Stephanie Olson, *Personal Jurisdiction and Foreign Corporation Registration Statutes: A Purple Haze, but the Sky Is Not Falling*, Perkins Coie (Jun. 29, 2023), https://perkinscoie.com/insights/update/personal-jurisdiction-and-foreign-corporation-registration-statutes-purple-haze-sky (explaining that, unlike Pennsylvania and Georgia, in many states, "mere compliance with a business registration statute is insufficient to grant courts personal jurisdiction over a corporation").

261. *See Does a Corporation Consent to the General Jurisdiction of a State's Courts by Registering to Do Business There?*, Wolters Kluwer, https://www.nass.org/sites/default/files/2024-02/CT-Issue-Paper-NASS-Winter24.pdf (suggesting that in 2023, no state enacted a statute providing that a corporation consents to jurisdiction by registering to do business in a state, which could be explained by the fact that it is not in states' best interests to enact such statutes, as it could deter out-of-state corporations from doing business in the state).

262. *See* Andrew Rhys Davies, *3 Personal Jurisdiction Questions Mallory Leaves Unanswered*, WilmerHale (Oct. 18, 2023), https://www.wilmerhale.com/insights/publications/20231025-3-personal-jurisdiction-questions-mallory-leaves-unanswered (stating that the majority in *Mallory* insisted that *Mallory* was consistent with *International Shoe*, which, according to them, merely staked out "an additional road to jurisdiction over out-of-state corporations... without supplanting other roads, such as consent").

In most instances, the right wing of the Court has invoked originalism in its various forms to expand rights like Second Amendment rights[263] and to narrow other rights like the right to procreative choice.[264] That is, most often, originalism has served to advance the right-wing agenda.[265] In *United States v. Rahimi,* the Court's most recent Second Amendment case, justices on the right disagreed among themselves about the original understanding of the Second Amendment.[266] If the Court returns to the original understanding of due process as it relates to personal jurisdiction, what will that look like?

The answer to the previous question is that one can only guess. Suits against wealthy defendants, including far flung corporations, were possible in the earliest days if the defendants had property in the forum state.[267] The plaintiff could begin a proceeding in rem by attaching the property. Would an originalist justice vote to overrule *Shaffer* to allow such suits without compliance with traditional notions of fair play and substantial justice? Would the Court overrule cases like *McGee,* where out-of-state defendants are subject to suit in the plaintiff's home state based on activity within the state or would those plaintiffs be forced to sue in defendants' home states?[268]

Even Justice Scalia, one of the fathers of the originalist movement, acknowledged that the Court had adopted modern forms of asserting jurisdiction. For example, while he asserted that tradition was sufficient to explain the result in *Burnham*, he did not urge the abandonment of the *International Shoe* framework across the board.[269] Instead, he was content to limit state's power to compel a defendant to answer suit in a

---

263. *See* N.Y. State Rifle & Pistol Ass'n v. Bruen, 597 U.S. 1 (2022); *See also The Second Amendment & Originalism*, Talks On Law, https://www.talksonlaw.com/briefs/the-second-amendment-originalism (explaining that "Second Amendment rights have emerged from often conflicting constitutional interpretations, but none has shaped its modern understanding more than the doctrine of Originalism.").

264. *See* Dobbs v. Jackson Women's health Org., 597 U.S. 215 (2022).

265. *See* Madiba K. Dennie, The Originalism Trap (Random House 2024)

266. *See* United States v. Rahimi, 602 U.S. 680 (2024).

267. *See Pennoyer*, 95 U.S. 714.

268. As developed in *Daimler*, one reason for general jurisdiction in the pre-*International Shoe* era was so that a plaintiff had somewhere to sue the defendant. *Daimler*, 134 S. Ct. at 758 n.9. Would justices rethinking the Court's approach to personal jurisdiction go back to such early rules more suited to a pre-Industrial Revolution era?

269. *See Burnham*, 495 U.S. at 605.

state by requiring that the defendant direct purposeful activity to the state in specific jurisdiction cases.[270]

Less certain is how the new generation of originalist justices would view personal jurisdiction through an originalist lens. The concern is that many of the right-wing justices have voted so often to favor corporations.[271]

I do not suggest that the justices on the right wing of the Court consciously decide to favor corporations at the expense of plaintiffs. Scholars debate the extent to which justices are aware of biases when they decide cases. For purposes of this book, I do not need to resolve that question. But justices have value preferences that animate their views. Former President Obama's critics attacked his comments about Justice Sotomayor when he suggested that her life's experience would be an advantage on the Court.[272] Some critics cried foul, invoking the myth that the judge's role is limited to interpreting the law, not making the law. Some invoked Chief Justice Roberts' rather remarkably disingenuous comment that he would act as an umpire, objectively interpreting the law.[273] And if anyone doubts that justices' experiences are relevant to their decision-making, he or she should read Justice Kennedy's *Iqbal* opinion in which he called on judges to rely on their common sense and life's experiences in determining whether a plaintiff's claim is plausible.[274]

A few parting thoughts: one wonders how Fourteenth Amendment due process has been invoked to protect states' rights, even as recently as 2017 in Justice Alito's *BMS* opinion. That certainly does not sound like an original understanding of a constitutional amendment aimed at limiting states' powers. In addition, a further retrenchment, based on an original understanding of the Constitution or otherwise, would seem particularly pro-defendant in an era of increasingly rapid communication and transportation. That retrenchment comes at the expense of in-

270. *Asahi*, 480 U.S. at 109 (Justice Scalia joined the part of Justice O'Connor's plurality opinion in which she explained that "minimum contacts must have a basis in 'some act by which the defendant purposefully avails itself of the privilege of conducting activities within the forum State'").

271. *See Daimler*, 134 S. Ct. 746; *Bristol-Myers Squibb*, 582 U.S. 255.

272. *See infra* Chapter 6, Section B.

273. Bruce Weber, *Empires v. Judges*, New York Times (July 11, 2009) http://www.nytimes.com/2009/07/12/weekinreview/12weber.html?_r=0.

274. *Iqbal*, 556 U.S. 662.

jured plaintiffs. Finally, Justice Alito's suggestion in *Mallory* that the defendant should argue that Pennsylvania's exercise of jurisdiction over it violated the dormant Commerce Clause suggests two things: one, that at least some members of the Court's right wing want to usher in a new set of rules limiting plaintiffs' ability to choose a convenient forum. Two, Justice Alito is willing to invite an argument with little historical support. His view of the dormant Commerce Clause has little support as a matter of the Framers' original intent, despite his adherence to originalism in various contexts.[275]

275. Vitiello & Croxall, *supra* note 1 at 266.

FOUR

The Complaint

A. Introduction

Many years ago, an experienced lawyer said something to me about the Federal Rules of Civil Procedure that did not resonate until I had taught Civil Procedure for the second or third time. He commented that lawyers do not appreciate the philosophy underlying the Federal Rules of Civil Procedure (or any other system of procedural rules, I imagine). Without appreciating that philosophy, students are likely to approach pleading, discovery, summary judgment, and related issues with minimal curiosity at best. Lawyers who fail to understand that fact as well may miss important arguments in support of their positions.

This chapter focuses on the philosophy underlying Federal Rule of Civil Procedure 8(a)(2), dealing with pleading in the federal system. That also requires some discussion of the history leading to adoption of the Federal Rules of Civil Procedure, including an evaluation of earlier pleading systems. It also revisits the Supreme Court's substantive due process activism. Further, it explores how the drafters of the Rules lowered the bar at the pleading stage and relied on other Rules to weed out non-meritorious claims. It then turns to two important Supreme Court cases that have rewritten Rule 8(a)(2). At a minimum, students should see that important policy questions animate pleading rules. In addition, the two leading Supreme Court cases on point, *Bell Atlantic Corp. v. Twombly*[1]

1. Bell Atl. Corp. v. Twombly, 550 U.S. 544 (2007).

and *Ashcroft v. Iqbal*,[2] provide another example where the Court, especially its right wing, made access to federal courts more difficult.

At times, liberals and progressives have rued the ease with which plaintiffs could bring suit in federal court.[3] A notable example explored in this chapter is Paula Jones's suit against then-President Bill Clinton. But for the most part, the Court's new heightened pleading standard disfavors civil rights plaintiffs and generally favors corporations and governmental entities over plaintiffs.

This chapter also reviews two developments since the first edition of this book. As developed below, the Court's *Twombly* and *Iqbal* decisions suggested that the Court was revising Rule 8(a)(2) inappropriately. Consistent with the overall theme of this book, that revision seemed to favor corporate and other defendant groups at the expense of injured plaintiffs. This chapter examines empirical data that suggests the not-so-hidden political bias in the Court's decisions. But the chapter also circles back to Professor Mullenix's suggestion that I am a "procedural Cassandra." Here, the results are mixed. The Supreme Court has backed away from what seemed to be the clear message of *Twombly* and *Iqbal* to impose a much higher burden on the plaintiff to get to discovery. But not to concede too much to Professor Mullenix, an examination of lower court opinions suggests that some right-wing judges have interpreted *Twombly* and *Iqbal* as an invitation to make access to justice more difficult for some categories of plaintiffs.

B. The Historical Perspective

(1) Earlier Systems

Imagine a case in which a man and a woman went back to her apartment after having had dinner together. Once in her apartment, the man made an unwanted sexual advance. During his attempts to kiss her, her head banged into a book case, causing her serious injuries. Also imagine that at some later date, he ran his car into hers, again causing her injuries.

---

2. Ashcroft v. Iqbal, 556 U.S. 662 (2009).

3. *See generally* Joe Conason & Gene Lyons, The Hunting of the President 126 (2000) (referencing a publication claiming the complaint was "poorly drafted" and "dismissible on its face.").

How should the woman proceed if she decides to sue the man for her various injuries? That depends on the pleading system in the court where she chooses to file her action.

The history of pleading in the United States is relatively short: we have had three dominant procedural systems in place. Ending in the twentieth century, the earliest system of pleading focused on the form of action that a plaintiff had. Inherited from English common law, the writ system required a plaintiff to select a particular writ that fit the form of action she hoped to bring. Writs that students may come across in their basic courses include the writ of assumpsit (in Contracts), the writ of trespass, and the writ of trespass on the case (both of the latter in Torts). The writ of trespass was the proper writ for someone claiming one of the five intentional torts that developed in early common law—assault, battery, trespass to chattels, trespass to land, and false imprisonment. Negligence actions evolved from the writ of trespass on the case.[4] The system was highly technical, allowing, for example, a litigant to join multiple unrelated claims if they were all within one writ (e.g., trespass to chattel and battery), but not related claims that did not derive from the same historical writ.

So, in the hypothetical above, the plaintiff had to choose whether her claim was that the defendant assaulted her by making sexual advances or whether her injuries resulted from his negligence. If she sought the writ of trespass, however, she could not advance her negligence theory. But she could add a second trespass tort, even if the second tort was unrelated to the first tort. Hence, if in the second case, her claim was that the man rammed his car into her intentionally, she could join that as a battery. Further, if the plaintiff filed under the writ of trespass but the court found that the defendant's conduct was negligent, not a trespass, the plaintiff would lose her case.[5]

Most students introduced to these kinds of arcane distinctions in the writ system understand why jurisdictions abandoned it. It produced results that are hard to justify. For instance, in the previous example, the defendant could not claim any prejudice in defending himself. Reading the original complaint told him what he did that the plaintiff found objectionable. At least in that simple fact pattern, he could deny that he did

4. *See* William Prosser & W. Page Keeton, The Law of Torts 30 (5th ed. 1984).

5. *Id.* at 29.

what the plaintiff alleged; perhaps he could argue that he did not intend the contact to be offensive; or he could contend that the plaintiff overstated the damages. Often, the results of hyper-technicalities benefit defendants, as in this example.[6] Even if the plaintiff could refile her action by getting a writ of trespass on the case, any recovery would be delayed by years.

Arcane systems that result in highly technical decisions also favor the parties who can hire the most skilled lawyers. Typically, defendants are more likely to be able to do so than are plaintiffs. That is especially true if the defendant is a large institutional entity and the plaintiff is an injured individual. The net result is a system that favors wealthy litigants because of their wealth, not because of the merits of the case for or against them. Indeed, it is undemocratic. In many cases, judges resolved disputes without a jury ever getting to hear the case.[7]

By the mid-nineteenth century, reform efforts were in place. The most impressive "modern" code was the product of David Dudley Field's efforts. David Field, the brother of Supreme Court Justice Stephen Field (the author of *Pennoyer v. Neff*), drafted a code that the New York Legislature adopted in 1848. Among other important features (including merging law and equity), the Field Code ("code pleading") abandoned the writ system and its forms of action. The code adopted a pleading standard for the complaint that required the plaintiff to include in the complaint a "plain and concise statement of the facts constituting a cause of action without unnecessary repetition...."[8] The code also introduced the transactional unit as the basic unit of joinder as well.[9] That is, unlike the writ system, a person could join two distinct claims as long as they derived from the same transaction, i.e., from events closely related in time and place.

Applied to the hypothetical above, the code would allow the plaintiff to bring her claim for damages caused by the unwanted touching in a

6. McCaughey v. H. C. Schuette, 117 Cal. 223 (1897).

7. *E.g.*, Arthur R. Miller, *From* Conley *to* Twombly *to* Iqbal: *A Double Play on the Federal Rules of Civil Procedure*, 60 Duke L.J. 1, 16 (2010) (analyzing the effects of the two Supreme Court decisions in *Bell Atlantic Corp. v. Twombly* and *Ashcroft v. Iqbal* against the already established Federal Rules of Civil Procedure).

8. Jack H. Friedenthal, Mary Kay Kane & Arthur R. Miller, Civil Procedure 249 (5th ed. 2015).

9. *Id.* at 250.

single action. Whether the second injury was properly before the court turned on whether the court could characterize the two sets of events as a single transaction or occurrence.

Despite the obvious hope of adopters of the code that it would reduce arcane rules governing access to court, many state courts interpreted the code hyper-technically. Both the meaning of "facts" and "cause of action" could beguile attorneys.[10] Most important for this discussion are the cases interpreting the term "facts."

Most contemporary civil procedure casebooks include examples of state law cases interpreting that term. For example, an edition of Friedenthal, Miller, Sexton, and Hershkoff's Civil Procedure casebook includes two seemingly indistinguishable cases. In *Gillispie v. Goodyear Service Stores,*[11] a case arising in North Carolina (a code state), a plaintiff alleged as follows:

> [T]he defendants, without cause or just excuse and maliciously came upon and trespassed upon the premises occupied by the plaintiff as a residence, and by the use of harsh language and threatening language and physical force directed against the plaintiff assaulted the plaintiff and placed her in great fear, and humiliated and embarrassed her by subjecting her to public scorn and ridicule, and caused her to be seized and exhibited to the public as a prisoner, and to be confined in a public jail, all to her great humiliation, embarrassment and harm.[12]

Under North Carolina precedent, a pleader must disclose "issuable facts" and allege "material, essential and ultimate facts upon which plaintiff's right of action is based." The court found that the cited allegations were mere legal conclusions. Terms like "assault" and "trespass" did not allow the opposing party to respond or the court to declare the law as it related to the facts.[13]

The Friedenthal casebook then discusses a similar case, arising in Maryland, also a code state. There, the plaintiff alleged,

---

10. *Id.* at 249.

11. Gillispie v. Goodyear Serv. Stores, 128 S.E.2d 762 (N.C. 1963); FRIEDENTHAL ET AL., *supra* note 8, at 32.

12. *Id.* at 765.

13. *Id.* at 764.

> [The defendants] did then and there falsely maliciously, and without just cause...arrest [plaintiff]...on charges[s] of disorderly conduct and resisting arrest... [they took him] to the police station where he was forceably [sic] imprisoned, kept, detained and restrained of his liberty... [but upon trial he] was acquitted.... [Defendants] well knew that the prosecution was false, groundless, and without probable cause....[14]

Unlike the court's holding in *Gillispie*, the Maryland court in *Robinson v. Board of County Commissioners* found the complaint stated facts sufficient to state a cause of action.[15]

Casebooks also often include a case or cases in which a plaintiff has alleged that a defendant was negligent. Quite often, the courts reject such pleadings because negligence is not a fact, but a legal conclusion. And editors introduce students to other critical distinctions that courts have adopted in interpreting code pleading standards. Thus, a plaintiff should not plead conclusions of law; instead, she must plead "operative facts," and cannot plead "evidentiary facts."[16]

Casebook editors may also introduce students to the procedural consequences of pleading improperly. For example, does the plaintiff have an opportunity to re-plead or is the complaint dismissed with prejudice? The Sixth Edition of Freer and Perdue's *Civil Procedure: Cases, Materials, and Questions* includes a discussion of *McCaughey v. Schuette*,[17] which was decided by the California Supreme Court. There, after the plaintiff won in the trial court below, the defendant appealed and alleged that the pleading in the complaint alleged legal conclusions, not facts as required by the code.[18]

The message in presenting this material is not merely that courts have created confusing distinctions, often in direct contradiction to other cases. But more importantly, the discussion of such cases should lead to a further inquiry as to whether such technicalities matter. If a

---

14. Robinson v. Board of County Comm'rs, 278 A.2d 71 (Md. 1971).

15. *Id.* at 75.

16. *See, e.g.*, Richard D. Freer & Wendy Collins Perdue, Civil Procedure: Cases, Materials, and Questions 293–94, (6th ed. 2012); *accord.* Friedenthal et al., *supra* note 8, at 557.

17. McCaughey v. H. C. Schuette, 117 Cal. 223 (1897).

18. Freer & Perdue, *supra* note 16, at 293.

court adopts an arcane distinction because sound policies support the distinction, so be it. That is not the case if the distinction lacks a sound foundation.

When I teach the preceding material, I tease out whether the defendant is at a disadvantage when it receives such a complaint. For example, in discussing *Gillispie*, I ask students what corporate counsel would do upon first reading the complaint. Presumably, counsel would contact the manager of the Goodyear store and ask the manager what occurred between store employees and the plaintiff. As an aside, having lived in the rural south for a period of time, I know that, at least in the past, Goodyear stores sold appliances as well as tires. In many communities, they sold goods on-time. I imagine that the plaintiff failed to pay an installment or multiple installments and Goodyear employees attempted to repossess the goods from the plaintiff. Certainly, if my imagined scenario is correct, defense counsel would have no difficulty figuring out what was at stake in *Gillispie*.

Similarly, assume that a plaintiff and defendant were involved in an automobile accident. The plaintiff may not be aware what the defendant was doing at the time of the accident. She may have been texting; she may have fallen asleep; or she may have hit her gas pedal instead of her brake in attempting to stop. If the plaintiff filed an action alleging that the defendant was negligent in operating her vehicle—inadequate under most court's interpretations of code-fact pleading—again, would the defendant be unable to figure out what the complaint was about? Indeed, she might have a much better idea what caused the accident than would the plaintiff.[19]

The point of the previous discussion is that the kinds of allegations that courts might reject as inadequate under the code satisfy basic notice requirements. But those courts may be concerned about other issues. For example, making the plaintiff's job too easy may encourage frivolous lawsuits. They may want plaintiffs to invest in pre-filing investigation before allowing them to waste the time of both defendants and courts. But requiring heightened factual pleading does not seem well-suited to preventing frivolous suits from being filed. And the relevant informa-

19. Miller, *supra* note 7, at 40–41.

tion may be beyond the plaintiff's reach even if she does engage in pre-filing investigation.[20]

In the simple auto accident example, the defendant might not cooperate with the plaintiff's investigator. Only if the investigator can get the defendant under oath can he get relevant information. In addition, forcing a plaintiff to state ultimate facts, not legal conclusions or evidentiary facts, does not guarantee that the plaintiff will not file a frivolous lawsuit.[21]

The *Gillispie* case is a bit trickier. Assume the facts are as I hypothesized and that Goodyear attempted to repossess the appliance from the plaintiff. The law may authorize the defendant to use self-help to repossess the appliance. Further, the law may allow the defendant to use reasonable force to do so and may deny the person dispossessed from using force to resist. As a result, Goodyear might have been entitled to a motion to dismiss if Gillispie had more thoroughly alleged facts surrounding the dispute.[22]

Obviously, if a plaintiff alleges information that does not allow recovery under the law, she should not be able to proceed past the pleading stages. Thus, if a state does not recognize the tort of negligent infliction of emotional distress and if all that a plaintiff alleges is that the defendant negligently inflicted emotional distress on the plaintiff, the court should dismiss the suit with a minimum of time and effort on behalf of the court and defendant. But in *Gillispie*, North Carolina law almost certainly included other devices whereby the defendant could put relevant facts in front of the court with little additional effort on its behalf. Minimal discovery between the parties would have made the case ripe for summary judgment, for example, if Goodyear's employees were attempting to repossess Gillispie's appliance. Alternatively, if that material revealed that Gillispie was claiming that Goodyear's employees used excessive force, then the case should go to trial. Real factual disputes are not likely to reveal themselves at the pleading stages.[23]

20. *Id.* at 45, 53.

21. *See* Bell Atl. Corp. v. Twombly, 550 U.S. 544, 575 (2007); *see also* Miller, *supra* note 7, at 53–54 (describing the motivations behind *Twombly* and *Iqbal* as to filter out meritless claims).

22. *See generally* PROSSER & KEETON, *supra* note 4, at 140 (defenses to intentional interference).

23. *E.g.*, CHARLES ALAN WRIGHT & MARY KAY KANE, LAW OF FEDERAL COURTS 467 (7th ed. 2011).

As often noted, pleading systems can serve four functions. My earlier discussion mentions two that are valuable: providing notice and weeding out meritless claims. But pleading does not do a good job of determining the parties' view of the facts, nor does it do well narrowing the issues.[24] As discussed above, in many cases, one party simply does not have access to facts within the possession of the other party to allow her to develop a view of the facts. In a simple case, she may not know that the other driver was texting while driving. In a complex case, defendants may have conspired in private, leaving no trail for members of the public. Without access to that kind of information, narrowing the issues may be implausible as well.

(2) The Federal Rules of Civil Procedure

(A) BACKGROUND

The failures of the writ system help one understand what the Field Code hoped to achieve. But before turning to the specific changes in the federal rules, this section discusses the politics that led to the adoption of the Federal Rules of Civil Procedure. And as with significant changes to the law, this change resulted from an interesting political coalition.

For much of the latter half of the nineteenth century and the first third of the twentieth century, federal courts were business-friendly courts. They often supported business and conservative interests through judicial activism seldom rivaled in our history. Most often, the Supreme Court advanced those interests through creation or denial of substantive rights.[25]

Many law students and some political science students are familiar with the Supreme Court's substantive due process jurisprudence. During a period of progressive politics that dominated in many states, state legislatures attempted to regulate wages and working conditions. The Court routinely struck down progressive legislation on constitutional grounds. Similarly, when Congress passed early New Deal legislation, the Court

---

24. *See id.* (discussing the four functions of the pleading system); *see also* FRIEDENTHAL ET AL., *supra* note 8, at 257 ("[N]otice pleading makes it less likely that the pleadings themselves will narrow issues. . . .").

25. *See* EDWARD A. PURCELL, JR., BRANDEIS AND THE PROGRESSIVE CONSTITUTION 15 (2000).

struck down statutes aimed at stimulating economic recovery. Further, the Court developed rules of general federal common law, most often favoring business interests as well. The effect of some of the Court's holdings was to create rights favoring conservative interests and placing them beyond Congress' power to substitute its judgment for that of the Court.[26] As is the case today, those kinds of decisions attracted the public's attention. Members of the public understood what was at stake.[27]

Frustration with the Court eventually led to one of the more brazen attempts to undercut the Court's decisions when President Roosevelt proposed increasing its membership. His "court-packing" legislation would have created a new position on the Court for every justice over 70 years old, up to a total of 6 new seats. Given the ages of the Justices at that point, Roosevelt would have been able to achieve a majority of less conservative Justices within a short period of time.[28]

Even earlier, conservative and business interests were urging procedural reform. At the same time, Progressives favored substantive and procedural reform. Professor Edward A. Purcell, Jr.'s informative book *Brandeis and the Progressive Constitution* provides a detailed account of the political factors that led to procedural reform.[29] For example, he explores how William Howard Taft attempted to subvert the Progressives' call for judicial reform:

> While still president of the United States, he began a sedulous campaign to defeat Progressive judicial reform by galvanizing the profession behind a calculated and narrow reform program of its own. Subsequently, as law professor, president of the ABA, and chief justice of the United States, Taft continued to preach the twin gospels of preemptive procedural reform and protection of the federal judiciary.[30]

The federal judiciary that Roosevelt inherited was a business-friendly, anti-Progressive institution. But Taft shared concerns with Progressives

---

26. *Id.* at 12–15.

27. *See, e.g.*, Lochner v. New York, 198 U.S. 45 (1905) (holding for the business over the employee who had worked over 60 hours a week because a business' right of contract is a liberty protected by the Fourteenth Amendment).

28. *See* Purcell, *supra* note 25, at 35.

29. *Id.*

30. *Id.* at 27.

that procedures should be simplified, consistent with many reformers of their day.[31]

In the early part of the twentieth century, conservative organizations, like the American Bar Association, advanced procedural simplification at a time when large law firms were beginning to represent interstate corporations. (Given the contemporary claim that the ABA is now a liberal organization, one should not doubt that it was conservative during the years under discussion. It routinely opposed Progressive legislative reforms, including efforts to outlaw child labor and to provide for minimum wages.) While conservative lawyers favored federal courts because they were defense oriented, practice under the 1872 Conformity Act[32] was inefficient. Under that act, a federal court (unless sitting in equity) applied the procedural rules of the state in which the court sat. Beginning in the early part of the twentieth century, the ABA took up Taft's call for procedural reform. The bill it proposed, like the Rules Enabling Act,[33] shifted to the Supreme Court the authority to create rules of practice and procedure.[34]

Again as Professor Purcell demonstrates, many supporters of the ABA bill were motivated by highly political concerns. Procedural reform deflected "attention from substantive legal issues and egregious inequalities in the distribution of legal services, to identify proper legal reform with politically arcane issues beyond the competence of the public, and to demonstrate the civic virtue of the legal elite."[35] Despite Taft's hopes and the ABA's support for reform, their efforts were frustrated by Progressive Democratic Senator Thomas Walsh from Montana. Walsh was a powerful member of the Judiciary Committee. By 1930, reform efforts seemed dead.[36]

Walsh was slated to become the Attorney General of the United States, but he died before his appointment in 1933. His replacement, Homer Cummings, ended up leading efforts to get the Rules Enabling Act passed in 1934. Even prior to 1934, Progressives divided on whether

31. *Id.* at 28.
32. 1872 Conformity Act, 17 Stat. 197.
33. Rules Enabling Act, 28 U.S.C. § 2072 (2012).
34. PURCELL, *supra* note 25, at 28–31.
35. *Id.* at 24–28.
36. *Id.* at 31.

they should back procedural reform. Many Progressive academics favored reform, while many plaintiffs' lawyers were satisfied with state procedural rules, applicable in federal court. Among Progressives who favored reform were Second Circuit Judge Learned Hand and Yale Law School Dean Charles E. Clark, who was later appointed to the Second Circuit as well.[37]

Judge Clark would make his mark on procedural reform. Influenced by an article written by Clark, Chief Justice Hughes named Clark the Reporter when he also named the Advisory Committee in charge of drafting the Rules. His Progressive fingerprints are all over the rules as eventually promulgated by the Court.[38]

(B) FEDERAL RULE OF CIVIL PROCEDURE 8(A)(2)

Despite the odd bedfellows who crafted the Federal Rules of Civil Procedure, the pleading rules were quite plaintiff friendly and self-consciously rejected many aspects of Code pleading. Rule 8(a)(2) states that "a claim for relief must contain: . . . a short and plain statement of the claim showing that the pleader is entitled to relief. . . ."[39] The drafters avoided the use of the terms "facts" and "cause of action," terms used in the Field Code that resulted in the kind of confusing distinctions discussed above. Thus, if a plaintiff were to state that the defendant injured her through his negligence, the defendant could not object on the ground that the plaintiff alleged a legal conclusion. The drafters eliminated any doubts about that by including sample forms. Complying with the forms, according to Rule 84, amounted to sufficient pleading. And the forms included a sample pleading for a negligence action, which demonstrated a model pleading: "On [Date], at [Place], the defendant negligently drove a motor vehicle against the plaintiff."[40]

The role of the complaint was to provide notice to the defendant. In some narrow circumstances, a plaintiff's minimal pleading might allow a motion to dismiss for the failure to state a claim for relief. But such instances would be rare. Other rules satisfied additional goals that other

37. *Id.* at 31–32.

38. *Id.* at 31, 221.

39. Fed. R. Civ. P. 8(a)(2).

40. Fed. R. Civ. P. Rules Appendix of Forms, Form 11; *see also* Friedenthal et al., *supra* note 8, at 291.

procedural systems sought to advance at the pleading stage. Rule 11, for example, provided for sanctions against a party who submitted frivolous pleadings.[41] That guaranteed some factual investigation prior to filing. While some motions on the pleadings might narrow issues, the overall design of the rules gave a plaintiff whose attorney had done enough factual investigation to avoid sanctions to get to discovery. After discovery, a defendant could file for a summary judgment, in whole or in part, thereby getting rid of non-meritorious cases and narrowing the dispute between the parties. Other devices, like requests for admissions and pretrial orders, also helped narrow issues between the parties.[42]

That these rules are plaintiff friendly from their inception is beyond serious debate. As indicated, Judge Charles E. Clark was the Reporter for the Advisory Committee that drafted the rules.[43] Six years after the effective date of the Federal Rules of Civil Procedure, Judge Clark wrote an opinion, reproduced in many leading casebooks, demonstrating how Rule 8(a)(2) was supposed to work. In *Dioguardi v. Durning*,[44] Johnny Dioguardi filed a pro se complaint in the federal district court. His complaint was, at best, confusing. The district court granted the defendant's motion to dismiss Dioguardi's initial complaint with leave to amend. Thereafter, Dioguardi filed an amended complaint, which again the district court found wanting. In dismissing the complaint, the district court stated that the complaint failed "to state facts sufficient to constitute a cause of action."[45]

Judge Clark's opinion for the Second Circuit reads like a primer for lawyers unfamiliar with the new pleading standards. It compares the district court's statement with the language of the new rule and hints that the lower court had not bothered to review the language of the rule. Further, Judge Clark made clear other important changes ushered in by the rules: the party who sought to have the complaint dismissed carried the burden of showing that the complaint was inadequate, effectively reversing the approach under Code pleading, where failure to comply with hyper-technical pleading rules led to dismissal of the complaint.

---

41. Fed. R. Civ. P. 11(c)(1).

42. Mary J. Davis, *Summary Adjudication in United States Civil Procedure*, 46 Am. J. Comp. L. 229, 247 (1998).

43. Purcell, *supra* note 25, at 220–21.

44. Dioguardi v. Durning, 139 F.2d 774 (2d Cir. 1944).

45. *Id.*

Judge Clark also sifted through Dioguardi's poorly written complaint to suggest possible legal bases for recovery despite the pleader's failure to mention those theories.[46]

The Court's opinion made clear that without the assistance of counsel, Dioguardi would likely lose on remand. Dioguardi had refused legal assistance in the trial court. As Judge Clark stated, "It is the plaintiff's privilege to decline all legal help; but we fear that he will be indeed ill advised to attempt to meet a motion for summary judgment or other similar presentation of the merits without competent advice and assistance."[47] His solicitous attitude towards the plaintiff might have led one to believe that *Dioguardi* was limited to cases of self-representation. Subsequent cases made clear that was not the case. The Federal Rules of Civil Procedure intentionally ushered in a new era of liberalized pleading.[48]

No doubt, the district court judge and the court of appeals panel judges must have known that Dioguardi would lose at trial. And he did.[49] Forcing a case like Dioguardi's to trial comes with costs. Unless a defendant can get the case dismissed on a motion for summary judgment, a defendant must bear the cost of a defense and the public pays for the cost of the legal system. But the adopters of the rules made a policy choice summarized in Wright & Kane's federal courts treatise:

> Those who criticize the result in the *Dioguardi* case necessarily must believe that 'good pleading' is a sufficiently important goal that even possibly meritorious claims should be dismissed if they are not properly pleaded. [Such a position] is contrary to the fundamental notion of all modern procedural reform, that the object of procedure should be to secure a determination on the merits rather than to penalize litigants because of procedural blunders.[50]

As stated in Rule 1, the rules were designed to "secure the just, speedy and inexpensive determination of every action and proceeding."[51] If a

---

46. *Id.* at 775.

47. *Id.*

48. Friedenthal et al., *supra* note 8, at 244–45.

49. *Dioguardi*, 139 F.2d at 775–76; *see* Oliver L. McCaskill, *The Modern Philosophy of Pleading: A Dialogue Outside the Shades*, 38 A.B.A. J. 123, 126 (1952).

50. Wright & Kane, *supra* note 23, at 469.

51. Fed. R. Civ. P. 1.

defendant knows what the plaintiff contends he did to harm her, and such conduct is actionable, the complaint has served its purpose. Thus, drafters of the rules were leveling the playing field, away from the wealthy who could afford high-priced lawyers adept at hyper-technical rules, towards ordinary litigants who deserved their day in court.[52]

Dioguardi was also consistent with what, for many years, was the Supreme Court's view of the role of pleading. In *Conley v. Gibson*,[53] Black union members brought a class action against their union. The class action complaint alleged a breach of the duty of fair representation. The union moved to dismiss, in part, on the ground that the complaint failed to state a claim for relief. The unanimous Court stated that, "In appraising the sufficiency of the complaint we follow, of course, the accepted rule that a complaint should not be dismissed for failure to state a claim unless it appears beyond doubt that the plaintiff can prove no set of facts in support of his claim which would entitle him to relief."[54] While that statement suggests an extreme deference to a plaintiff's allegations, in context, the plaintiffs' complaint stated an entirely plausible set of facts. The plaintiffs alleged that their railroad employer fired them because of their race and that the union did not protect their jobs whereas it did protect white union members' jobs. Further, they alleged that the union did not help them pursue grievances against the railroad. As the Court observed, proof of those allegations would show a clear breach of the union's duty of fair representation.[55]

Elsewhere in its opinion, the Court also dispensed with the defendant's contention that the complaint failed to state sufficient facts to support the general allegations of discrimination. In addition to observing that the rules do not require a statement of facts—but instead, only a plain statement of the claim—the Court stated that the rules required that the pleadings give defendant "fair notice of what the plaintiff's claim is and the grounds upon which it rests."[56] It characterized this kind of pleading as "notice pleading."[57]

---

52. *See* Miller, *supra* note 7, at 8–9.
53. Conley v. Gibson, 355 U.S. 41 (1957).
54. *Id.* at 45–46.
55. *Id.* at 46–47.
56. *Id.* at 47.
57. *Id.*

Both aspects of *Conley*—the statements about the plausibility of the complaint (no set of facts) and notice to the defendant—could mislead. As developed below, the "no set of facts" language may have overstated a defendant's burden in winning a motion to dismiss.

The statement concerning "notice pleading," if taken out of context, could lead to misunderstanding. Taken literally and out of context, the statement might mean only that a defendant had to know that the plaintiff believed that the defendant harmed her and that the defendant should compensate her for her injuries. In context, the Court's statement made clear that the plaintiff's allegations had to provide notice of much more than that. The short plain statement had to show "what the plaintiff's claim is and the grounds upon which it rests."[58] *Conley* illustrates the difference. The plaintiffs had to allege more than that the union breached its duty of fair representation. The plaintiffs had to—and did—allege enough information so that, if proven, the plaintiffs would win. Their short plain statement did allege enough to demonstrate the grounds upon which their claim rested and to show that they had a cognizable legal theory upon which they could prevail.[59] Of course, to some degree, the rule as designed included some ambiguity: a statement had to be both short and plain but detailed enough to show that the pleader was entitled to relief. But the overall theme was clear: the drafters of the rules favored access to the courts over hyper technical pleading requirements.

As a general matter, liberals favor federal pleading as designed. They favor access to the courts as supportive of the rule of law. Pleading hurdles prevent plaintiffs from bringing wrongdoers to justice.[60] But the next section considers a counterexample, one that demonstrates some of the mischief that liberal pleading can do.

---

58. *Id.*

59. *Id.* at 48.

60. A. Benjamin Spencer, *Essay: The Restrictive Ethos in Civil Procedure*, 78 Geo. Wash. L. Rev. 353, 344 (2010) (describing the "Liberal Ethos" in civil procedure as motivating the promotion of accessibility in the drafting of the Federal Rules of Civil Procedure).

C. *Jones v. Clinton*[61]

Current law students may have little memory of Paula Jones's lawsuit against then-President Bill Clinton or the enormous ramifications for the nation. I find that students benefit from some background about the case, as Professor Nan Hunter captured in her book *The Power of Procedure*.[62]

According to allegations in her complaint, Paula Jones was working for an Arkansas state agency. When her agency was sponsoring a conference in a Little Rock hotel, she was working at the registration desk when a state trooper gave her a note with a room number where Clinton was staying. At the time, Clinton was the governor of Arkansas. The trooper explained that Clinton wanted to meet Jones. Once Jones was in the governor's suite, Clinton attempted to engage in sexual activity with her; at one point, he lowered his trousers and exposed his penis. She rejected his offer, and as she was leaving his suite, Clinton looked at her sternly and told her that they should keep their encounter between themselves.[63]

Some Clinton supporters have argued—with some force—that the lawyers who brought the lawsuit against Clinton did so for improper reasons. Some of his long-time political enemies had a role in helping Jones locate attorneys to bring the case. And later in the litigation, after her original attorneys dropped out of the case after failed settlement talks, her new attorneys seemed to keep the litigation going in order to set a perjury trap for the President after they had learned about Monica Lewinsky.[64] But courts have difficulty imposing Rule 11 sanctions in cases where a plaintiff has an underlying theory that has factual support.[65] Whether Jones' claim had factual support is a complicated question.

Were the only factual disputes whether Clinton fondled Jones and exposed himself, the case would present no significant legal issues. Such factual disputes almost always require a trial. But Jones' main claim was that Clinton violated her constitutional rights. By the time Jones found an attorney, any claim under Title VII for sexual harassment was time

61. Jones v. Clinton, 990 F. Supp. 657 (E.D. Ark. 1998).

62. Nan D. Hunter, The Power of Procedure (2002).

63. *Id.* at 7–9.

64. *See, e.g.*, Robert W. Gordon, *Imprudence and Partisanship: Starr's OIC and the Clinton-Lewinsky Affair*, 68 Fordham L. Rev. 639, 705 (1999).

65. Fed. R. Civ. P. 11(b)(3).

barred. But by reframing her claim as a violation of her constitutional rights, she was able to invoke the longer statute of limitations for § 1983 claims. (Congress failed to create a statute of limitations for § 1983 claims. As a result, the Court has held that the trial court must borrow the most closely analogous statute of limitations from state tort law.) In effect, however, by framing her claim as a violation of her equal protection and due process rights, Jones had to prove the same elements that she would have had to prove had her claim been under Title VII.[66]

Title VII recognizes two main theories of sexual harassment. The first theory is a quid-pro-quo theory, whereby a defendant is liable if he conditioned employment or an employment benefit on the plaintiff's sexual acquiescence. The second theory turns on a showing of a hostile work environment. Thus, an employer who makes repeated sexual jokes or allows employees to do so may be liable under the hostile work environment theory.[67]

Jones' complaint provided a great deal of detail concerning some aspects of the case, including conduct in Clinton's suite, statements she made to others after the event, and her reaction to a story that appeared in the right-wing publication *The American Spectator* mentioning a sexual encounter between Clinton and a woman named Paula. But allegations relating to elements of Jones' hostile workplace and quid-pro-quo claims were thin.[68]

With regard to the hostile work environment claim, Jones' complaint stated, she was in constant fear of retaliation and her enjoyment of her employment was severely diminished. Her complaint then stated, "In fact, she was treated in a hostile and rude manner by certain superiors in her agency."[69]

With regard to the quid-pro-quo theory, the complaint stated that Clinton punished Jones for not engaging in sex with him by making sure that she was denied merit raises. Thus, her complaint stated, "[A]fter her maternity leave she was transferred to a position which had no responsible duties for which she could be adequately evaluated for earn advancement.... In addition, the job in which she was placed called for a higher

66. Hunter, *supra* note 62, at 2–5.

67. *Id.* at 31–32.

68. *Id.* at 7–17.

69. *Id.* at 14.

grade and pay, yet she was not paid more money than she received in her previous position. Although other employees received merit raises, Jones never received a raise beyond a cost of living increase."[70]

In moving to dismiss pursuant to Rule 12(c) (judged by the same standard in this case as a Rule 12(b)(6) motion), Clinton's counsel raised a number of arguments. One argument particularly relevant to this discussion was that Jones' allegation of a hostile work environment was insufficient because she only alleged a subjective perception about the hostile work environment. Instead, in reliance on Supreme Court precedent, the memorandum argued that she failed to demonstrate that a reasonable person would have found the environment hostile.[71]

As to the quid-pro-quo theory, the memorandum argued that Jones failed to allege that Clinton made any promises to her if she did comply with his sexual demands. Further, counsel argued that the complaint did not allege a tangible job detriment. Jones, Clinton's counsel argued, did not allege any threats. Further, pointing to the facts alleged in the complaint, the memorandum argued that some of the facts alleged undercut her sexual harassment claims. Finally, the memorandum argued that Jones did not allege facts giving rise to an inference that Clinton took steps to bring about the changes in her working conditions or that he spoke to anyone about the hotel room incident in any way that affected her job situation.[72]

Some of Clinton's statements in the memorandum are clearly not appropriately framed. Thus, the insistence that Jones' complaint failed to allege sufficient facts is wrong for the same reason that it was wrong in *Dioguardi*. The drafters of the rules quite consciously rejected the need to plead facts. Insofar as her complaint contained factual allegations that seemed to undercut her own theory, again as *Dioguardi* suggested, the court's job is to see if, read in the light most favorable to the pleader, she has stated a claim for relief. Further, because the plaintiff's lawyer, not the litigant, signs the pleading, a litigant's statements do not have the same effect as would a sworn statement. Judged by Code pleading standards, Jones' complaint could have been found wanting. In a Code pleading system, the failure to plead sufficient ultimate facts might have

70. *Id.* at 11.

71. *Id.* at 22–24.

72. *Id.*

led to the dismissal of the complaint. Further, courts read ambiguous pleadings in favor of the moving party, not the pleader.[73]

Despite the sufficiency of Jones' complaint under the federal rules, especially in light of facts that came out during Jones' deposition, the pleadings were thin on specifics. During Jones' deposition, Clinton's attorney asked her if she had gotten merit raises. After some confusing back and forth, she admitted that she did not know the difference between merit and cost-of-living raises. When questioned whether she had gotten merit raises, Clinton's lawyer had records to show that she had indeed gotten merit raises.[74]

After the fact, Jones' case looked especially weak. One might ask if her counsel failed to do an adequate factual investigation before filing suit. For example, assuming that attorneys based the statement in the complaint that Jones received no merit raises on their interview with her without doing any further investigation, one might wonder whether such cursory acceptance of their client's statement complied with Rule 11.[75] Without a good bit more information, however, I doubt that a court would—or should—have found her attorneys' investigation inadequate. Further, attorneys often must rely on their clients' version of the facts absent other readily available sources. Perhaps Jones' attorneys had her employment records—for example, her employer may have sent her confirmation of her raises. But absent some clear contradiction between her statements to them and information in their hands, counsel complied with Rule 11's reasonable investigation requirement. That was especially true because Jones approached counsel near the end of the statutory period, requiring them to act quickly.[76]

One might point to one other possible Rule 11 problem with Jones' complaint. The previous paragraph suggests some areas where counsel may not have had information but alleged facts anyway. Thus, the attorneys may have lacked information about whether Clinton retaliated against their client. Rule 11(b)(3) instructs counsel to indicate in the pleading that counsel does not have evidentiary support for allegations, but believes such support is likely to be available after a further oppor-

---

73. FRIEDENTHAL, KANE & MILLER, *supra* note 8, at 554–55.

74. HUNTER, *supra* note 62, at 91.

75. WRIGHT & KANE, *supra* note 23, at 486.

76. HUNTER, *supra* note 62, at 2–3.

tunity for investigation or discovery.[77] Attorneys are hesitant to highlight their lack of evidentiary support because it signals the weakness in their cases. Despite the language in Rule 11, treatises report few instances where courts have sanctioned attorneys based on the failure to comply with that subsection.[78]

Although *Jones v. Clinton* ended up leading to the divisive impeachment and trial of the President, critics should not fault the federal rules' approach to pleading. Something untoward went on in the Excelsior Hotel room. Jones believed that she was the target of discrimination. Facts supporting that discrimination were not readily available to her. As developed more fully in the chapter on discovery, the drafters believed that discovery was essential to assuring the just resolution of disputes. That belief has been a hallmark of our civil justice system since the adoption of the Rules. Even more so than liberal pleading requirements, discovery levels the playing field between the parties.[79]

As unfortunate as was *Jones v. Clinton*, the fault did not lie with the Federal Rules. The occasional hard case does not prove that the law is wrong. Further, insofar as liberals might have seen liberal pleading as part of the problem in *Jones v. Clinton*, as developed below, critics of liberal pleadings far more often have a conservative agenda, making access to court more difficult for injured plaintiffs.

D. Lower Courts' Efforts to Reform Liberal Pleading

The Advisory Committee's description of the pleading rules in the mid-1950s probably summarizes the views of most commentators, judges and lawyers. Apart from some minor criticisms, "the consensus favors the rule and the reported cases indicate that it has worked satisfactorily and has advanced the administration of justice in the district courts."[80] But critics do exist.

---

77. Fed. R. Civ. P. 11(b)(3).

78. *See, e.g.*, Friedenthal, Kane & Miller, *supra* note 8, at 272.

79. *Id.* at 280.

80. Wright & Kane, supra note 23, at 472.

Periodically, lower courts have created exceptions to Rule 8(a)(2)'s liberal pleading standard. For example, courts created heightened pleading requirements for antitrust cases and shareholder derivative actions. Supporters of heightened pleading in those cases imagined that imposing greater pleading requirements would somehow save work for busy courts. Civil rights cases often flood federal courts, where prisoners' rights cases are especially nettlesome. The drafters imagined Rule 11 as a filter to prevent plaintiffs from filing frivolous claims. Similar restraints do not deter prisoners. At least some lawyers and commentators believed that some judges were hostile towards civil rights plaintiffs, not just prisoners. Instead, judges who were hostile to civil rights plaintiffs were making access to court more difficult for disfavored plaintiffs by "legislating" heightened pleading requirements.[81]

No matter how tempting it might be to use pleadings to screen out non-meritorious claims, the courts had little support for the creation of heightened pleading standards in subsets of cases. Congress has the power to legislate special rules in specific cases, as it did when it enacted special rules for securities fraud cases. The Rules include Rule 9, which established instances when litigants must conform to heightened pleading standards. Even when courts had to wade through prisoner complaints, they could find little support in the Court's case law, which had insisted that courts should test pro se complaints by less stringent standards than appropriate when a lawyer filed the complaint. Despite that, courts did develop special pleading standards.[82]

The Supreme Court seemingly put an end to that kind of judge-made rulemaking in *Leatherman v. Tarrant County Narcotics Intelligence & Coordination Unit*.[83] There, the Court rejected a heightened pleading standard developed by lower courts in civil rights cases alleging municipal liability under § 1983. The Court was unanimous. Chief Justice Rehnquist stated that it was impossible to square heightened pleading with the liberal pleading standard established by the Federal Rules of Civil Procedure. His opinion included an unfortunate dictum, when he

---

81. *Id.* at 487.

82. Friedenthal et al., *supra* note 8, at 260, 289–95; *see also* Fed. R. Civ. P. 9.

83. Leatherman v. Tarrant County Narcotics Intelligence & Coordination Unit, 507 U.S. 163 (1993) (holding that the federal courts were not permitted to apply a "heightened pleading standard" more stringent than the usual pleading requirements of Fed. R. Civ. P. 8(a) in civil rights cases alleging municipal liability under 42 U.S.C. § 1983).

speculated "if Rules 8 and 9 were rewritten today, claims against municipalities under 1983 might be subjected to the added specificity requirement of Rule 9(b)."[84] While the Chief Justice also observed that change should come through the process for amending the Rules, some courts expressed uncertainty whether the Court was still open to judicially-created exceptions.[85] And things were about to get much worse.

E. Rewriting Rule 8(a)(2)

In 1984, American Telephone & Telegraph was forced to give up local telephone service, which was then vested in several "Baby Bells." Initially, the Baby Bells had monopolies on local service and were forbidden from competing in the long distance market. The 1996 Telecommunications Act attempted to increase competition among the various entities by allowing them to offer long-distance service if they permitted competition for local service as well. The Baby Bells entered the long-distance market but did not enter other Baby Bells' local markets.[86]

In *Bell Atl. Corp. v. Twombly*, the plaintiffs brought a class action law suit against the Baby Bells. The plaintiffs alleged a conspiracy to violate the Sherman Antitrust Act,[87] which prohibits conspiracies in restraint of trade. The defendants moved to dismiss on the ground that the complaint failed to state a claim for relief.[88]

No doubt, an outside observer might suspect that the Baby Bells agreed not to compete within their respective local markets. Such a conspiracy would violate the Sherman Act. An economist might draw a different conclusion and might argue that competition for local service

---

84. *Id.* at 168.

85. For example, the Sixth Circuit established a requirement that a prisoner suing to challenge conditions of confinement had to allege specifically that he first attempted to resolve the dispute through available administrative remedies, a requirement imposed by the Prison Litigation Reform Act. In *Jones v. Bock*, 549 U.S. 199 (2007), the Court rejected the Sixth Circuit's approach. The prisoner's failure, if he did fail to seek administrative remedies, is an affirmative defense, which the defendant must plead.

86. Bell Atl. Corp. v. Twombly, 550 U.S. 544, 549 (2007) (reversing the U.S. Court of Appeals for the Second Circuit and holding that the plaintiffs failed to state a claim upon which relief can be granted).

87. Sherman Antitrust Act, 69 Stat. 282 (1955).

88. *Twombly*, 550 U.S. at 581.

outside of their network was uneconomical.[89] Further, under the prevailing substantive law, a plaintiff could not prevail merely by showing that the various defendants engaged in parallel conduct. But viewed in light of Rule 8(a)(2) and the prevailing case law, one would have expected the case to proceed to discovery.

The district court granted the defendants' motion to dismiss. Not surprisingly, though, the Second Circuit Court of Appeals vacated and remanded.[90]

The district court found that the allegations in the complaint amounted to no more than conscious parallelism. It found the complaint devoid of any of the "plus factors" required under the Supreme Court's antitrust precedent that would have supported the conclusion that the parallel conduct was the result of a conspiracy. The district court recognized the tension between dismissal at the pleading stage and the requirements of Rule 8(a)(2). But the court found that the complaint alleged nothing more than parallel conduct and did not give defendants notice of the plaintiffs' theory of the conspiracy. The district court concluded that the complaint failed to allege facts "suspicious enough to suggest that defendants are acting pursuant to a mutual agreement rather than their own individual self-interest."[91]

Often missed in discussions of *Twombly* is that the complaint did include a good bit more factual material than a bald conclusion that the defendants conspired. For example, it cited a statement from a representative of one of the defendants that entering the local market would have been in the company's short-term interest as evidence that the defendants were not merely acting in the company's self-interest. The district court disagreed with the plaintiffs' contention. It found that the plaintiffs' theory was erroneous because it assumed that operating a telephone business as a Baby Bell was similar to operating as a Competitive Local Exchange Carrier. Thus, two aspects troubled the district court: the

89. *Id.* at 591.

90. Twombly v. Bell Atl. Corp., 425 F.3d 99 (2d Cir. 2005) (vacating the district court's decision because it applied a heightened pleading standard and holding instead that the plaintiffs were only required to plead substantial facts from which to draw an inference).

91. Twombly v. Bell Atl. Corp., 313 F. Supp. 2d 174, 179 (S.D.N.Y. 2003) (granting the defendant's motion to dismiss for failure to state a claim when a class of consumer plaintiffs claimed the companies conspired to prevent competitive entry into the markets, which violates the Sherman Act, thus requiring a heightened pleading standard).

pleading of a conspiracy was too general; but even beyond that, the court disagreed with the plaintiffs' characterization of the factual information included in the complaint.[92]

Few, if any, commentators were surprised with the Second Circuit's decision overruling the district court. Examined closely, the district court was, in effect, requiring heightened pleading on the plaintiffs' behalf. The Second Circuit relied on Supreme Court and appellate court decisions restating the fundamental principles reflected in Rule 8(a)(2). It also discussed in some detail whether the same rules applied in antitrust cases and concluded again, based on ample authority, that the same liberal pleading standards apply, despite the fact that the Second Circuit found the complaint to be poorly drafted. Further, it stated that the kinds of problems identified by the district court are properly resolved on summary judgment. That is, after the parties have had an opportunity for discovery, the plaintiffs would have to come forward with more than general allegations that would be sufficient at the pleading stages. The district court's disagreement with the assessment of the plaintiffs' characterization of the factual information alleged seemed inappropriate, certainly at the pleading stage. As discussed above, *Conley* made clear that pleading is sufficient as long as the plaintiff can prevail on any set of facts.[93]

The Supreme Court disagreed with the Second Circuit. Justice Souter wrote for seven Justices. Figuring out just what the plaintiffs failed to do is difficult to determine. The Court began with a statement concerning the controlling substantive law: a plaintiff cannot prevail by asking the factfinder to draw an inference from parallel conduct. A Sherman Act conspiracy "must include evidence tending to exclude the possibility of independent action."[94] But the Court recognized that the issue presented in *Twombly* was the sufficiency of pleading, not proof at trial. The Court identified the controlling legal standard:

> "[T]he pleading must contain something more... than... a statement of facts that merely creates a suspicion [of] a legally cognizable right of action", on the assumption that all the allegations in the complaint are true (even if doubtful in

92. *Id.* at 183–84.

93. Miller, *supra* note 7.

94. Bell Atl. Corp. v. Twombly, 550 U.S. 544, 544 (2007).

> fact)...("Rule 12(b)(6) does not countenance...dismissals based on a judge's disbelief of a complaint's factual allegations");...(a well-pleaded complaint may proceed even if it appears "that a recovery is very remote and unlikely").[95]

The Court made several other statements: the complaint needs to include "enough factual material (taken as true) to suggest that an agreement was made."[96] The standard is not a plausibility standard; instead, the allegations should raise a reasonable expectation that discovery will reveal evidence of an illegal agreement. The case should go forward even if a "savvy judge" believes the allegations are improbable.[97] But a "bare assertion of conspiracy" plus an assertion of parallel conduct is insufficient. Thus, the allegations must be "placed in a preceding agreement, not merely parallel conduct...." The complaint must include more than just a "naked assertion of a conspiracy," and that requires more than an assertion of parallel conduct.[98]

Justice Souter rejected the argument that "a claim just shy of a plausible entitlement to relief...can be weeded out early in the discovery process."[99] He expressed concerns about the defendant being forced to settle a dispute because of the threat of discovery expenses, even if the plaintiffs' case is weak. He also rebutted the plaintiffs' reliance on *Conley* and the Second Circuit's interpretation of that case (the "no set of facts" language): they were too literal in their interpretation. On that literal reading, "a wholly conclusory statement of claim would survive a motion to dismiss"[100] whenever a plaintiff might later discover the facts to support its theory. But here, the complaint did not suggest a single fact in support of the existence of a conspiracy.[101]

The Court then rejected the broad reading of *Conley*'s no-set-of-facts language. Instead, the correct standard is that "once a claim has been

95. *Id.* at 555–56.
96. *Id.* at 556.
97. *Id.*
98. *Id.* at 557
99. *Id.* at 559.
100. *Id.* at 551.
101. *Id.* at 561–62.

stated adequately, it may be supported by showing any set of facts consistent with the allegations in the complaint."[102]

Finally, the Court agreed with the district court. The complaint alleged only parallel conduct, not on any independent allegation of actual agreement among the Baby Bells. The Court characterized the other allegations as "a few stray statements [that] speak directly of a conspiracy... on fair reading these are merely legal conclusions resting on the prior allegations." Rejecting the argument that the Court was requiring heightened pleading, it concluded it required "only enough facts to state a claim for relief."[103]

For readers who focused closely on the discussion of the history of Rule 8(a)(2), much of *Twombly* should come as a surprise. For example, Justice Souter insisted that the complaint failed to state sufficient *facts*, seemingly harking back to the Code pleading morass that the Rules drafters sought to avoid. In addition, the drafters rejected distinctions between evidentiary facts, ultimate facts, and legal conclusions. Also contrary to the traditional understanding of federal practice was the Court's very close examination of the allegations. Seemingly, it read them in the light most favorable to the defendants, not to the plaintiffs. That is contrary to the standard in cases like *Dioguardi* and Supreme Court cases as well. Finally, the Rules contain a vehicle for testing weak cases. The pleading stage comes too early for dismissal in most cases. Instead, if a party cannot establish an essential element of its case after an opportunity for discovery, the opposing party should win a summary judgment motion.

Justice Souter recognized some of the problems discussed above, some of which Justice Stevens identified in dissent. Justice Souter's answers appear in a series of footnotes. Justice Stevens accused the majority of reinstituting the arcane distinction between ultimate facts and legal conclusions.[104] Indeed, until the Court got rid of Rule 84 in 2015, compliance with the Forms was sufficient pleading. The idea that one had to plead facts, not legal conclusions, seemed inconsistent with Form 9 (later changed to Form 11, basically requiring a statement of the time and place of an accident and a statement that the defendant's neg-

102. *Id.* at 563.

103. *Id.* at 564–66, 570.

104. *Id.* at 574–75 (Stevens, J., dissenting).

ligence caused the accident), prescribing pleading a negligence action. In footnote 10, Justice Souter attempted to reconcile *Twombly* with the forms. In a simple case, like the one described in the Form (a single car accident), the defendant would know how to answer the allegation in the complaint.[105]

One can certainly question the conclusion that the defendants in *Twombly* would not know how to answer the complaint, even though the expense of answering the complaint might have been substantial. Presumably, upon receiving the complaint, corporate counsel could investigate whether any high-ranking managers engaged in conspiratorial behavior. In fact, Justice Souter seemed sensitive to that cost question when he made note of the high cost of antitrust cases. At the same time, Justice Souter denied that the Court was creating a heightened pleading standard or even overruling *Conley*.[106]

The Court made a big deal out of the conclusory nature of the pleading in the complaint and downplayed specific facts that were alleged, facts that were consistent with the plaintiffs' theory of the case. The problem was that, even when considering those facts, the plaintiffs did not state a claim "plausible on its face."[107] But how can a court determine whether a claim is plausible at the pleading stage? The plaintiffs' complaint did allege a conspiracy along with some specific facts. Is it not plausible that large corporations engage in conspiracies to restrain trade? The district court believed that the plaintiffs' allegations were more consistent with a self-interested business decision to avoid entering other Baby Bell territories than with a conspiracy, and the Supreme Court agreed. Such a conclusion is troubling. At the pleading stage, a court's view of the merits is not controlling because the judge does not serve as the factfinder and because the parties have not had time to collect and submit evidence supporting one's claim. While some plaintiffs make such bizarre claims that they do not warrant any court's time, courts must be careful to allow close cases to proceed. That is especially true at the pleading stage where the parties have not had the benefit of discovery.[108]

---

105. *Id.* at 563 (majority opinion).

106. *Id.* at 558.

107. *Id.* at 570.

108. *Id.* at 552–54.

Think back to *Dioguardi*. Judge Clark more than hinted that Dioguardi would lose at trial without the aid of counsel. But using a dismissal on the pleadings was inappropriate under the design of the federal rules.

Perhaps because an overly broad reading of *Twombly* would be such a radical revision of Rule 8(a)(2), some commentators and courts read it narrowly, suggesting, for example, that it was limited to antitrust cases. The Court also focused on the special substantive aspects of antitrust law, also suggestive that the decision would be narrowly construed.[109]

That conclusion seemed true when the Court decided a more typical case, one involving a pro se prisoner's claim against prison officials for failing to provide adequate medical care. Decided only a few weeks after *Twombly*, *Erickson v. Pardus*[110] reversed a dismissal of the complaint.

Any idea that the Court intended to cabin *Twombly* ended with the Court's decision in *Ashcroft v. Iqbal*.[111] The case arose after the September 11, 2001, terrorist attack when the F.B.I. picked up over 1,000 suspects. The government imposed restrictive convictions of confinement on "high-interest" detainees. Iqbal, who was detained as a suspect of "high-interest," alleged that Attorney General John Ashcroft and F.B.I. Director Robert Mueller "knew of, condoned, and willfully and maliciously agreed to subject Plaintiff to . . . [extremely harsh] conditions of confinement as a matter of policy, solely on account of [his] religion, race, and/or national origin and for no legitimate penological interest."[112] Further, his complaint stated that Ashcroft was the "principal architect" of the discriminatory policy and Mueller was "instrumental" in its implementation.[113]

Attorney General Ashcroft and Director Mueller raised the defense of qualified immunity and moved to dismiss for failure to state a claim for relief. A closely divided Court held that the complaint failed to state a claim for relief. Justice Kennedy's opinion did not suggest that the holding was tied in any way to the qualified immunity defense. Instead, he

---

109. *Id.* at 558–59.

110. Erickson v. Pardus, 551 U.S. 89 (2007) (using *Conley v. Gibson* language as the pleading standard with no mention of "plausibility").

111. Ashcroft v. Iqbal, 556 U.S. 662 (2009).

112. *Id.* at 662.

113. *Id.* at 669.

resolved the question left open after *Twombly*—whether that case applied only in antitrust cases. It did not.[114]

Iqbal set out blackletter law that, as developed below, has produced considerable confusion and litigation. Justice Kennedy stated that *Twombly* rested on two underlying principles: first, the policy that "a court must accept as true all of the allegations in a complaint is inapplicable to legal conclusions. Threadbare recitals of the elements of a cause of action, supported by mere conclusory statements, do not suffice."[115] A court is "not bound to accept as true a legal conclusion couched as a factual allegation"; and second, "only a complaint that states a plausible claim for relief survives a motion to dismiss."[116] A court determining whether a claim is plausible must "draw on its judicial experience and common sense." Iqbal's complaint failed to meet that standard. Nor did it matter that the district court could have limited discovery, focusing discovery on whether Attorney General Ashcroft and Director Mueller had the requisite intent to violate the law required to get past a qualified immunity defense.[117]

Twombly and especially *Iqbal* have been the topic of considerable criticism for both underlying principles identified above.[118] With regard to the first principle, I offer an example that I have used in teaching Civil Procedure. For many years, I used a simulation book that I wrote, one involving a question whether an Internet blogger conspired with one of the plaintiff's former co-workers or a member of a local police department to violate the plaintiff's right to privacy. The complaint suggests that the conspiracy took place in a fairly narrow window of time. The defendant has filed a motion to dismiss under Rule 12(b)(6). I asked students to prepare a memo for the court. On occasion, I specified further that students should justify the denial of the motion. Alternatively, I specified that students should make competing arguments. In effect, I signaled that the issue is not clear cut.[119]

---

114. *Id.* at 664.

115. *Id.* at 678.

116. *Id.* at 679.

117. *Id.*

118. Friedenthal et al., *supra* note 8, at 264.

119. Michael Vitiello, Civil Procedure Simulations 30 (2012).

Applying the first principle, students must determine whether a "conspiracy" is a legal conclusion. That question is complicated. In some contexts, a "conspiracy" is a mixed question of law and fact; in some contexts, it is the ultimate fact to be proven by an underlying agreement and, depending on the definition of "conspiracy," perhaps an overt act as well. But lay people use the term in common parlance. Lower courts often disagree on how to characterize such terms. After *Iqbal*, if it is a legal conclusion—dressed up as a factual statement—the district court must ignore it.[120]

The hypothetical complaint pleads the conspiracy in the alternative. I created that uncertainty for a number of reasons. Most notably, the plaintiff has not had a chance for discovery, and absent that opportunity, has little chance to uncover a conspiracy. Further, given the explicit provision allowing alternative pleadings, the Rules contemplate such uncertainties.[121]

In this example, the literal application of *Twombly* and *Iqbal* led many students to conclude that the court should dismiss the complaint. But that can't be! The forms and the history of the drafting of the Rules make clear that the drafters wanted to get district courts out of making such fine distinctions between conclusions of law and ultimate facts: the distinctions were not worth the salt. Instead, the question at the pleading stage should be whether the defendant had sufficient notice to know how to answer the complaint and whether, as alleged, the plaintiff had grounds upon which she could recover. Quite obviously, in my example, the defendant is in a much better position than the plaintiff to know whether he conspired. Further, under the relevant substantive law in the simulation that I created, a defendant is liable if he conspired to violate the plaintiff's right to privacy.[122]

The exercise, in effect, invites students to see how they can distinguish *Twombly* in particular because it involved a conspiracy charge. Justice Souter suggested at one point that the problem for the Baby Bells was the inability to answer the complaint because of the imprecise time frame (a

---

120. Sydney Beckman, Susan Crump & Fred Galves, Evidence: A Contemporary Approach 484, 493 (2nd ed. 2012) (referencing Federal Rules of Evidence 701 and 702 which state that a lay person can give only their general opinion of what they saw first hand, whereas an expert is required for any scientific or technical testimony).

121. Fed. R. Civ. P. 8(d)(2).

122. Vitiello, *supra* note 119, at 30.

many-year conspiracy with potentially numerous unidentified participants). Elsewhere, he suggested that the problem was the cost of discovery in antitrust cases, creating a fear of settlement to avoid that cost even in a weak case. The simulation poses neither problem. The complaint identifies the defendant as a participant. He must know whether he conspired. Further, discovery in a fairly small case does not present the concern of a strike suit in an antitrust case. But nothing in *Iqbal* suggests a narrow interpretation of the Court's holdings.

The Court's second principle is as troubling as its first principle. Judges have a limited role in reviewing a complaint. The Court has repeated often that the district court must view allegations in a light most favorable to the non-moving party. The rule serves an important purpose. Without an opportunity to assemble one's case, including through discovery, a party has not had the chance to present evidence to the ultimate factfinder. The Rules' drafters contemplated a low threshold for pleading, an opportunity for discovery, and then, if the complaining party lacked evidence, a motion for summary judgment.[123] The Court eventually rejected the scintilla of evidence standard at the summary judgment stage in favor of a substantial evidence test, which focuses on whether a reasonable jury could find for the nonmoving party.[124] Despite that, as developed in a later chapter, in close cases, judges should let cases go to juries. That is equally true at the pleading stage, where inviting judges to impose their view of the merits on the case may lead to its improper dismissal, a situation where reasonable jurors could disagree how the case should be resolved.

Dioguardi again offers a classic example of how the Rules drafters thought the pleadings rules should work. Judge Clark made clear his doubts about the merits of Dioguardi's claim, but he sent the case back for trial. Dioguardi lost; but could he have won? Of course he could have. Similarly, could Attorney General Ashcroft and Director Mueller have set up discriminatory policies without penological purposes? Justice Kennedy seems to believe that, after 9/11, the defendants were attempting to uncover additional plots, not to discriminate against Arabs and Muslims. I might be inclined to agree but would want more infor-

123. *See* Miller, *supra* note 7, at 5.

124. Anderson v. Liberty Lobby, Inc., 477 U.S. 242, 255–56 (1986).

mation before jumping to that conclusion. One can find numerous examples of governmental officials who have acted illegally.

A prominent hornbook includes the following discussion to make the previous point even more clearly:

> Consider the routine automobile accident case where an injured pedestrian sues the driver of the car that struck him. Such a case is dealt with by Form 11 of the Federal Rules which under Rule 84 is deemed sufficient to state a case. As to liability, Form 11 requires only that plaintiff state "On *date*, at *place*, the defendant negligently drove a motor vehicle against the plaintiff." How can such a simple allegation stand in the face of the plausibility requirement?[125]

The authors then list numerous explanations that preclude a finding of the defendant's negligence.[126] Because the defendant could have caused the accident without having been negligent, is it possible that a court would find that the plaintiff failed to meet the plausibility standard? Before *Twombly* and *Iqbal*, the question was not worth considering: the pleading was sufficient. But all bets are off since the Court rewrote Rule 8(a)(2). And the Court did so without following procedures for amending the Rules.

The Court made matters worse by abandoning Rule 84 and the forms. Since the inception of the Rules, the drafters included the Forms and made explicit that compliance with the forms satisfies the pleading standard. Repealing Rule 84 leaves uncertain the level of specificity required to meet Rule 8(a)(2)'s standard.[127]

Even before the abandonment of Rule 84, lower courts have struggled with the meaning of *Twombly* and *Iqbal*. A few judges have seemingly ignored the Supreme Court's new pleading requirements. Others have tried to make sense out of those cases. For example, at least one court has allowed less precise pleading of factual matters if the information is solely within the defendant's possession. Some courts have compared the explanations (on the pleadings as a whole) provided by the two par-

125. FRIEDENTHAL ET AL., *supra* note 8, at 265.

126. *Id.*

127. *Id.*

ties and selected the more plausible explanation—surely, risking intruding on the jury's function.[128]

Swanson v. Citibank, N.A. offers a particularly clear example of the uncertainty that the Supreme Court has created.[129] Seventh Circuit Judge Diane Wood wrote the majority opinion, which Judge Frank Easterbrook joined. Judge Richard Posner dissented. The biographies of the three judges read like a who's-who in the federal judiciary. Apart from a host of professional accomplishments, all served as professors on the University of Chicago Law faculty.[130]

The plaintiff sued three defendants for racial discrimination after Citibank refused her a home-equity loan. Her complaint alleged her account of why she believed that the defendants' conduct was discriminatory. Among her allegations were facts relating to the low appraisal given by one of the defendants for the value of her house, lower than an independent evaluation that she secured shortly thereafter.[131]

Judge Wood posed the problem as follows. The Court's new pleading requirements raised the pleading standard, but the key question was by how much? She also pointed out some of the Court's contradictory statements: while the Court has adopted a plausibility standard, it has insisted that it is not requiring fact pleading. In effect, she was unwilling to find that the Court was engaged "in a *sub rosa* campaign to reinstate the old-fashion pleading system called for by the Field Code or even more modern codes."[132] She concluded that the plaintiff met the standard when she presented a "story that holds together."[133] Judge Wood identified some extraneous facts in the complaint but found that, apart from those facts, the plaintiff's story held together.[134]

---

128. *See, e.g.*, Miller, *supra* note 7, at 107 n.411.

129. Swanson v. Citibank, N.A., 614 F.3d 400 (7th Cir. 2010).

130. *The Faculty*, University of Chicago Law School, http://www.law.uchicago.edu/people/faculty (last visited June 28, 2016). Judge Wood, now retired from the bench, serves as the Director of the American Law Institute. Christopher Roberts, *Judge Diane P. Wood '75 Named New American Law Institute Director*, The University of Texas at Austin School of Law (Jan. 20, 2023), https://law.utexas.edu/news/2023/01/20/judge-diane-p-wood-75-named-new-american-law-institute-director/.

131. *Swanson*, 614 F.3d at 403.

132. *Id.* at 404.

133. *Id.*

134. *Id.* at 407.

By comparison, Judge Posner looked far more closely at what the plaintiff said in her complaint. He concluded from examining the facts alleged that the reason for the denial of her loan was the low evaluation of her property, not racial discrimination. Unlike Judge Wood, he relied on some of the contradictory facts that she alleged. He read *Twombly* and *Iqbal* as responding to concerns about the expense of discovery and as reflecting a demand that a plaintiff conduct a more extensive pre-filing investigation than in the pre-*Twombly-Iqbal* era.[135]

Not only are lower courts uncertain how to apply the new pleading standards, but those standards have produced winners and losers. *Twombly* and *Iqbal* are not value-neutral. Instead, typically, increasing the pleading bar favors the powerful over the less powerful. Data suggest that the weight of those cases falls most frequently on plaintiffs in civil rights cases, such as employment and housing discrimination cases and in cases involving disabilities.[136]

Many academic lawyers certainly recognized the negative implications of *Twombly* and *Iqbal*. The academic literature largely criticized the Court, especially for its holding in *Iqbal*.[137] As developed in the next section, perhaps because of broad criticism or perhaps because the Court never intended to effectuate a pleading revolution, the Court seems to have backed off from the broad reading of *Twombly* and *Iqbal*. But also, as developed below, many lower courts have not gotten the memo!

F. Recent Developments

Two weeks after the Court announced its *Twombly* decision, without mentioning *Twombly*, the Court handed down an opinion that seemed to suggest that *Twombly* applied only in particularly complex cases, where a defendant might not have fair notice based on generalized pleading and faced significant discovery costs. In *Erickson v. Pardus*, the Court upheld a prisoner's complaint that alleged that public officials vi-

135. *Id.* at 408, 411–12 (Posner, J., dissenting).

136. *See* Douglas, *Election Law Pleading*, 81 GEO. WASH. L. REV. 1966, 1980–84 (2013); *see also* Miller, *supra* note 7, at 10.

137. *See* David L. Noll, *The Intermediacy of* Iqbal, 99 GEO. L. J. 117, 119 n.12 (2010) (citing over a dozen comments critical of *Iqbal*).

olated his constitutional rights by demonstrating deliberate indifference to his medical needs.[138] A broad reading of *Twombly* might have led to dismissal of the complaint. After all, "deliberate indifference" is a legal conclusion akin to the conspiracy alleged in *Twombly*. Examining the rest of the complaint might have allowed the Court to conclude that the prisoner did not negate an alternative explanation for the medical provider's decision not to provide the prisoner with the treatment that he alleged he was denied. Without citing *Twombly*, the Court remanded the lower court's dismissal of the complaint and noted, consistent with prevailing pleading principles, that "[s]pecific facts are not necessary; the statement need 'only give the defendant fair notice of what the... claim is and the grounds upon which it rests.'"[139]

Of course, the Court decided *Iqbal* two years later, seemingly abandoning that traditional understanding of pleading. Or did it? Since *Iqbal*, the Court has decided other pleading cases that seem more in line with traditional pleading rules. Indeed, the editors of a leading Civil Procedure casebook have stated, "[t]he Court may be shying away from a strict reading of *Iqbal*. In subsequent cases, it has given more favorable signals to plaintiffs."[140] The editors include citations to three cases decided post-*Iqbal*, all more in accord with the pre-*Twombly* and *Iqbal* caselaw.

Perhaps, I, along with other scholars, were overly pessimistic about the Court's efforts to close the courthouse door. As I mentioned above, some lower courts may not agree with Professors Freer, Perdue, and Effron.

Professors Burbank and Farhang have conducted two empirical studies concerning access to justice. Their 2020 research focused on lower courts' handling of Rule 23 class certifications. As reported in that paper, the authors found a strong association between political party of appointing president and certification outcomes, with all-Democratic panels producing pro-certification outcomes almost three times more than all-Republican panels.[141]

---

138. 551 U.S. 89 (2007).

139. *Id.* at 93.

140. Richard D. Freer et al., Civil Procedure: Cases, Materials, and Questions 334 (9th ed. 2024).

141. Stephen B. Burbank & Sean Farhang, *Politics, Identity, and Class Certification on the U.S. Courts of Appeals*, 119 Mich. L. Rev. 231, 260–61 (2020).

More recently, Professors Burbank and Farhang conducted an extensive study of appellate court decisions interpreting *Twombly* and *Iqbal.*[142] They measured various factors, but for purposes of this chapter, here are some key findings. As a general rule, three-judge panels with a majority of judges who were appointed by Democratic Presidents found for plaintiffs in 38% of cases involving *Twombly* and *Iqbal* pleading issues. That compared with a pro-plaintiff rate of 24% when Republican appointed judges had a majority on three-judge panels.[143]

G. Concluding Thoughts

As discussed in earlier chapters, the Court has narrowed substantive rights in some areas. But the Court's ability to deny a plaintiff a substantive right that Congress has established has outer limits.[144] The Court can achieve the same result by making more difficult, if not impossible, a plaintiff's ability to get into court. Think back to the dispute in *Twombly.* Did the Baby Bells conspire? How could the plaintiffs have uncovered information supporting the conspiracy? One can imagine sets of circumstances where the plaintiffs might have gotten inside information from a whistleblower. But as a general matter, the facts present a classic example where the defendant's records may contain evidence of its illegality that may remain beyond discovery if a plaintiff must come forward with detailed pleadings.[145]

Liberal pleading comes with a cost. It may allow some marginal cases to go forward; it may require defendants to bear discovery costs. But the drafters of the Rules recognized those costs and favored access to court over using pleading as a crude tool to weed out weak cases. The Rules included other provisions intended to fulfill that need. In *Twombly* and *Iqbal,* not only did the Supreme Court rewrite Rule 8(a)(2); it did so

---

142. Stephen B. Burbank & Sean Farhang, *Politics, Identity, and Pleading Decisions on the U.S. Courts of Appeals,* 169 U. Penn. L. Rev. 2127 (2021).

143. *Id.* at 2162–63.

144. Some commentators have argued, I believe, correctly, that the current Court, which includes the three appointments made by President Trump, is less constrained by precedent. But as argued earlier, members of the public react to such decisions, sometimes with repercussions at the ballot box.

145. *See* Miller, *supra* note 7, at 16.

without going through the normal channels for amending the rules. Perhaps, on balance, critics of liberal pleading could have shown that the cost of liberal pleading was too great. But *Twombly* and *Iqbal* short-circuited the normal law-making process.[146]

As a result, as Justice Stevens' *Twombly* dissent pointed out, the defendants never had to deny whether they had conspired, and the plaintiffs never had a chance to discover information exclusively within the defendants' control.[147]

As discussed above, concerns about excessive discovery may have influenced the Justices. But of course, that ignored ways in which district courts could have dealt with excessive discovery. And that also ignored further efforts to limit discovery, making efforts by plaintiffs to uncover wrongdoing even more difficult. As result, even when *Twombly* and *Iqbal* have kept the courthouse door open for plaintiffs, are injured plaintiffs still able to engage in liberal discovery or have the courts made access to proof more difficult as well?

But that is the subject of the next chapter.

---

146. *See* Jack H. Friedenthal, Arthur R. Miller, John E. Sexton & Helen Hershkoff, Civil Procedure Cases and Materials 574 (10th ed. 2009); *see also* Miller, *supra* note 7, at 84–86.

147. Bell Atl. Corp. v. Twombly, 550 U.S. 544, 593 (2007) (Stevens, J., dissenting).

FIVE

Discovery

A. Introduction

As developed in the previous chapter, the drafters of the Federal Rules of Civil Procedure lowered the bar for plaintiffs seeking access to court. They rejected the approach taken by courts in many Field Code states that could frustrate a litigant's attempt to get past pleading stages. As long as a pleader included enough information to indicate that the pleader had a claim for relief, the drafters of the Rules believed that the parties should engage in discovery. Only then, if a party lacked evidence to prove her claim, should her case be dismissed.[1]

Liberal discovery proved so successful that most states eventually adopted provisions based on the federal rules approach. For more than thirty years, lawyers and lawmakers generally accepted the value of liberal discovery. As one commentator stated in the late 1960s, "[T]he present federal discovery rules enjoy the predominant support of the Bar."[2]

And the drafters of the Rules did envision liberal discovery. But for many years, various groups, including business groups, argued that plaintiffs abused discovery. At various times over the past forty-plus years, those claims have been examined and largely rebutted. Over

1. Jack H. Friedenthal, Mary Kay Kane & Arthur Miller, Civil Procedure 380 (5th ed. 2015).

2. Charles Alan Wright & Mary Kay Kane, Law of Federal Courts 578 (7th ed. 2011).

time, the Advisory Committee recommended, and the Court adopted minor changes to the discovery rules to try to address claims of abuse. In 2015, however, the Court adopted more significant changes to the discovery rules.[3]

Both sides of a lawsuit may abuse discovery. But the 2015 changes are tilted towards perceived abuses by plaintiffs. The not-so-hidden message of the amendments to the discovery rules is that district courts should limit discovery by plaintiffs in any number of cases. The net effect is to deprive plaintiffs of a useful tool to uncover misbehavior by defendants.[4]

This chapter explores liberal discovery, including some of its history and some notable examples of the kinds of information that discovery can reveal. Often, courts enforcing discovery rules have forced litigants to hand over evidence that is best characterized as a smoking gun. Thereafter, it turns to some of the claims made about discovery abuses. That section focuses closely on claims made by business-friendly groups about the costs associated with discovery. It raises questions as to whether the problem is with the cost of discovery or with compliance with important progressive policies enacted by Congress and the states. The chapter then turns to the tweaking of the rules that the Court has engaged in over time. The chapter also explores the authority that judges have always had to narrow the scope of discovery. Finally, this chapter views the 2015 changes to the discovery rules and explores the impact of those changes. In doing so, I review an empirical study that my colleague Professor Daniel Croxall and I did. We examined cases raising proportionality challenges to determine if one could predict whether a judge would grant a proportionality challenge based on which President appointed the judge. As developed below, we found a strong correlation

---

3. *Id.* at 580–86; *Rule 26 Duty to Disclose, General Provisions Governing Discovery*, Legal Information Institute, https://www.law.cornell.edu/rules/frcp/rule_26 (last visited Jan. 9, 2025).

4. *See, e.g.*, Bentley v. Highlands Hosp. Corp., 2016 U.S. Dist. 23539 (E.D. Ky. Feb. 23, 2016) (denying sixteen of the plaintiff's eighteen requests for discovery in a medical negligence action because they were not proportional under the amended Rule 26(b)); *see also Significant Changes to the Federal Rules of Civil Procedure Expected to Take Effect December 1, 2015: Practical Implications and What Litigators Need to Know*, Jones Day (Sept. 2015), http://www.jonesday.com/significant-changes-to-the-federal-rules-of-civil-procedure-expected-to-take-effect-december-1-12015-practical-implications-and-what-litigators-need-to-know-09-25-2015/.

with Republican appointed judges favoring defendants, while Democratic appointed judges favor plaintiffs.

B. A Short History of Discovery: The Case for Liberal Discovery

The previous chapter focused on the changes that the Rules made to Code pleading. While the drafters intended a significant departure from the overly technical pleading requirements lower courts had imposed, the discovery rules represented an even greater departure from existing practice. Indeed, as a prominent federal courts treatise states, "The broad and flexible provisions in Rules 26 to 37 for discovery were the most significant innovation in civil procedure when the rules were adopted in 1938."[5]

Earlier practice in the United States did not include much in the way of discovery. Pleadings provided some information, but litigants had to rely on their own resources to discover information useful at trial. A litigant could file an action in equity for some discovery, but again, that was quite limited.[6] That state of affairs suggests an obvious inequity; injured parties with limited resources might not be able to gain access to court.[7]

The drafters of the Rules radically departed from historical practice. Under the Rules, a party seeking discovery was entitled to disclosure of all relevant information in possession of anyone, (even non-litigants), unless the information was privileged. The drafters clearly rejected the "sporting theory of justice,"[8] whereby one party might win a lawsuit not because of the merits of the case but because the opponents lacked access to relevant information. The original drafters of the Rules envisioned liberal discovery, but because some lower courts read the rules narrowly, amendments to the Rules were required in 1946 to give full

5. Wright & Kane, *supra* note 2, at 577.

6. Friedenthal et al., *supra* note 1, at 380.

7. *Id.*

8. Tiedman v. American Pigment Corp., 253 F.2d 803, 808 (4th Cir. 1958).

effect to liberal discovery.[9] At least by the end of the 1940s, as one commentator stated:

> [D]iscovery in civil litigation was intended to be an essentially cooperative, self-regulating process for which the parties would take responsibility, with little intervention required. Significant benefits were anticipated (and substantially achieved) from the provisions of procedures for avoiding dispositions on the basis of technicalities of pleading, eliminating from trials the element of unfair surprise, asserting instead that cases would be decided on their merits or compromised according to their strengths and weaknesses, and eliminating systematic unfairness resulting from disparities of wealth and power by prescribing means by which less powerful litigants could obtain the information necessary to prove their claims.[10]

As was the case with pleading, the drafters advanced progressive values through the Rules—here, through the discovery rules.

Instead of relying on pleadings to eliminate unsubstantiated claims, the drafters of the Rules envisioned an opportunity for full and fair discovery. If at that point, a litigant lacked sufficient information to establish a claim or defense, her opponent should prevail on summary judgment. The drafters recognized that a party might use discovery improperly. Sub-rules like Rule 26(c) gave a litigant an opportunity to challenge his opponent's discovery requests as improper. The Rules also gave courts discretion on handling discovery matters, including imposing orders limiting discovery or controlling the time of discovery. Thus, if a plaintiff claims to have personal injuries but is fearful that the defendant has an impeaching video demonstrating plaintiff engaged in vigorous activity, the district court may order disclosure of the video after the defendant has deposed the plaintiff.[11]

One can measure the success of the federal discovery rules by the fact that nearly every state adopted broad discovery rules, often mod-

---

9. John H. Beisner, *Discovering a Better Way: The Need for Effective Civil Litigation Reform*, 60 DUKE L.J. 547, 558–60 (2010).

10. John S. Beckerman, *Confronting Civil Discovery's Fatal Flaws*, 84 MINN. L. REV. 505, 513–14 (2000).

11. WRIGHT & KANE, *supra* note 2, at 582–83.

eled on the federal rules.[12] As one scholar has stated, what started as a "mere procedural rule" became the cornerstone of the American civil litigation system.[13]

When I teach discovery in Civil Procedure, I give students discovery material that includes evidence damning to their client. Many are stunned when they realize that they must hand over such incriminating evidence. Some students invoke the Fifth Amendment right not to incriminate oneself or other arguments why the discovery rules seem unfair. That is understandable. Indeed, the United States is unique among nations around the world in allowing such liberal discovery. Typical of other nations, the German Supreme Court has stated that "it is fundamental that no party is obligated to help its adversary to victory by furnishing him with information that he does not already have."[14] While many nations allow discovery when necessary to preserve evidence, only the United States and some parts of Canada allow the use of pre-trial depositions for gathering evidence.[15]

Many defend liberal discovery as developed in the Rules. As indicated above, liberal discovery supports greater access to justice by leveling the playing field. It prevents "gotcha justice" by forcing parties to reveal their evidence in advance of trial.[16] Such openness should force rational settlement of cases as well. Liberal discovery also advances other democratic values. In *Discovery in Global Perspective: Are We Nuts?*, Professor Stephen Subrin offered additional justifications for liberal discovery: "Consider our historic distrust of concentrated power. Our doctrines of federalism and separation of powers, the right to a jury trial, and the adversary system, including party control, reflect our historic distrust of residing power in one person or limited groups."[17] Discovery promotes transparency by revealing information about government and corporate practices. Professor Paul Carrington has offered a related explanation for

12. Friedenthal et al., *supra* note 1, at 380.

13. Geoffrey C. Hazard, Jr., *From Whom No Secrets Are Hid*, 76 Tex. L. Rev. 1665, 1694 (1998).

14. Michael Vitiello, Civil Procedure Simulations 97 n.1 (2012).

15. Thomas O. Main, Global Issues in Civil Procedure 34 (2005).

16. Justice Larry V. Starcher, *A Judicial Philosophy: People-Oriented Justice*, 111 W. Va. L. Rev. 411, 443 (2009).

17. Stephen N. Subrin, *Discovery in Global Perspective: Are We Nuts?*, 52 DePaul L. Rev. 299, 309 (2002).

liberal discovery: private litigants serve as private attorneys general. He stated, "Every day, hundreds of American lawyers caution their clients that an unlawful course of conduct will be accompanied by serious risk of exposure at the hands of some hundreds of thousands of lawyers, each armed with a subpoena power by which misdeeds can be uncovered."[18]

Those are some of the theoretical justifications. Discovery has advanced the public good and helped litigants in many cases. The following examples involve cases where litigants have tried to hide smoking guns—no doubt, had they provided the documents in a timely manner consistent with the discovery rules, the cases would have settled. I use the examples to demonstrate what I see as the virtue of liberal discovery. Few, if any, will want to defend the conduct of the defendants in these cases. Their conduct was in clear violation of the law.[19]

Tobacco use has cost millions of Americans their lives and cost the nation billions in healthcare costs. For years, plaintiffs failed in their suits against the tobacco industry. That changed in the 1990s when several states pursued the industry on the new theory that the industry caused states damages through the states' obligations to pay for healthcare costs of their citizens. The states were able to take on the industry and its usual scorched earth discovery strategy, including the industry's willingness to attempt any strategy to withhold damning information. While the litigation brought by Minnesota, for example, also demonstrates some of the notable discovery abuses, the states' litigation against the tobacco industry eventually resulted in the disclosure of documents demonstrating the full extent of the industry's knowledge of the harm caused by its product. Revelation eventually resulted in a multibillion-dollar settlement, providing states with resources for healthcare and to provide anti-smoking educational programs.[20]

A leading Civil Procedure casebook includes a case decided by the Washington Supreme Court that is widely reported. The state modeled its discovery rules after the federal rules. The case offers another example of the kind of information that a party who should unequivocally be

---

18. Paul D. Carrington, *Renovating Discovery*, 49 Ala. L. Rev. 51, 54 (1997).

19. Fed. R. Civ. P. 26(a) (specifying required disclosures to other parties at the start of a case).

20. Michael V. Ciresi et al., *Decades of Deceit: Document Discovery in the Minnesota Tobacco Litigation*, 25 Wm. Mitchell L. Rev. 477, 479 & n.5, 480–81, 487–88 (1999).

liable may have in its possession. Again, while we may understand why such a party may want to withhold the information, this demonstrates the value of liberal discovery; it advances a just result where a defendant's clearly culpable conduct caused severe injury.[21]

A pediatrician prescribed a drug manufactured by Fisons Corporation for a sick child. The two-year-old suffered seizures, resulting in permanent and severe brain damage. The child's parents sued the pediatrician and Fisons. Tests demonstrated that an excessive amount of a particular chemical caused the infant's injuries. At issue in the case was whether Fisons had notice of the harm that its product could cause.[22] The pediatrician and the infant's parents sought discovery of Fisons' documents relating to the particular ingredient in the prescribed drug that caused the infant's incapacitation. Years into the litigation, an anonymous source sent the infant's parents a document that blew the case wide open. Fisons had sent a letter to a small group of influential doctors and stated that the particular ingredient could be a "capricious drug."[23] The parents and doctor moved for sanctions against Fisons.[24]

After the hearing on sanctions, Fisons handed over 10,000 documents. Among those was a memorandum from a communications director to a sales and marketing vice president. Like the letter, the memorandum contained evidence demonstrating beyond question that Fisons knew of the serious risk of toxicity when doctors prescribed the drug consistent with recommended dosages.[25]

The Washington Supreme Court's decision explored Fisons' evasive conduct. In effect, under its hyper-technical reading of any of the plaintiffs' discovery requests, Fisons did not have to turn over the documents. The court rejected Fisons' expert evidence that its lawyers were simply playing by the rules of discovery. The court made clear that the rules are not to be applied hyper-technically.[26]

---

21. Washington State Physicians Ins. Exch. & Ass'n v. Fisons Corp., 858 P.2d 1054 (Wash. 1993); Richard D. Freer & Wendy Collins Perdue, Civil Procedure: Cases, Materials, and Questions 421 (6th ed. 2012).

22. *Fisons*, 858 P.2d at 306–08.

23. *Id.* at 308.

24. *Id.*

25. *Id.* at 308–09.

26. *Id.* at 353–55.

As was the case with the tobacco litigation, one party did not abide by the rules. But once its misbehavior came to light, the parties settled the case. That was the drafters' intent; full and fair discovery should lead to informed settlements. Even in the criminal context, some commenters believe that the Fifth Amendment right to be free from compelled testimony obstructs just results. If the goal is to produce just results, forcing a civil litigant to hand over incriminating evidence is not unfair as long as a litigant does not face possible criminal sanctions. Under state law, Fisons' liability was clear. Gamesmanship should not frustrate the truth in such cases.[27]

One can find myriad cases where defendants, whether on their own or after their opponents' motions to compel, have handed over damning evidence. I have used two cases where defense counsel fought hard, and unfairly, to withhold damning evidence. I take that subject up below. Those cases demonstrate the kind of evidence that parties are supposed to hand over to their opponents.[28]

C. Limiting Discovery Abuses

Some critics argue that litigants routinely abuse discovery. Most often, critics include business groups, some of which have called for dramatic reductions in discovery or other measures that would alter the liberal discovery model in meaningful ways. Often, examined closely, those proposals are clearly pro-business and anti-plaintiff.[29]

Defining discovery abuses in and of itself poses definitional problems. As one writer observed, attorneys can identify their opponents' abuses but are less able to recognize their own misuse of discovery.[30]

---

27. *Id.* at 355–57.

28. *See, e.g.*, Arista Recs. LLC v. Usenet.com, 633 F. Supp. 2d 124, 142 (S.D.N.Y. 2009) (sanctioning Defendants for "bad faith spoliation of documents and other evasive discovery tactics"); Collisson & Kaplan v. Hartunian, 21 Cal. App. 4th 1611, 1618 (1994) (sanctioning Defendants after finding that their antics were either an attempt to "obscure a deliberate indifference to responsibility in discovery" or at the very least that they "[displayed] a propensity to engage in sophistry worthy of a theologian of the Middle Ages").

29. Patricia W. Hatamyar Moore, *The Anti-Plaintiff Pending Amendments to the Federal Rules of Civil Procedure and the Pro-Defendant Composition of the Federal Rulemaking Committees*, 83 U. Cin. L. Rev. 1083 (2015).

30. Beckerman, *supra* note 10, at 597.

While one might fine-tune definitions even further, some commentators identify two common forms of discovery abuse: overuse of discovery and evasive practices. Typically, plaintiffs are more likely than defendants to be guilty of overuse of discovery. They do so because generating discovery requests, like interrogatories, are inexpensive, but responding to them is expensive. That gives plaintiffs leverage in forcing settlements; buying off a plaintiff may be cheaper than responding to her discovery requests.[31]

Evasive practices include the use of boilerplate responses to discovery requests rather than answering consistent with the spirit of the rules. They also include hyper-technical readings of opponents' requests. In general, evasive practices involve resistance to legitimate discovery requests. The tobacco litigation and the Fisons case offer classic examples of evasive practices. As in those cases, defendants are more likely than plaintiffs to engage in such practices.[32]

Because of efforts to narrow discovery, organizations interested in civil litigation practice have studied the extent of discovery abuse. Various studies have come largely to the same conclusions about abuse. As demonstrated by two empirical studies in the late 1990s, "[D]iscovery problems ... are most likely to be concentrated in a minority of lawsuits," comprising roughly a third of the federal courts' civil docket.[33] In addition, the studies concluded that discovery worked "effectively and efficiently" in most civil cases.[34] At least one author suggested that reported cases involving discovery disputes have been on the rise.[35] Cases where observers report abuses tend to involve more complex issues with a great deal at stake in the outcome. Satellite litigation in those cases is often extensive and expensive.[36]

As suggested earlier, explaining why attorneys may engage in discovery abuses when they occur is not hard. The Rules' drafters' goals to some extent were aspirational, perhaps idealistic. My students often express surprise when they realize that they must hand over a smoking

31. *Id.* at 507–09, 543; Charles W. Sorenson, Jr., *Disclosure Under Federal Rule of Civil Procedure 26(A)—"Much Ado About Nothing"?*, 46 Hastings L.J. 679, 699 (1995).

32. Beckerman, *supra* note 10, at 552; Sorenson, *supra* note 31, at 699.

33. Beckerman, *supra* note 10, at 506.

34. *Id.* at 507.

35. *Id.* at 509.

36. *Id.* at 509, 550.

gun. Indeed, some critics of liberal discovery believe that it is contrary to the norms of the profession. Although many judges have railed against incivility among lawyers, the stereotype, especially of the litigator, is defined by aggression. Lawyers are, after all, hired guns. And at least as widely assumed, the obligations foisted on lawyers by the Rules run contrary to the ethical obligation of zealous representation of one's clients. I suspect that few lawyers enjoy explaining to their clients that the client and lawyer must find and hand over damning evidence; that is no doubt especially true when the lawyer charges many hundreds of dollars an hour. Also lamented by some lawyers, attorneys used to be counselors, explaining to clients why the clients cannot engage in certain activities. Today, clients expect lawyers to find ways for the clients to do what they intend to do. Evading handing over damning evidence no doubt is what many clients expect.[37]

The popular understanding of what it means to be a zealous advocate is often incorrect. Attorneys are officers of the court, whereby the system imposes duties on attorneys that may be at odds with the clients' interests. Even rules governing confidentiality yield in some instances, including fraud. Most importantly, the Federal Rules of Civil Procedure impose obligations on attorneys that trump any claim of duty to one's client. The Advisory Committee, Supreme Court, and Congress have effectively decided that when there is a conflict between a client's interest and the attorney's obligations under the Rules, the Rules must prevail.[38]

From my perspective, the problem is not that attorneys have conflicting obligations to the system and their clients. As indicated, that has been resolved. Instead, one needs to speculate why sanctions do not prevent discovery abuses. After all, most observers of our system still value the original goals of the Rules' drafters. And few, if any of us, want to argue that violators of legal obligations should avoid liability. Judges, however, are slow to impose sanctions.[39]

---

37. *Id.* at 516–17, 523–24.

38. *See, e.g.*, FED. R. CIV. P. 26(b)(3)(A) (one example of when an attorney must disclose otherwise privileged information to opposing counsel).

39. Sorenson, *supra* note 31, at 700; *see, e.g.*, Living Color Enters. v. New Era Aquaculture Ltd., 2016 U.S. Dist. LEXIS 39113 (S.D. Fla. Mar. 22, 2016) (denying plaintiff's motion for sanctions after defendant negligently failed to turn off the automatic deletion feature of his cell phone because the court determined the loss of the messages did not result in sufficient prejudice to warrant sanctions); Bry v. City of Frontenac, 2015 U.S.

The rules, including Rule 26(g) and Rule 37, give the district court a wide range of possible sanctions. Some are quite severe, including having an issue resolved against a party in violation of the Rules. The Supreme Court has limited lower courts' ability to impose the most severe sanctions, in effect, requiring a finding of subjective fault. But the case law shows that courts are very hesitant to impose serious sanctions even when intentional misconduct is obvious. Commentators have offered various explanations, and some make sense. Thus, if the overall goal of the rules is for a timely disposition on the merits of the case, a court should hesitate to use sanctions as a way to end the litigation.[40]

The district court's opinion in *Zubulake v. UBS Warburg, LLC*[41] has become the leading case on requirements for handling electronically-stored data. It is also illustrative of a district court's authority to impose sanctions and of a judge's hesitation to impose severe sanctions. From an outsider's perspective, I wonder why the judge was not willing to impose more severe sanctions than she did and why she did not impose those sanctions sooner. There, the plaintiff filed a claim of gender discrimination. The defendant's employees had notice of the suit months before the plaintiff filed. In-house and outside counsel instructed key players in the suit and told them of their obligations to preserve relevant documents, including e-mails. Despite that, e-mails between various employees, including the plaintiff's immediate supervisor, were destroyed. In response to the plaintiff's efforts to get production of material that was deleted from the defendant's server, the defendant sought a protective order and claimed that it should not have to produce the requested evidence. Over the course of more than two years, the district court decided five different issues involving the destruction and reconstruction of the e-mails of several of the defendant's employees.[42]

The defendant's employees' conduct seems to have been deliberate. Destruction of at least some of the e-mails came after counsel warned key players to retain their e-mail files. The information in those e-mails almost certainly was damning. Reading all five of the district court's

---

Dist. LEXIS 169286 (E.D. Mo. Dec. 18, 2015) (denying plaintiff's motion for sanctions alleging spoliation of ESI records of on-duty police because the court was not fully convinced the evidence had ever existed).

40. *Id.*

41. Zubulake v. UBS Warburg LLC, 229 F.R.D. 422 (S.D.N.Y. 2004).

42. *Id.* at 424–30.

opinions leaves one with the impression that the defendant was attempting to exhaust the plaintiff's resources to avoid liability at all, or to settle for pennies on the dollar.[43]

In light of the protracted, deliberate, and unjustified conduct, the district court could have imposed the most severe sanctions allowed under Rule 37. Here, that would have a finding of liability against the defendant. Instead, the court imposed several sanctions that were less severe than the nuclear option. The court required the defendant to pay for re-depositions of relevant personnel, restoration of certain documents, and reasonable attorneys' fees connected with the motion before the court. But instead of a finding on liability, the court indicated that it would give a jury instruction allowing the jury to draw an inference unfavorable to the defendant. Specifically, the jury could find from the defendant's conduct that facts alleged by the plaintiff were true.[44]

As indicated, judges faced with similar misconduct are generally slow to impose severe sanctions. One response to concerns about discovery abuses might be to direct judges to impose more severe sanctions early in the litigation. Keep in mind that in some instances, the conduct of the party seeking to evade discovery amounts to the crime of obstruction of justice. Federal law includes several obstruction of justice provisions. A person may violate the most commonly used provision, § 1503,[45] in a number of ways. For example, a person who destroys documents or interferes with production of documents may be guilty of the offense. Obviously, the crime includes other elements, including knowledge that proceedings were pending. A prosecutor would have to prove mens rea and the other elements of the offense. But in at least some instances of discovery abuse, the offender would almost certainly come within these technical elements.[46]

I recognize risks associated with over-criminalizing conduct in civil litigation. My point, however, is that courts and federal prosecutors have tools to address the most egregious instances of discovery abuse. Even modest enforcement of existing laws—both rules governing sanctions and the criminal law—would almost certainly reduce evasive dis-

---

43. *Id.*

44. *Id.* at 436–38.

45. 18 U.S.C. § 1503.

46. Ellen S. Podgor et al., White Collar Crime 164–75 (2013).

covery practices. Proponents of reform seldom urge such an aggressive approach.[47]

The lack of enthusiasm for amped-up sanctions may be for good reasons. One wonders whether it might lead to increased satellite litigation as occurred during the 1980s when parties routinely attempted to use motions for sanctions as a way to intimidate their opponents. But at root, it may reflect a kind of tolerance for aggressive lawyering behavior. As counsel for Fisons argued, the evasive tactics were really the way attorneys practiced law. Fisons introduced evidence from prominent lawyers and professors to that effect. Members of the Court and Advisory Committee may simply be unwilling to take on the likely pushback from many members of the Bar.[48]

Remember though that critics of discovery often list evasion as one of its evils. And yet many of its critics are not interested in eliminating evasion, I suspect. Instead, they are foes of liberal discovery in the first instance. Some groups, especially pro-business, pro-defendant groups, have called for radical impairment of liberal discovery. They often rely on overstating the extent of abuses as a justification for reform. For example, during the first President Bush's presidency, business groups pushed for significant reforms. The Competitiveness Commission, led by Vice President Dan Quayle, believed that discovery made American businesses uncompetitive. Apparently, its members did consider urging repeal of the federal discovery rules.[49]

Articulate representatives of corporate America have written about discovery abuses. One commentator on those abuses, John Beisner, a partner at a large law firm and active member in organizations supporting corporate defendants, described what appear to be the excesses of discovery today:

> [I]t has fallen well short of these laudable goals. Instead, the pretrial discovery process is broadly viewed as dysfunctional, with litigants utilizing discovery excessively and abusively. Plaintiffs' attorneys routinely burden defendants with costly discovery requests and engage in open-ended "fishing expeditions" in the hope of coercing a quick settlement. As a result,

---

47. Moore, *supra* note 29, at 1116.

48. *See* Sorenson, *supra* note 31, at 696 n.52.

49. Moore, *supra* note 29, at 1084.

> discovery frequently becomes the focus of litigation, rather than a mere step in the adjudication process. By some estimates, discovery costs now comprise between 50 and 90 percent of the total litigation costs in a case. Discovery abuse also represents one of the principal causes of delay and congestion in the judicial system.[50]

Beisner was a participant in an important conference that Duke Law School hosted on discovery practice in 2010 where he presented his above-quoted paper on behalf of the right-leaning U.S. Chamber Institute for Legal Reform.[51]

Beisner's presentation, published in the Duke Law Journal, made a powerful case against current discovery practices. There, he contended that excessive discovery, especially as a result of electronic discovery, costs American businesses billions of dollars. Complying with discovery requests is expensive by itself. But businesses also waste billions of dollars to settle frivolous cases because the cost of discovery exceeds the settlement value of those cases. The cost of discovery especially—what some call a "litigation tax"—"hampers productivity and innovation."[52] The litigation tax hampers our international competitiveness and deters foreign countries from investing in the United States.[53]

After reviewing several recent efforts to reform the discovery rules and concluding that those changes have failed to curb abuse, Beisner proposed a set of reforms. His first proposal was to shift costs of electronic discovery to the party seeking discovery, "thereby creating incentives for parties to make requests that are better calculated to lead to the discovery of relevant evidence."[54] His paper also proposed a set of factors to determine when to shift costs. Further, he would have the party seeking discovery of electronic documents "not reasonably accessible... be required to bear the costs of doing so." That includes requests for seeking data backup tapes and similar material. A similar rule in effect in Texas, according to Beisner, has limited discovery costs.[55]

---

50. Beisner, *supra* note 9, at 549.
51. *Id.* at 547.
52. *Id.* at 575.
53. *Id.* at 576–77.
54. *Id.* at 585.
55. *Id.* at 586.

Although Beisner mentioned evasive practices in passing, his proposed remedies do not address evasion. His proposals are all likely to add to litigation costs for plaintiffs and to reduce costs for defendants. Typically, those who point to over-discovery identify plaintiffs as the chief culprits. If the result of discovery reform adds to the cost for plaintiffs, fewer plaintiffs will have access to the courts. Few injured plaintiffs can bear the significant cost of discovery; even plaintiffs' lawyers who fund litigation expenses will turn down cases where the ultimate return is not great enough to cover the additional discovery costs.[56]

At a minimum, proposals like Beisner's demonstrate the potential for closing the courthouse door on many prospective plaintiffs. Imagine a case like Zubulake's in a system that had adopted Beisner's limitations on discovery. Instead of ordering the defendant to pay for restoring backup tapes, the court would have to impose that cost on the plaintiff. Unable to bear such costs, the plaintiff would have had to accept a meager settlement or drop her case. While the various *Zubulake* opinions did not reveal what evidence eventually emerged from those tapes, the strong suggestion is that the evidence was damning. Alternative discovery was not likely to reveal the damning evidence either; the plaintiff's lawyer had already taken depositions that had not revealed it, as indicated by the court's order requiring the defendant to pay for retaking depositions.[57]

According to Beisner, his discovery reforms would force parties seeking discovery to make requests better calculated to lead to discovery of relevant information. No doubt that would force the party seeking discovery to do more investigation outside the discovery process, again increasing costs. But Beisner's proposal poses a far greater risk to the plaintiff's ability to uncover damning evidence. Parties seeking discovery, most often plaintiffs, word discovery requests broadly. From a defendant's perspective, that may be to increase the burden on the defendant. But that ignores the need for broadly worded discovery requests; a party seeking discovery does not know how to describe what her opponents possess, and describing a document or other information too specifically will allow the opponents to refuse to provide information be-

56. *Id.* at 584–94.

57. *Id.* at 585–86.

cause the discovery request does not describe the document in the defendant's possession.[58]

Consider *Fisons*, discussed above, as a case study in evasion. At every turn, attorneys for Fisons made hyper-technical responses to avoid handing over damning evidence. And the discovery rules in effect in Washington at the time of the litigation did not include the kinds of narrowing requirements envisioned by Beisner.[59]

Beisner and others who focus on the overall cost of discovery fail to address one basic fact: often, evasion runs up the costs of discovery. *Zubulake* and *Fisons* provide case studies. The defendant in *Zubulake* knew the plaintiff's suit was pending and that it had an obligation to preserve electronic information. Its employees failed to comply with a clear legal obligation. The defendant dragged out discovery for two years through dilatory motions. At best, the defendant engaged in conduct that was in violation of the Rules and may have violated federal law governing obstruction of justice.[60] At least some corporate defendants would rather pay higher costs to avoid production than simply to provide the requested information.

I offer another reason to question whether excessive discovery, rather than a settled course of evasion, explains the high cost of discovery. Imagine what in-house counsel would do in a case like *Zubulake* or *Fisons* upon receipt of the complaint. To answer the complaint (at least as envisioned by the Rules), counsel would have to confer with a corporate representative who would need to collect information necessary to answer the allegations in the complaint. What should that conversation sound like? Surely, in *Fisons*, counsel would have to ask about the drug that the plaintiffs alleged caused their child's impairment and specifically inquire about the collective corporate knowledge of the drug's toxicity. And a corporate employee would have to search Fisons' files to find out what they revealed on that question. Presumably, a reasonable investigation would uncover the damning "Dear Doctor" letter and other material that ended up dooming Fisons.[61]

58. *Id.* at 585.

59. Wash. State Physicians Ins. Exch. & Ass'n v. Fisons Corp., 858 P.2d 1054 (Wash. 1993).

60. Zubulake v. UBS Warburg LLC, 229 F.R.D. 422 (S.D.N.Y. 2004).

61. *Fisons*, 858 P.2d at 1081.

All of the foregoing information should have been within counsel's possession long before the plaintiffs' discovery requests. Handing over the documents in conformity with the law would have saved the parties and the court significant time and effort. Any claim that those costs resulted from excessive discovery is false; evasion caused those costs due to the course of conduct chosen by the defendant.[62]

Similarly, the defendant's gamesmanship in *Fisons* resulted in protracted satellite litigation. It dragged on for over seven years until the Washington Supreme Court remanded the case to the trial court for a hearing on sanctions. At that point, Fisons and its lawyers paid $350,000 as sanctions for discovery abuses. No doubt, in current dollars, the cost of discovery from start to finish in a case like *Fisons* (including sanctions) would exceed a million dollars. That would, almost certainly, cut into Fisons' bottom line, as suggested by Beisner.[63]

But wait. Supporters of limiting discovery would be hard-pressed to justify the defendant's conduct in either *Zubulake* or *Fisons*, at least as long as our system allows discovery of damning evidence from one's opponents. Had the defendants in those cases wanted to avoid the high cost of discovery, they could have done so by complying with the law. I do not doubt the high cost of discovery identified by Beisner, but I have not been able to find reliable empirical evidence concerning how much of the cost of discovery results from excessive discovery or from evasion by parties seeking to avoid discovery. Beisner aggregates both costs and then argues that the cost is excessive. That skews the data.[64]

Beisner and other proponents of limiting discovery also fail to address the fact that some of their clients have engaged in tortious and illegal conduct. One can disagree about how often corporate America engages in criminal conduct, but one cannot deny that such conduct takes place. Liberal discovery encourages plaintiffs to become private attorneys general, helping to enforce the law when other agencies lack the resources to pursue investigations. The result of imposing stringent

62. *Id.* at 1077.

63. *Id.* at 1085; Beisner, *supra* note 9, at 595.

64. Beisner, *supra* note 9, at 549–50.

discovery limitations is obvious: it erodes protections against corporate misconduct.[65]

Indeed, pro-defendant commentators like Beisner contend that foreign corporations do not open operations in the United States, in part, because of discovery costs. On that view, liberal discovery costs Americans good jobs that would result from foreign investment in the United States. One should at best be agnostic when considering such a claim. More likely, foreign corporations do not invest in the United States for the same reasons that many American corporations have moved offshore. Compliance with environmental regulations is expensive. Labor costs in foreign markets like Mexico, China, and other emerging economies remain far lower than in the United States.[66]

As conceived by liberal reformers, plaintiffs can function as private attorneys general by bringing suit against defendants who have violated laws regulating the environment, wages, and other similar progressive policies. Liberal discovery often yields proof that corporations violate those rules. Making discovery difficult simply immunizes that kind of illegality.[67]

Another way of thinking about the dispute over liberal discovery is to see it as another example where a successful corporate strategy will exacerbate income inequality. Reduced litigation costs will benefit corporations' bottom lines, and limited discovery will leave more victims of misbehavior uncompensated. Given the current direction of the American economy, corporate health does not inure to the benefit of workers. Wage growth lags behind corporate wealth.[68]

One might argue that federal agencies and law enforcement can compel compliance with relevant policies. The government lacks resources to compel anywhere near full compliance with the law. In addition, many of the same forces that urge limitations on discovery seek to gut

---

65. *See, e.g.*, Érica Gorga & Michael Halberstam, *Litigation Discovery and Corporate Governance: The Missing Story About the «Genius of American Corporate Law»*, 63 EMORY L.J.1383, 1493 (2014) (suggesting that the 2015 amendments would have negative effects on corporate governance controls and would incentivize spoliation); *see also* Abraham Pomerantz, *New Developments in Class Actions—Has Their Death Knell Been Sounded?*, 25 BUS. LAW 1259, 1259 (1970).

66. Beisner, *supra* note 9, at 595.

67. *See, e.g.*, Ciresi et al., *supra* note 20.

68. *See, e.g.*, *Income Inequality*, INEQUALITY.ORG, http://inequality.org/income-inequality/ (last visited Jan. 9, 2025).

agencies like the Environmental Protection Agency, a bugaboo of the right wing in this country.[69]

Most proponents of discovery reform do not also argue that our system abandon the ability to discover damning evidence, a move that would bring our system in line with most countries around the world. Most likely, they do not urge that change because the basic goals of liberal discovery are imbedded in our system. Many advocates of reform, like Beisner, are also active in tort reform and other reforms that limit plaintiffs' ability to recover meaningful damages. They also often advocate for severely curtailing class actions and enforcing arbitration agreements. The net effect of this host of reforms is that injured plaintiffs have either no remedies or grossly inadequate remedies. The lack of effective remedies erodes the deterrent effect of the law.[70] At the end of the day, a claim to be a society that honors the rule of law appears hollow.

D. Reforming the Discovery Rules

The Advisory Committee and the Court have modified discovery rules to limit abuse. This section reviews many of those changes and also reviews tools available to district court judges to limit discovery abuse.

Despite widespread support for the federal discovery rules, criticism in the late 1970s focused on "undue and uncontrolled discovery."[71] As the authors of the leading federal courts treatise have stated, "For some in the profession it became an article of faith—though with little empirical proof—that discovery is being widely abused."[72] During the 1980s, when reform efforts focused on abuse, as indicated, the evidence did not support claims of substantial abuse. As a result, during the 1980s, the drafters of the Rules made modest changes to the discovery rules. Most importantly, the drafters made limited changes to Rules 33 and 34 and strengthened judicial control over discovery. The district court now was to be involved in having the parties form a discovery plan. In 1983, the

---

69. Jane Mayer, Dark Money 274–75 (2016).

70. *See, e.g.*, John H. Beisner, *Big Defense Win in* Whirlpool, *But Everyone Still Loses*, Law360 (Dec. 4, 2014) (in an article for his corporate defense firm, Beisner advocates for stringent class certification, among other restrictions).

71. *Herbert v. Lando*, 441 U.S. 153, 177 (1979).

72. Wright & Kane, *supra* note 2, at 578–79.

drafters amended the rules to add presumptive limits on the frequency of discovery.[73]

The drafters of the Rules flirted with perhaps the most effective way to control discovery abuse in the 1990s when the Advisory Committee proposed a rule mandating automatic disclosure. This proposed amendment would require that the parties engage in automatic disclosure before they engage in formal discovery. The drafters included any material relating "to disputed facts alleged with particularity in the pleadings."[74] The proposal was truly revolutionary. A party had to review its files and determine information that may help its opponent with the opponent's case.[75]

The proposal produced an extraordinary coalition of organizations opposing its passage. "[D]isparate groups including the Clinton Justice Department, big-firm lawyers, big business, manufacturers, insurers, Justices Scalia and Thomas, public interest groups, professors, many judges, most organized bars, and both plaintiff and defense lawyers all rallied against the new disclosure requirement...."[76] Despite widespread criticism, including a claim that automatic disclosure might violate counsel's duty to her client, the Court adopted the rule. Passage was possible because the Advisory Committee amended the rule to allow individual federal districts to opt out of the provision.[77]

Supporters of automatic disclosure argued that the primary effect of the rule was to speed up the handing over of information that the party from whom discovery was sought would have to share eventually. By forcing parties to participate in automatic disclosure, the drafters of the amended rule anticipated that discovery would be less expensive. Thus, its proponents were responding directly to one of the primary criticisms of discovery practice. Further, other 1993 changes, limiting the presumptive number of interrogatories and depositions, were to shorten the discovery process. A party should need fewer interrogatories, for

---

73. *Id.* at 580–81.

74. Fed. R. Civ. P. 26(a)(1) (repealed 2000).

75. *See* David J. Waxse, *"Do I Really Have To Do That?" Rule 26(a)(1) Disclosures and Electronic Information*, 10 Rich. J.L. & Tech. 50 (2004).

76. Rogelio A. Lasso, *Gladiators Be Gone: The New Disclosure Rules Compel a Reexamination of the Adversary Process*, 36 B.C. L. Rev. 479, 481–82.

77. Waxse, *supra* note 75, at 2.

example, because much of that information would be forthcoming through automatic disclosure.[78]

Continued criticism of the Rule led to its reformulation in 2000. While the Rule no longer allows districts to opt out of automatic disclosure, a litigant needs to hand over only information that supports that party's claim or defense. That party's opponents must still make discovery requests to receive information that supports the opponent's case.[79]

The drafters of the rule included a second amendment in 2000 aimed at addressing discovery abuses. For years, Rule 26(b) defined the scope of discovery broadly: A party could request any non-privileged information as long as it related to the subject matter of the dispute and was reasonably calculated to lead to admissible evidence. Critics claimed, especially in light of liberal pleading rules, that plaintiffs engaged in fishing expeditions. They could plead generally and then search for evidence of wrongdoing, even though they had no plausible basis for believing that their opponents had engaged in wrongdoing. The amendment narrowed discovery by stating that one could request information relating to claims or defenses. Only upon a showing of good cause could a litigant expand the scope of discovery.[80]

As pointed out by commentators and courts, the change in the scope of discovery did not amount to a significant change. It did little to alleviate pressure to amend the discovery rules.[81]

Prior to 2015, the other major change to the discovery rules occurred in 2006. In effect, the 2006 amendments tweaked various discovery rules to make clear that electronically-stored documents came within the rules governing discovery.

Earlier changes have not radically reformed discovery practice. But then, given the data that suggests that discovery abuses are limited to relatively few cases, opponents of liberal discovery have not made a

---

78. *Id.* at 2 (citing FED. R. CIV. P. 26 advisory committee's note, subdivision (a) (1993)).

79. *Id.*

80. FED. R. CIV. P. 26(a)(1) (repealed 2000).

81. *See, e.g.*, JOHN BEISNER, U.S. CHAMBER INST. FOR LEGAL REFORM, THE CENTRE CANNOT HOLD: THE NEED FOR EFFECTIVE REFORM OF THE U.S. CIVIL DISCOVERY PROCESS 22 (2010); Thomas D. Rowe, *A Square Peg in a Round Hole? The 2000 Limitation on the Scope of Federal Civil Discovery*, 69 TENN. L. REV. 13, 24–25 (2001).

compelling case for that reform. Despite that, efforts to curtail discovery have been ongoing.

The 2015 amendments to the discovery rules have their origin in a conference hosted by the Duke University School of Law in 2010. The invitation-only gathering of about 200 judges, lawyers, and academics focused on the costs of discovery and possible solutions to the perceived problem.[82]

As one scholar has argued, the starting point of organizers of the conference was that federal court litigation was unacceptably expensive and time-consuming. In preparation for the conference, empirical studies were commissioned despite the fact that many similar studies had already been conducted. Under the 1990 Civil Justice Reform Act, federal district courts had developed civil justice delay plans. Those inquiries demonstrated that the expansion of the federal courts' criminal docket caused the delay in civil cases. In addition to that data, the Administrative Office of the United States Courts maintains statistics about pending cases. Its data did not support the conclusion that federal courts faced a rising docket or increased disposition time. Instead of hard empirical studies, the "empirical studies" prepared in conjunction with the Duke conference focused on opinion surveys of lawyers, a far cry from hard data on the realities of whether discovery was out of control.[83]

The Duke conference led to several proposed changes to the rules. The Advisory Committee took up that basic package of proposed changes. After hearings and comments on those proposed amendments, the Advisory Committee advanced them to the Court, which signed off on them. Congress's failure to act led to passage of those changes, effective in 2015.[84]

Several changes affect access to justice. But for one change, which dealt with production of documents, all of the amendments are pro-corporate defendant. For purposes of this chapter, most important are the changes to Rule 26, which altered the scope of discovery.

---

82. *2010 Civil Litigation Conference*, UNITED STATES COURTS, http://www.uscourts.gov/rules-policies/records-and-archives-rules-committees/special-projects-rules-committees/2010-civil (last visited Jan. 9, 2025).

83. *Id.* (providing links to the commissioned studies under the "Empirical Research" heading).

84. *Rules of Civil Procedure*, UNITED STATES SUPREME COURT 1 (2015), https://www.supremecourt.gov/orders/courtorders/frcv15(update)_1823.pdf.

To put those changes in context, think back to the earlier discussion of discovery abuses. Where they exist, abuses by plaintiffs include excessive discovery. Similarly, defendants who abuse discovery do so typically by evasion. The 2015 amendments largely ignore the latter type of abuse or, in some instances, make sanctions more difficult.[85]

One of the themes of the Duke conference was that discovery should be proportional to what is at stake in the litigation. That responds directly to the claim that plaintiffs often make unreasonably burdensome discovery requests to coerce defendants to settle rather than absorbing those costs. Prior to 2015, district courts had the power to limit discovery. Indeed, since the 1980s, Rule 26 included language making clear that a court should consider proportionality in deciding whether to limit discovery.[86]

The 2015 change moves proportionality into the primary section, Rule 26(b), defining the scope of discovery. The Advisory Committee made that change because it found that district courts did not apply proportionality sufficiently. As observed by one critic of the changes to the rules, "This assertion appears to be based upon anecdotal impressions rather than a review of case law."[87] Some data suggests the contrary—that lawyers have right-sized discovery.[88]

Despite substantial opposition to the proposed changes, largely from plaintiffs' groups and academics, the Advisory Committee did advance changes to the Court. The pre-2015 version of Rule 26(b) included two important sections. Rule 26(b)(1) set out the scope of discovery "in general." That allowed discovery of any information not privileged that related to any claim or defense in the case. Rule 26(b)(2) gave the district court discretion to limit discovery in light of criteria set out in the rule.[89]

The new version of Rule 26(b)(1) states:

> Unless otherwise limited by court order, the scope of discovery is as follows: Parties may obtain discovery regarding any nonprivileged matter that is relevant to any party's claim or

85. *See, e.g.*, *id.* at 12–13 (adding the restriction on the scope of discovery that it be "proportional to the needs of the case").

86. Waxse, *supra* note 75.

87. Moore, *supra* note 29, at 1113.

88. *Id.* at 1113–14.

89. Waxse, *supra* note 75.

> defense and proportional to the needs of the case, considering the importance of the issues at stake in the action, the amount in controversy, the parties' relative access to relevant information, the parties' resources, the importance of the discovery in resolving the issues, and whether the burden or expense of the proposed discovery outweighs its likely benefit.[90]

Although members of the Advisory Committee contended during hearings on the proposed changes to the rules that the proposed language did not change the burden of proving proportionality, many plaintiffs' lawyers believe that the rule intends that result. As one commentator pointed out, the original Committee notes state that the rule "is revised to limit the scope of discovery to what is proportional to the needs of the case."[91] At least if federal courts read the rule in light of that stated intention, a party seeking discovery has an added burden of proving proportionality, not merely relevance.[92]

How might lower courts view the new rule in light of insistence by the Advisory Committee that it has not changed the existing burden of proof? In an effort to "mollify plaintiffs' lawyers," the Advisory Committee added a note that stated that the proposed change does not add to the burden of the party seeking discovery "of addressing all proportionality considerations."[93] Even that reassurance is limited; obviously, the party seeking discovery has the burden of prevailing on some of the proportionality factors.[94]

In addition, Chief Justice Roberts appointed members of the Advisory Committee. Federalist Society members dominate the committee. No doubt, many are adherents to the late Justice Scalia's interpretative philosophy. Were Justice Scalia alive and faced with an interpretation of the new Rule 26(b)(1), he would ignore the Committee notes in reliance only on the clear text of the rule. That suggests that the rule really does

90. Fed. R. Civ. P. 26(b)(1).

91. Moore, *supra* note 29, at 1114.

92. *Id.* at 1116.

93. *Id.*

94. *Id.*; *See, e.g.*, *Wilmington Trust Co. v. AEP Generating Co.*, 2016 U.S. Dist. LEXIS 28762 (S.D. Ohio Mar. 7, 2016) (denying plaintiffs' request for production because they did not adequately explain that their need for the documents was proportional).

limit the scope of discovery by forcing the party seeking discovery to satisfy the proportionality inquiry.[95]

The second change that the Advisory Committee made to Rule 26(b)(1) drops from the rule the long-standing language that a party may seek information as long as it is relevant to the subject matter of the dispute. Even when the Court adopted the amended version of the rule in 2000—limiting discovery to claims or defenses—it allowed parties to petition the court to expand discovery to include any matter related to the subject matter involved in the action. The Committee deleted that language. Anecdotally, according to the Committee, parties rarely invoked that subsection of Rule 26(b)(1).[96]

At least one scholar has questioned the Advisory Committee's conclusion. According to Professor Patricia H. Moore, case law proves otherwise. She raises concerns that district courts may read the rule to eliminate the possibility of expanding the scope of discovery even for good cause.[97]

The changes discussed thus far invite efforts to limit discovery. On various defense-oriented websites, one can find discussions suggesting that the rules have affected significant changes as well as arguments that lawyers should make to narrow discovery.[98] But one other change may signal difficulty for parties seeking discovery. That is the change to Rule 26(c).

Historically, in the run-of-the-mill discovery dispute, the parties bear their own costs. Rule 26(c)(1)(B) may have changed that. Rule 26(c)(1)

---

95. *Id.* at 1117 n.157. I have not discussed two other changes to Rule 26(b). The new rule does not include language that made clear that a party seeking discovery could ask questions relating to "the existence, description, nature, custody, condition and location of any documents or other tangible things...." While the Advisory Committee insisted that the deletion does not change the meaning of the rule, Professor Moore has raised questions about that conclusion. *Id.* at 1119. The other change that does not seem to have made a significant change to the rule is the deletion of the language making clear that discovery relates to any matter, not privileged, that is reasonably calculated to lead to admissible evidence. One might read the language as tightening the connection between admissibility and discovery, but the new text includes language rebutting that conclusion.

96. Moore, *supra* note 29, at 1117.

97. *Id.* at 1117–18.

98. *See, e.g.*, Jones Day, *supra* note 4; Lee Mickus, *FRCP 26(b) Amendment Will Change the Culture of Discovery*, Snell & Wilmer (May 13, 2015), https://www.swlaw.com/blogs/product-liability-update/2015/05/13/frcp-26b-amendment-will-change-the-culture-of-discovery/.

(B) now provides that the court may enter an order protecting a party from discovery and in doing so, may specify terms on discovery "including time and place or the allocation of expenses, for the disclosure or discovery. . . ."[99] The Advisory Committee notes state that this power has been implicit in the rules for some time and should not be read as recommending that cost-shifting should become common practice.[100]

Anticipate aggressive invocation of Rule 26(c)(1)(B). As discussed above, the defense industry and corporate-oriented organizations have advocated cost-shifting for years. Given the new emphasis in the rule, I suspect cost-shifting motions will become commonplace, even if district courts resist granting such motions. A great deal is at stake for plaintiffs and defendants. Injured plaintiffs often lack resources to pay such costs, and even if a plaintiff's attorney funds discovery costs, that lawyer will take fewer cases because the cost of discovery may make the case too expensive to pursue.[101]

E. Future Implications Updated

At the end of 2015, Chief Justice Roberts filed his annual report on the judiciary. In it, he urged "a change in our legal culture." He called for lawyers to "avoid antagonistic tactics, wasteful procedural maneuvers and . . . brinkmanship."[102] Further, he saw the amendments to the federal rules as a welcome change. The Chief Justice "cannot believe that many members of the bar went to law school because of a burning desire to spend their professional life wearing down opponents with creatively burdensome discovery requests or evading legitimate requests through dilatory tactics."[103] Limiting discovery to what is proportional to the

---

99. FED. R. CIV. P. 26(c)(1)(B).

100. Moore, *supra* note 29, at 1121.

101. *See, e.g.*, Chad A. Readler, *The Bitter and Sweet of the* Wal-Mart/Comcast/Halliburton *Triumvirate: More Grounds for Defeating Class Certification, But More Exposure to Discovery* (Jan. 2015), http://www.jonesday.com/the-bitter-and-sweet-of-the-walmartcomcasthalliburton-triumvirate-more-grounds-for-defeating-class-certification-but-more-exposure-to-discovery-01-29-2015/.

102. Adam Liptak, *Chief Justice's Report Praises Limits on Litigants' Access to Information*, NEW YORK TIMES (Dec. 31, 2015) http://www.nytimes.com/2016/01/01/us/politics/chief-justices-report-praises-limits-on-claimants-access-to-information.html?_r=0.

103. *Id.*

needs of the case, according to the Chief Justice, would advance civility and reduce wasted resources.[104]

Note closely that the Chief Justice criticized both excessive discovery and evasiveness in resisting discovery. What he failed to point out was that the 2015 amendments did little to sanction evasiveness. In fact, one change to Rule 37 may make evasiveness even easier. That sub-provision makes a party's burden in a case like *Zubulake* more difficult. I refer anyone who doubts that to Judge Scheindlin's opinion in *Sekisui American Corporation v. Hart*.[105] Judge Scheindlin helped develop spoliation standards in *Zubulake*. In footnote 51 in *Sekisui*, she explained how the new rule would make sanctions for destruction of evidence much more difficult and called for public comments to oppose what was then the proposed rule.[106]

Other commentators have recognized that the new Rule 37(e) has indeed changed the law. For example, one article discussed how the rule, in effect, overrules the standard developed in the Second Circuit.[107]

The change to Rule 37 is similar to changes discussed earlier in this chapter. The changes are significant and largely one-sided. Corporate-defense interests basically cleaned the table.[108]

One might ask whether the changes to the rules fit within my overall thesis; that is, the right wing of the Court did not draft those changes. True enough, but the Court is involved in reforming the rules. Not only can the Court refer matters to the Advisory Committee, but the Court must sign on to proposed changes before Congress has a role in the process.[109]

And the Advisory Committee is not a randomly selected group of judges. The Chief Justice appoints its members, and its current composition leans heavily to the right. Not only is it defense-oriented, but a

---

104. *Id.*

105. Sekisui Am. Corp. v. Hart, 945 F. Supp. 2d 494 (S.D.N.Y. 2013).

106. *Id.* at 503 n.51.

107. H. Christopher Boehning & Daniel J. Toal, *New Rule 37(e) Overrules Second Circuit on Sanctions for Loss of ESI*, New York Law Journal (June 3, 2014), http://www.paulweiss.com/media/2523632/3june14nylj.pdf.

108. United States Supreme Court, *supra* note 84, at 24–26.

109. *How the Rulemaking Process Works*, United States Courts, http://www.uscourts.gov/rules-policies/about-rulemaking-process/how-rulemaking-process-works (last visited Jan. 9, 2025).

majority of its members have Federalist Society affiliation. Given efforts dating back to the Federalist Society's origins to shape the federal judiciary, one should not be surprised at the number of lower court judges who have an affiliation with the organization.[110]

Beyond the composition of the Advisory Committee is the reality that reforming federal rules, especially those governing liberal discovery, has long been part of the Federalist Society's agenda. The reasons that its members favor those reforms are not hard to find; increasingly, it has coordinated its activities with a host of defense-oriented groups, including groups that favor tort reform. The net effect, as argued throughout this chapter, is that such reforms close the courthouse door on many injured parties.[111]

One might reasonably ask if my negative view of the politics animating discovery is borne out by data. The Federalist Society's influence on reshaping the federal judiciary is now widely acknowledged. Republican Presidents for many years have appointed judges with strong Federalist Society affiliations.[112] Would it surprise anyone if such judges viewed plaintiffs' discovery requests with jaundiced eyes?

My colleague Daniel Croxall and I set out to test whether one could predict how a federal judge would decide a proportionality challenge by knowing whether a Republican or Democratic President appointed the federal judge. In *Proportionality and the Federal Rule 26(b)(1): An Empirical Inquiry,* we described our methodology.[113] Initially, we focused only on district court cases, not magistrate or special masters cases because magistrates and special masters are not presidential appointees.

---

110. David Fontana, *A Small Right-Wing Conspiracy: The Federalist Society*, Daily Beast (June 11, 2013), https://www.thedailybeast.com/a-small-right-wing-conspiracy-the-federalist-society/.

111. *See, e.g.*, Patricia W. Moore, *"Corporate and Defense Perspective" Prevails in the Proposed Step Toward Cost-Shifting in Rule 26(c)*, Law Professor Blogs Network (Sept. 11, 2014), http://lawprofessors.typepad.com/civpro/2014/09/corporate-and-defense-perspective-prevails-in-the-proposed-step-toward-cost-shifting-in-rule-26c.html.

112. Michael Avery & Danielle McLaughlin, The Federalist Society: How Conservatives Took the Law Back from Liberals 12–13 (2013). *See also* Zoya Haq, *How the Federalist Society Shaped America's Judiciary*, Yale Daily News (Nov. 4, 2024), https://yaledailynews.com/blog/2024/11/04/how-the-federalist-society-shaped-americas-judiciary/.

113. Daniel Croxall & Michael Vitiello, *Proportionality and the Federal Rule of Civil Procedure 26(b)(1): An Empirical Inquiry*, 93 U. Cinn. L. Rev. 645, 659 (2025).

Our original search term, "proportional 26(b)(1)", limited to cases after the amendment to the rule, yielded about 400 potential cases. We further narrowed our sample, as explained here:

> At that point, we reviewed all cases in the search results and identified cases that focused exclusively or primarily on the proportionality analysis developed by case law. Those cases that specifically relied on proportionality for at least one of their holdings were carefully included. We also included cases that focused on the burden versus expense component of proportionality because that analysis is the part of the test where potential bias would most likely be apparent. Thus, cases that did not specifically apply Rule 26(b)(1)'s proportionality mandate were excluded.[114]

The final sample, although smaller than we would have liked, was about 60 cases. But we believe that the sample allows fair generalizations about the correlation. We avoided asking who appointed the judge until after we did a further examination of the case law. We did so to avoid outcome bias.[115]

As expected, we found a meaningful correlation between the President who appointed the judge and how the judge ruled on the proportionality motion:

> As a broad conclusion, we found that following the 2015 amendments to the Federal Rules of Civil Procedure, Republican-appointed judges tend to limit discovery—particularly in disputes involving business or corporate defendants—under Rule 26(b)(1) significantly more than their Democrat-appointed counterpart judges. Conversely, we also observed that Democrat-appointed judges tend to allow for more liberal discovery when they conduct a proportionality analysis under Rule 26(b)(1) in cases involving business or corporate defendants.[116]

Here is a more granular view of the data:

---

114. *Id.* at 660.

115. *Id.*

116. *Id.* at 661.

> Cases where Republican-appointed judges limited discovery in favor of defendants based on proportionality equated to 35% of our sample set. Cases where Democrat-appointed judges allowed discovery in favor of plaintiffs despite a proportionality objection or motion for a protective order equated to 38% of our sample set. Combining Categories One and Two equates to 73% of the sample set that was consistent with our hypothesis. And while we do not assert that a causal effect exists, we do assert a correlative conclusion. Practitioners can make a fairly safe prediction about how a discovery dispute will be resolved based on who appointed the judge and what side of the discovery debate the appointing President was on.[117]

Be clear: judges who limit discovery based on a proportionality challenge may be preventing disclosure of information that would leave a defendant open to punitive damages.[118] Further, in torts cases involving unliquidated damages, courts have limited power to overturn generous jury awards.[119] But the effect of aggressive use of the proportionality review allows judges to substitute their judgment concerning the value of the plaintiff's injuries for that of the jury.

Famously, during hearings on Chief Justice Roberts' nomination to the Court, he stated that the role of a justice was to call balls and strikes, not to substitute his personal opinions for the law.[120] Members of the public are increasingly cynical about the Court as a political institu-

---

117. *Id.* at 676.

118. *See, e.g.*, John L. Diamond, Lawrence C. Levine & Anita Bernstein, Understanding Torts 386 (7th ed. 2023) (explaining that punitive damages are available when a defendant acts with malice and that they operate both to deter such conduct and provide retribution).

119. Diamond et al., *supra* note 119, at 387 (surveying cases in which the Supreme Court has upheld punitive damage awards when substantive due process is not violated); *see also* Honda Motor Co. v. Oberg, 512 U.S. 415, 425 (1994) (suggesting that the common law standard allows judicial review of damage awards in cases where the size of the award indicates "passion or prejudice" on the part of the jury).

120. *Chief Justice John Roberts—Nomination Process*, United States Courts, https://www.uscourts.gov/about-federal-courts/educational-resources/supreme-court-landmarks/nomination-process/chief-justice-roberts-statement-nomination-process (last visited Jan. 9, 2025).

tion.[121] Sadly, Professor Croxall and my study suggests that the Court's critics are correct.

121. *See, e.g.*, Joseph Copeland, *Favorable Views of Supreme Court Remain Near Historic Low*, Pew Rsch. Ctr. (Aug. 8, 2024), https://www.pewresearch.org/short-reads/2024/08/08/favorable-views-of-supreme-court-remain-near-historic-low/ (finding that 51% of Americans currently hold an unfavorable view of the Supreme Court); *Trust in U.S. Supreme Court Continues to Sink*, Annenberg Pub. Pol'y Ctr. (Oct. 2, 2024), https://www.annenbergpublicpolicycenter.org/trust-in-us-supreme-court-continues-to-sink/ (noting a steep decline in trust of the Court after the 2022 *Dobbs* decision, researchers found that 34% of people surveyed in 2024 did not trust the Court to act in their best interest).

SIX

Taking Cases from the Jury

A. Introduction

Are justices on the Court activists? Often, critics of liberal justices on the Court accuse them of judicial activism. Sometimes, members of the Court accuse their fellow justices of activism.[1] Mark R. Levin, lawyer and right-wing radio talk show host, sees the Court as having subverted democracy in favor of its liberal agenda. For example, he stated in *Men in Black: How the Supreme Court is Destroying America* that: "Judicial activists are nothing short of radicals in robes—contemptuous of the rule of law, subverting the Constitution at will, and using their public trust to impose their policy preferences on society."[2]

Is that true? Such claims were in evidence when former President Obama nominated Judge Sonia Sotomayor to replace Justice Souter on the Supreme Court. The debate surrounding her appointment to the Supreme Court provides a case study in how badly many commentators and some members of the Senate contribute to the public's misunder-

1. *See, e.g.*, Obergefell v. Hodges, 135 S. Ct. 2584, 2642 (2015) (Scalia, J., dissenting) (alleging that the majority's decision to recognize same-sex marriage was "far beyond the outer reaches of this Court's authority"); Adam Liptak, *Court is 'One of Most Activist,' Ginsburg Says, Vowing to Stay*, New York Times (Aug. 24, 2013) (Justice Ginsburg, describing the current Court, stated it was "one of the most activist courts in history.").

2. Mark R. Levin, Men in Black: How the Supreme Court is Destroying America 22 (2006).

standing of the Supreme Court process. Over time, confirmation hearings have degenerated into, at best, political theater. The first President Bush appointed then-Judge Sotomayor, a former prosecutor, to the federal District Court in 1992, a sign that she was no radical reformist. Despite that, when President Obama nominated her to the Supreme Court, her right-wing opponents grabbed onto a statement that she had made in a speech about her Latina background and attempted to demonstrate that she would be a liberal activist. Some of those comments demonstrated a profound misunderstanding of how judges and justices work. No serious commentator believes that justices' backgrounds do not inform their decisions. At the same time, most commentators believe that justices should not and do not merely follow personal predilections in deciding cases.[3]

This chapter explores questions about identifying when justices may be substituting their personal ideology or personal views inappropriately. Initially, this chapter focuses briefly on the debate surrounding Justice Sotomayor's nomination to the Supreme Court. The special focus is on the right's attempt to portray her as a liberal activist based on a quotation about her Latina heritage (taken out of context). Some of the pundits suggested that a judge's background does not influence that judge's decision-making. They then argued that Sotomayor was unqualified because her comments reflected that her background would influence her decision-making. Thereafter, this chapter turns to a brief discussion about why "judicial activism" is not a particularly good way to describe the way justices decide cases and borrows from a thoughtful book on the topic. Professor Kermit Roosevelt's *The Myth of Judicial Activism: Making Sense of Supreme Court Decisions* attempts to offer an alternative way to assess when justices decide cases inappropriately. Next, this chapter reviews the role of summary judgment under the Federal Rules of Civil Procedure. In reliance on the approach urged in *The Myth of Judicial Activism*, it then turns to two instances in which the right wing of the Court has substituted its judgment for that of juries. Further, it explores the obvious biases in their views. Finally, it argues

3. *See, e.g.*, Brian Montopoli, *Early GOP Reaction to Obama's Supreme Court Pick*, CBS News (May 26, 2009, 11:42 AM), http://www.cbsnews.com/news/early-gop-reaction-to-obamas-supreme-court-pick; Caitlin Millat, *Rush Calls Sotomayor, Obama "Racist,"* NBC Washington (Jul. 13, 2009, 9:04 PM), http://www.nbcwashington.com/news/archive/NATL-Rush-Calls-Sotomayor-Obama-Racist.html.

that, while judges inevitably are the product of their pasts, the cases highlighted in this chapter represent unwarranted substitutions of the justices' values.

B. A Wise Latina Woman

Between 1994 and 2003, then-Judge Sotomayor made several speeches in which she discussed the relevance of her ethnic background. In a speech delivered at the University of California at Berkeley School of Law, she stated:

> [O]ur gender and national origins may and will make a difference in our judging. Justice O'Connor has often been cited as saying that a wise old man and wise old woman will reach the same conclusion in deciding cases.... I am... not so sure that I agree with that statement.... I would hope that a wise Latina woman with the richness of her experiences would more often than not reach a better conclusion than a white male who hasn't lived that life.[4]

That statement produced fireworks after President Obama nominated Judge Sotomayor for a position on the Supreme Court.

Talk show hosts like Rush Limbaugh went ballistic. Senators on the right were somewhat—but not much—more restrained. Former Fox media personality Megyn Kelly questioned Arizona Senator Jon Kyl about the approach he would take in questioning Judge Sotomayor. After suggesting that he would first determine if she really meant what she said, Senator Kyl stated as follows:

> [I]t's a matter of finding out what she really believes.... [I]f she really means by that, that members of the court who are persons of color, as she puts it, will make better decisions, and will make decisions based upon a particular agenda that they hold—and she encourages that there be more and more of those judges appointed to the court, that's a bad thing. As we all know, judges are supposed to be like umpires in a ball

---

4. Sonia Sotomayor, *A Latina Judge's Voice*, 13 La Raza L.J. 87 (2002).

> game, calling the balls and strikes, not changing the rules of the game....[5]

Many others on the right struck a similar tone. Senator Chuck Grassley stated that a Supreme Court Justice's job "is not to impose their own personal opinions of right and wrong."[6] Senator Lindsey Graham hinted at a theme struck by Rush Limbaugh that Sotomayor's remarks proved that she and President Obama were reverse racists when he said that if he made a similar statement (i.e., that he was a better decision maker because he was a Caucasian male), "they would have had my head."[7] Somewhat defensively, Sotomayor attempted to placate her critics when she responded to a question from Senator John Cornyn by observing that judges "can't change law. We [referring to judges] are not lawmakers."[8]

Over the course of the process, Justice Sotomayor stated that her comment was unfortunate. She did not make three other significant points: first, that her critics were taking her comment out of context. Her comments focused specifically on how her background could help her better understand race and sex discrimination cases. Even more importantly, she did not point out that Justices like Samuel Alito made similar comments during their nominations. To do so would have been inappropriate, of course; but Senators certainly heard Justice Alito's testimony, for example, about how his Italian-American roots influenced his judging. He stated, for example, that in immigration cases, he says to himself:

> You know, this could be your grandfather, this could be your grandmother.... When I get a case about discrimination, I

5. Tom Allison & Christine Schwen, *Media Still Can't Find Context of Sotomayor's "Wise Latina" Comment*, MEDIA MATTERS (July 13, 2009, 5:38 PM), http://mediamatters.org/research/2009/07/13/media-still-cant-find-context-of-sotomayors-wis/151975.

6. Chuck Grassley, *Grassley Opening Statement at Alito Supreme Court Nomination Hearing*, CHUCK GRASSLEY (Jan. 9, 2006), http://www.grassley.senate.gov/news/news-releases/grassley-opening-statement-alito-supreme-court-nomination-hearing.

7. CQ Transcriptions, *Sen. Lindsey Graham Holds a Hearing on the Nomination of Judge Sonia Sotomayor to Be an Associate Justice of the U.S. Supreme Court*, WASHINGTON POST (July 14, 2009, 5:13 PM), http://www.washingtonpost.com/wp-dyn/content/article/2009/07/14/AR2009071402782.html.

8. CQ Transcriptions, *Chairman's Opening Statements, Cornyn Questions Sotomayor at Supreme Court Nomination Hearings*, WASHINGTON POST (July 15, 2009, 9:37 AM), http://www.washingtonpost.com/wp-dyn/content/article/2009/07/15/AR2009071501255.html.

> have to think about people in my own family who suffered discrimination because of their ethnic background or because of religion or because of gender. And I do take that into account.[9]

While Clarence Thomas told the Senate that "those of us who become judges understand that we have to begin to shed the personal opinions we have,"[10] he and his backers made much of his humble beginnings in rural Georgia.

Justice Amy Coney Barrett provides an even more obvious example of someone whose views shape her view of the law. While a law professor at the Notre Dame Law School, Barrett explained to her students that they should see their careers "as but a means to an end...and that end is building the Kingdom of God."[11] She is a member of the People of Praise, a religious organization that adheres to views considered by most observers to be outside mainstream religious views.[12] During the nomination process, she claimed that, "It is never appropriate for a judge to impose that judge's personal convictions, whether they derive from faith or anywhere else on the law."[13] But can anyone seriously believe that President Trump and those advisors who advocated for her selection did not choose her for those beliefs? An examination of her votes on cases involving First Amendment liberty issues[14] and in the *Dobbs* case, overruling *Roe v. Wade,* undercuts any credibility that one might give to her statements.

---

9. CQ Transcriptions, *U.S. Senate Judiciary Hearing on Judge Samuel Alito's Nomination to the Supreme Court*, WASHINGTON POST (Jan. 11, 2006, 12:46 PM), http://www.washingtonpost.com/wp-dyn/content/article/2006/01/11/AR2006011101148.html.

10. Gary Wills, *Thomas's Confirmation: The True Story*, NY BOOKS (Feb. 2, 1995), http://www.nybooks.com/articles/1995/02/02/thomass-confirmation-the-true-story/.

11. Tom Gjelten, *Amy Coney Barrett's Catholicism is Controversial but May Not Be Confirmation Issue*, NPR (Sept. 29, 2020, 5:42 PM), https://www.npr.org/2020/09/29/917943045/amy-coney-barretts-catholicism-is-controversial-but-may-not-be-confirmation-issu.

12. Stephanie Kirchgaessner, *Amy Coney Barrett: Spotlight Falls on Secretive Catholic Group People of Praise*, THE GUARDIAN (Sept. 26, 2020, 8:29 AM), https://www.theguardian.com/us-news/2020/sep/26/amy-coney-barrett-supreme-court-donald-trump-people-of-praise.

13. Gjelten, *supra* note 11.

14. Ian Millhiser, *The Supreme Court Is Leading a Christian Conservative Revolution*, Vox (Jan. 30, 2022, 5:00 AM), https://www.vox.com/22889417/supreme-court-religious-liberty-christian-right-revolution-amy-coney-barrett.

Finally, Justice Sotomayor might also have made a third point: at least since *Marbury v. Madison*[15] and probably before, the Court has always made law, for example, by interpreting the Constitution when its meaning is open to debate. And until *Erie Railroad Co. v. Tompkins*, the Court declared rules of common law, just as do common law courts around the country.[16]

Nonetheless, critics of the Court raise important questions about the role of justices' personal philosophies and biases. At least in the public's perception, the Court has few constraints on their views. Given lifetime tenure, are justices free simply to impose their personal views in an anti-democratic fashion? As claimed by Mark Levin and similar critics, are the justices on the Court "contemptuous of the rule of law, subverting the Constitution at will, and using their public trust to impose their policy preferences on society"?[17]

C. Judicial Activism and All That Jazz

Objectivity may be a myth. Thus, Justices Sotomayor, Alito, Thomas, and Barrett's life experiences influence the way they understand the law. Before the Supreme Court decided *Obergefell v. Hodges*,[18] the *New York Times* ran a front-page article about former Justice Kennedy. The author suggested his long friendship with Gordon Schaber, the Dean of McGeorge School of Law who hired him to teach Constitutional Law when Justice Kennedy was a young Sacramento lawyer, explained Justice Kennedy's pro-gay rights stance.[19] So are justices simply imposing their policy preferences?

At least in the post-Legal Realism world, scholars and others examine various justices to measure bias. Critics on both sides of the political

15. Marbury v. Madison, 5 U.S. 137 (1803).

16. Erie R.R. v. Tompkins, 304 U.S. 64 (1938).

17. Levin, *supra* note 2, at 22.

18. Obergefell v. Hodges, 135 S. Ct. 2584 (2015).

19. Sheryl Gay Stolberg, *Justice Anthony Kennedy's Tolerance Is Seen in His Sacramento Roots*, New York Times (June 21, 2015), http://www.nytimes.com/2015/06/22/us/kennedys-gay-rights-rulings-seen-in-his-sacramento-roots.html.

spectrum level claims of judicial activism when the Court (usually deeply divided) rules contrary to the critics' view of the law.[20] So is an assessment of whether justices are acting improperly, merely a reflection of our agreement or disagreement with the result in a particular case?

Professor Kermit Roosevelt's *The Myth of Judicial Activism: Making Sense of Supreme Court Decisions* argued persuasively that "judicial activism" lacks a meaningful definition. As he summarized in an online discussion of his thesis, the term often means that "a judge has decided a case based on personal policy preferences rather than the law." He doubted that judges believe that they are deciding cases on that basis. He also argued that when a person accuses a justice of judicial activism, the critic seems to assume that the justice is ignoring a clear answer to the legal issue. Roosevelt argued that the Constitution, for example, seldom produces clear answers. His book offered numerous examples of when "plain language" simply does not answer a particular legal issue. For example, the First Amendment does not tell the Court what "speech" includes.[21]

Roosevelt argued that a better measure of appropriate judicial behavior should focus on "whether the Court is showing an appropriate level of deference to the government actor whose conduct it is reviewing."[22] That has a number of advantages, including the fact that it addresses the concern about the Court abusing its power. It is, after all, an unelected body with little accountability to other branches of the government. As Roosevelt stated, "[I]f we are concerned about courts abusing their power and usurping the policymaking function of other governmental actors, a lack of appropriate deference is the basic form that this abuse and usurpation would take."[23]

Determining when courts should defer, according to Roosevelt, depends on four factors, three of which are especially important for the discussion in this chapter: the first focuses on institutional competence. While Roosevelt focuses on legislatures, executives, and courts in his discussion, a similar analysis would focus on whether a judge or jury is

---

20. Kermit Roosevelt III, The Myth of Judicial Activism: Making Sense of Supreme Court Decisions (2008).

21. *Id.* at 41, 152, 211.

22. Kermit Roosevelt III, *Debate: Judicial Activism and Its Critics*, 155 U. Pa. L. Rev. PENNumbra 112, 113 (2006).

23. *Id.* at 114.

more competent to decide a particular question. The second factor of importance is what Roosevelt calls the lessons of history. That factor "considers whether particular actors have proven themselves trustworthy or untrustworthy in particular circumstances."[24] Finally, he looks to the cost of errors. If the Court rules in one fashion and causes harm, is a legislature likely to be able to remedy that harm? If the Court errs, will the decision impose very high costs on a small group of individuals? If so, the democratic process is not likely to address the harm.[25]

An advantage of Roosevelt's proposed analysis is that one can talk meaningfully about the various factors. That is less likely the case when critics toss around labels like "judicial activism." His analysis provides a useful tool in discussing many cases. For example, in examining when the Court overturned sections of the Voting Rights Act despite overwhelming support for the law in Congress, one can focus the discussion on whether the Court or Congress was in a better position to conduct factual inquiries into the continued existence of racism, requiring continued enforcement of the law.[26] In the next two sections, I use Roosevelt's analysis to focus on two cases where the right wing of the Court substituted its judgment for that of juries. The first involved a motion for summary judgment; the second involved a reversal of a jury finding on the ground that the jury verdict was wrong as a matter of law. As developed below, in both instances these cases demonstrate the Court's lack of deference to the jury in situations where the jury was the better governmental actor. Further, both decisions demonstrate the justices' willingness to impose their value preferences on the court system. Once again, as a result, injured plaintiffs find it more difficult to gain access to justice.[27]

24. *Id.*

25. *Id.* at 114–15.

26. *See, e.g.*, Shelby County v. Holder, 133 S. Ct. 2612 (2013).

27. Scott v. Harris, 550 U.S. 372 (2007); Anderson v. Liberty Lobby, Inc., 477 U.S. 242 (1986).

D. Summary Judgment Practice

By the time the Rules were enacted, the drafters envisioned a limited role for summary judgments. The drafters recognized that in cases involving failure to pay a debt, a defendant may have no defense, which would render a trial worthless. Even with regard to plaintiffs unable to prove essential facts, instead of relying on pleadings to weed out non-meritorious cases, the drafters envisioned summary judgment as the vehicle to do so. If a plaintiff, for example, has had a full opportunity for discovery but cannot come forward with any evidence on an element of her claim, she should not have an opportunity to get to trial. It is not immediately apparent, however, what the standard should be for granting a summary judgment.[28]

A summary judgment takes a case away from the jury. Indeed, granting summary judgment too liberally might violate the Seventh Amendment right to a civil jury trial. Further, a summary judgment motion adds cost to the parties and delays the trial.[29]

Anderson v. Liberty Lobby, Inc.[30] demonstrates some of the difficult choices about the relevant standard for granting a summary judgment. There, Liberty Lobby and its founder, Willis Carto, sued various defendants, including investigative reporter Jack Anderson, for defamation. The plaintiffs objected to two stories printed in the *Investigator*, a magazine published by Anderson, in which the magazine accused the plaintiffs of being neo-Nazi, anti-Semitic, racist, and fascist.[31]

After discovery, the defendants moved for summary judgment. Because the plaintiffs were public figures, they would have to prove actual malice at trial. The defendants attached considerable material to the motion for summary judgment, including an affidavit of the author of the articles in which he asserted his belief in their truthfulness. Also attached was an appendix listing the author's sources.[32]

The plaintiffs attempted to resist summary judgment by pointing to inaccuracies in the stories, and they claimed that the author had used

---

28. Fed. R. Civ. P. 56.

29. *See, e.g.*, Jack H. Friedenthal, Mary Kay Kane & Arthur R. Miller, Civil Procedure 447–50 (5th ed. 2015).

30. Anderson v. Liberty Lobby, Inc., 477 U.S. 242 (1986).

31. *Id.* at 244–45.

32. *Id.* at 245.

sources that were patently unreliable. They also presented evidence of one of the magazine's editors in which he supposedly said that the articles were "terrible" and "ridiculous." The district court granted the motion, but the court of appeals reversed in part.[33]

The Supreme Court resolved three questions: one, on summary judgment, should the district court consider the trial burden of proof? That is, because a plaintiff in a public figure defamation case has a higher standard of proof than in the typical civil action, is it easier for the defendant to meet its burden? The answer was yes. The third issue was whether a plaintiff can resist summary judgment in a case in which the defendant's state of mind is in issue. The Court said no. The second issue was the most important: can a plaintiff resist a summary judgment by showing only a scintilla of evidence, or must it demonstrate a higher standard?[34]

Anderson demonstrates how a different standard might work. For example, the plaintiffs did provide some evidence that might allow a jury to draw an inference of malice. The evidence from the *Investigator*'s editor that he thought the article was ridiculous, for example, might provide some evidence from which to draw the conclusion of malice. The alternative standard—could a reasonable jury find for the plaintiff (the substantial evidence test)—might not be met. The Court held that the standard was the substantial evidence test. It remanded the case and did not determine whether the plaintiffs' submissions met the standard. But surely, the message was clear that the plaintiffs would have a hard time meeting their burden.[35]

Some states reject the federal standard in favor of a scintilla of evidence standard. Further, some critics argue that *Anderson* invites the district court to weigh the evidence. Indeed, making sense of Justice White's opinion is challenging—he recognized that the court is not to weigh the evidence, but nonetheless, the standard requires the court to examine the caliber and quantity of the evidence. While the *Anderson* standard creates symmetry in the law governing summary judgments and judgments as a matter of law, some critics have argued that *Anderson*

33. *Id.* at 246–47.
34. *Id.* at 251–56.
35. *Id.* at 252–57.

and two other summary judgment cases that the Court decided in 1986 have resulted in an unfortunate decline in civil trials in federal courts.[36]

I do not propose resolving that debate. Beyond debate is that *Anderson* invited judges to take a greater role in determining whether a case is ripe for summary judgment: determining whether the nonmoving party has presented a scintilla of evidence makes the grant of summary judgment much more difficult than when the court must decide if a reasonable jury could find for the nonmoving party. With that in mind, I turn to two cases, one involving summary judgment practice and the other involving the review of a jury verdict. In both instances, the justices in the majority imposed their values and took the decision from the jury. Taking the decision from the jury may be appropriate in some instances, but whether the justices' imposition of their values is appropriate remains open to debate.

E. *Scott v. Harris*

(1) Take a Look for Yourself

Before reading further, go the following website and watch the chase that led to the suit in *Scott v. Harris*:[37] http://www.supremecourt.gov/media/media.aspx. At issue was whether the officer's decision to ram the suspect's vehicle was reasonable. More specifically, was the suspect's conduct endangering the lives of innocent bystanders?[38]

Even before the events in the video, an officer tried to stop Victor Harris for speeding—he was traveling at 73 miles per hour in a 55 mile per hour zone. Instead of stopping, he attempted to speed away, eventually leading officers on the chase on a country road. One officer, Timothy Scott, finally rammed the suspect's vehicle, resulting in serious injuries to the suspect and leaving him a quadriplegic. Scott had no idea why

36. *Anderson*, 477 U.S. 272; Celotex Corp. v. Catrett, 477 U.S. 317 (1986); Matsushita Elec. Indus. Co. v. Zenith Radio Corp. 475 U.S. 574 (1986); *see, e.g.*, Arthur R. Miller, *The Pretrial Rush to Judgment: Are the "Litigation Explosion," "Liability Crisis," and Efficiency Clichés Eroding Our Day in Court and Jury Trial Commitments?*, 78 N.Y.U. L. Rev. 982, 1004 n.110 ("Between 1990 and 2000, the number of federal civil trials declined by thirty-seven percent.").

37. Scott v. Harris, 550 U.S. 372 (2007).

38. *Id.* at 374.

other officers were pursuing Harris. He also realized the risk that he took when he rammed Harris' vehicle. The suspect, Victor Harris, sued Scott among others. In order to prove a § 1983 violation, Harris had to prove that Scott used excessive force, thereby violating his Fourth Amendment right to be free from an unreasonable seizure.[39]

Scott filed a motion for summary judgment based on a claim of qualified immunity. The district court denied the motion because, according to the court, facts were in issue. The court of appeals agreed. It found not only that facts were in dispute but also that the law was sufficiently well-settled that Scott was not entitled to qualified immunity. The Supreme Court resolved the case against Harris and found that Scott did not violate Harris' Fourth Amendment right to be free from an unreasonable seizure. Writing for eight justices, Justice Scalia acknowledged that the factual versions offered by the plaintiff and defendants differed substantially. But given the existence of the video, the case rested on different grounds: Harris did not contend that the video was altered or that the video did not represent what happened. "The videotape quite clearly contradicts the version of the story told by respondent and adopted by the Court of Appeals."[40]

After viewing the video, consider whether you agree with the Court's characterization of the events depicted there:

> The videotape tells quite a different story [from the one accepted by the Court of Appeals]. There we see respondent's vehicle racing down narrow, two-lane roads in the dead of night at speeds that are shockingly fast. We see it swerve around more than a dozen other cars, cross the double-yellow line, and force cars traveling in both directions to their respective shoulders to avoid being hit.[41]

Justice Scalia's account went further, but the previous paragraph gives the gist of his characterization of the incident. And in light of that description, the Court's conclusion is not surprising: Scott clearly did not violate Harris's Fourth Amendment right because his conduct was reasonable. The judge or jury deciding that question must balance the indi-

39. *Id.* at 375–76.

40. *Id.* at 375–76, 378.

41. *Id.* at 379.

vidual's Fourth Amendment interests against the government's interests that justify the intrusion. Scott was trying to prevent a significant risk of harm to innocent members of the public. Further, while Scott's conduct did result in Harris's severe injuries, the officer's conduct would not inevitably have led to those injuries. Thus, the risk to members of the public outweighed the risk to Harris. Only Justice Stevens dissented.[42]

(2) Take Another Look

At this point, I suspect that most of you who viewed the video side with the Court. But I am sure some of you disagreed with the Court, even if you did not read Justice Stevens' dissent. The *Scott v. Harris* majority invited the public to see for themselves whether Scott acted unreasonably: "We are happy to allow the videotape to speak for itself."[43] The Court posted the video on its webpage. Three law professors decided to test whether members of the public agreed with the Court's assessment. Their *Harvard Law Review* article contains some fascinating findings.[44]

Co-authors Dan Kahan, David Hoffman, and Donald Braman showed the video to 1,350 viewers to test whether a reasonable juror could find that Harris did not pose a deadly risk to the public. The authors drew the participants randomly; they ended up with a group that was 51% male; 9% Hispanic; 6% African-American; and 6% other minority. They also collected data relating to the subjects' socio-demographic characteristics. The authors placed the subjects in a trial-like situation and then showed them the video. While the authors edited footage from different police cameras, they kept the critical footage. The authors published their findings in an article entitled *Whose Eyes Are You Going to Believe?* Scott v. Harris *and the Perils of Cognitive Illiberalism.*[45] The results are noteworthy.

A significant majority of the subjects agreed with the Supreme Court's assessment of the risk that Harris posed. But 26% of the subjects believed that the use of deadly force was unjustified. Further, the authors

42. *Id.* at 389 (Stevens, J., dissenting).

43. *Id.* at 378 n.5 (majority opinion).

44. Dan M. Kahan, David A. Hoffman & Donald Braman, *Whose Eyes Are You Going to Believe?* Scott v. Harris *and the Perils of Cognitive Illiberalism*, 122 HARV. L. REV. 837 (2009).

45. *Id.*

found other differences. Here are a few of their findings: African-Americans were more pro-plaintiff than other subjects. Democrats were more pro-plaintiff than were Republicans, as were liberals and egalitarians as opposed to conservatives and "hierarchs." Low-income workers and residents of the Northeast also were more pro-plaintiff than their opposites. The authors acknowledged that the study did not include evidence other than the video or arguments by the lawyers. Hearing from witnesses and from lawyers could have influenced the subjects in various ways, depending on a host of factors, including the relative skills of the lawyers.[46]

(3) Think About Judges and Juries

Whose Eyes explores whether the authors' findings justify the grant of summary judgment. They concluded that their findings did not do so. Much of their discussion dovetails with Kermit Roosevelt's analysis of when the Court should defer to other decision-makers.[47]

In *Scott*, Justices Breyer and Ginsburg concurred and emphasized that their view depended on the facts of each case. The majority opinion was ambiguous as to whether it was creating a broader holding that officers were entitled to use the kind of force used by Scott in any high speed chase.[48] Assume for a moment that the Court was creating a bright line rule.

Especially during the 1970s and 80s, the Court rendered a series of decisions creating bright lines. The Court justified the creation of bright lines by reference to the need to give law enforcement officers clear guidance. Thus, when an officer makes a lawful custodial arrest, the Court made clear that an officer may conduct a full body search of the arrestee without regard to whether the officer believes the suspect is armed or

---

46. *Id.* at 859–60. For another example that demonstrates how witnesses can differ in their views about basic facts, examine this material: http://www.nytimes.com/interactive/2016/04/01/us/policebodycamvideo.html?_r=1&utm_campaign=Brookings+Brief&utm_source=hs_email&utm_medium=email&utm_content=27975443&_hsenc=p2ANqtz0mwdo_nZqgCPu8JrkJNpivsaDdDiAfgwwNzc1z_Mpu28u2SnTu8zvcwugKnJZgNsyK80fpFXkC9RiAdNlQjD2V6AHjv9mspmAnHqEHMMl-LPU4k&_hsmi=27975443.

47. Kahan, Hoffman & Brannan, *supra* note 44, at 905–06.

48. *Scott*, 550 U.S. 372.

has evidence of a crime on his person. Similarly, the Court held (and then eventually backed off from the position) that an officer may search the entire passenger compartment of a vehicle when the officer has arrested an occupant or recent occupant of the vehicle. Other examples include the Court's eventual position in its 1991 decision *California v. Acevedo*,[49] where the Court held effectively that police officers do not need a warrant when they search a vehicle. In such cases, one might argue that the Court is in the best position to articulate a bright line; that is, the Court may be the best governmental entity to declare the controlling law rather than leaving the issue to an ad hoc determination by juries. But bright lines come with a cost.[50]

Bright line rules have often resulted in searches that lacked justification. Thus, a search incident to a lawful arrest is reasonable because of concerns about officer safety and destruction of evidence. The result of a bright line rule allowing such a search may be to allow a search, in effect, without any justification.[51]

The question then is whether the Court should announce a bright line rule that officers may ram vehicles of fleeing suspects without the additional justification that a suspect's conduct is endangering officers or the public. That is not a sound rule. Imagine the myriad circumstances where a suspect is fleeing: what about a suspect speeding along an isolated country road, empty of other vehicles? What about a suspect traveling at a few miles above the speed limit? What about a case in which—as here—the original officer sought to stop Harris for a speeding violation? The officer was not in pursuit of an offender who had an outstanding warrant of any kind, no less a warrant for a serious felony. One can imagine many situations where a claim that the suspect represents a serious threat of harm to others is frivolous. And in cases like *Scott*, the police conduct represents a serious risk of harm to the suspect (and to the police officer). The law generally sets a high standard when a person engages in conduct that imperils human life. The same principles should apply in pursuit cases. As indicated above, at least if Justices

49. California v. Acevedo, 500 U.S. 565 (1991).

50. *Id.* at 580–81.

51. *See, e.g.*, Wayne R. LaFave, *The Fourth Amendment in an Imperfect World: On Drawing "Bright Lines" and "Good Faith,"* 43 U. Pitt. L. Rev. 307 (1982).

Ginsburg and Breyer were right, Justice Scalia did not intend to create a bright line rule.[52]

One might also argue that, at best, *Whose Eyes* demonstrates that observers who disagree with the Court's majority are outliers whose views are not worth consideration. That conclusion is unwarranted. Start with the fact that four lower court judges (the district court and the three judge court of appeals' panel) disagreed with the Supreme Court's assessment of the record. Beyond that, examine what one must argue to reject the data assembled by the authors of *Whose Eyes*. Those who disagreed with the majority are more African-American, liberal, and egalitarian. Can anyone seriously contend that their voices should not be heard? No one would seriously contend that citizens in our society can be excluded from jury service based on personal views, other than views that would prevent them from hearing the evidence fairly.[53]

My earlier question, of course, was rhetorical. But in partial answer, one might consider the *Batson v. Kentucky*[54] line of cases. In *Batson*, the Court found that a prosecutor violated an African-American's equal protection rights when he used peremptory challenges to exclude African-Americans from the jury. The Court expanded the doctrine in a series of cases and found that the rule applied in civil cases, in cases when the defendant was white, and in cases when defense counsel used peremptory challenges discriminatorily. Those cases raised complex issues, including where state action occurred in civil cases or in a criminal case when the defense used their peremptory challenges. Another significant issue arose when a prosecutor used peremptory challenges to exclude African-Americans when the defendant was white. That seemed to present a standing challenge. The Court's answer was that the prospective jurors' rights were being violated. The Court grounded the post-*Batson* decisions in the theory that participation of African-Americans is essential to establish public confidence in our criminal justice system. In addition, because the jury system works as a check on wrongful exercise of power by the state and prosecutor, racial discrimination damages that guarantee. Those same arguments should be

52. *Scott*, 550 U.S. at 386, 389.

53. Kahan, Hoffman & Brannan, *supra* note 44.

54. Batson v. Kentucky, 476 U.S. 79 (1986).

equally applicable in cases involving the excessive use of force by the police, like *Scott*.[55]

The Court decided *Scott* before the "Black Lives Matter" movement. The argument in favor of inclusion of African-American voices in our justice system has gained strength in light of that movement. Resolving the intractable issues of police use of force, especially in minority communities, must involve input from those communities and their participation in the process.[56]

Think back to the discussion of Professor Roosevelt's analysis. *Scott* was wrongly decided because the Court intruded on the role of a better governmental actor: the jury. The use of force by the police does not lend itself to bright lines. Because that is the case, one should focus on whether judges or juries are more adept at determining the particular legal issues likely to arise in cases like *Scott*.

Scott turned on whether force was excessive. In effect, that question involves an assessment of whether an officer's conduct was reasonable. Even as observed in *Scott*, the factfinder must balance competing interests. Outside the context of *Scott*, courts have found that juries are competent to make such determinations. In fact, in negligence actions—which, of course, turn on the question of reasonable conduct—courts almost never substitute their judgments for juries. A jury's determination is superior to a judge's assessment of negligence because it reflects community values. Viewed in that light, *Scott* begins to look more like an intrusion into the realm of a different governmental actor.[57] As developed in other chapters, here again the Court is closing the courthouse door to injured plaintiffs.

One might be tempted to argue that *Scott* is a narrow holding, based on a particularly graphic portrayal of the police chase, and therefore its impact on access to court is limited. Some scholars question that conclusion. For example, Professor Tobias Wolff has argued that lower courts have read language in *Scott* as an invitation to grant summary judgments in cases where they would have been clearly inappropriate prior to *Scott*.[58]

---

55. *Id.* at 86 n.8, 87–88.

56. *See id.* at 87; *see generally* Black Lives Matter, http://blacklivesmatter.com/ (last visited Jan. 9, 2025).

57. Scott v. Harris, 550 U.S. 372 (2007).

58. Tobias Barrington Wolff, Scott v. Harris *and the Future of Summary Judgment*, 15 Nev. L. J. 1351 (2015).

Given that the Court was all but unanimous, *Scott* does not seem to fit into my larger theme that it is the right wing of the Court that is closing the courthouse door. Rethink that argument after considering the next case, one that more clearly divided on ideological lines.

F. *Connick v. Thompson*

At the outset of this section, I want to provide full disclosure. As I have written in *Personal Reflections on* Connick v. Thompson,[59] I had two very minor roles in the *Connick* case reviewed in this section. As described below, John Thompson came close to being executed for murder. Evidence emerged shortly before Louisiana was going to execute Thompson that members of District Attorney Harry Connick's office covered up exculpatory evidence. The two young DAs identified as being involved in covering up exculpatory evidence were my former students. In addition, while working with an anti-death penalty organization charged with finding counsel for death row inmates, I contacted a close friend at Morgan, Lewis and Bockius and asked if his firm would represent Thompson during the post-conviction hearing phase. As discussed in detail in *Killing Time: An 18-Year Odyssey from Death Row to Freedom*,[60] dedicated lawyers from that firm doggedly represented Thompson and eventually secured his release from prison. Few disagree that *Connick v. Thompson* represents a travesty of justice.[61]

In late 1984, a member of a prominent New Orleans family was murdered. A few weeks later, three siblings were robbed at gunpoint by a single perpetrator. In a struggle that ensued, the robber was injured and left blood on his victim's pant leg. The police crime scene technician took the blood stained cloth back to the lab.[62]

---

59. Michael Vitiello, *Personal Reflections on* Connick v. Thompson, 11 Ohio St. J. Crim. L. 217 (2013). This section of Chapter Six relies heavily on that article.

60. John Hollway & Ronald M. Gauthier, Killing Time: An 18-Year Odyssey From Death Row to Freedom (2010).

61. Connick v. Thompson, 563 U.S. 51 (2011); *see, e.g.*, Andrew Rosenthal, *The Big Sleazy*, New York Times (Nov. 17, 2011, 10:00 AM), http://takingnote.blogs.nytimes.com/2011/11/17/the-big-sleazy/.

62. *Thompson*, 563 U.S. at 54–55.

In early 1985, police arrested Thompson for the earlier murder. When his picture appeared in the newspaper, one of the robbery victims believed he committed the robbery.[63]

Around that time, a member of New Orleans District Attorney Harry Connick Sr.'s office approved the robbery case for prosecution. On the paperwork, he indicated that the government may wish to perform a blood test on the swatch of cloth from the robbery victim's pants. The case was then sent to the DA in charge of the murder case. Meanwhile, the prosecutor sent the blood to the lab for testing and got back a report that the robber's blood was type B. That information was never given to the defense.[64]

Following normal procedure would have required the prosecutor's office to try the murder case first. Instead, the DA's office petitioned the trial court to allow the state to try Thompson for robbery first. Their motive was clear: securing a robbery conviction would reduce the chances that Thompson would take the stand in his murder trial. That is exactly what happened.[65]

The DA's strategy succeeded. Thompson did not take the stand in the murder trial. After his conviction, a member of the robbery victims' family testified at the sentencing phase, evidence that the state relied on heavily in its closing argument to secure the death penalty. After Thompson's right to counsel expired in 1989, two attorneys at Morgan, Lewis and Bockius took over Thompson's case pro bono. Their representation would continue for years.[66]

After his post-conviction petitions and appeals were exhausted, Thompson's execution was set for May 20, 1999. His attorneys informed him that he was out of options. In late April of that year, still on the job, a defense investigator found a microfiche copy of the report indicating that the robber's blood was type B. Thompson was then tested and found to have type O blood, meaning that he could not have been the robber. The DA's office agreed to a stay of execution.[67]

---

63. Thompson v. Connick, 553 F.3d 836, 843 (5th Cir. 2008).

64. *Id.* at 844.

65. *Id.* at 843–44.

66. *Id.* at 844–45.

67. *Id.* at 845.

An ensuing investigation revealed that in 1994, Gerry Deegan, then a DA involved in the case, told a fellow DA that he had intentionally suppressed the blood evidence. This was a clear ethical and legal violation. Deegan made his confession shortly before his death from cancer. Sadly, the other DA did not come forward until 1999 when the defense found the blood evidence. It took four more years after the discovery of the withheld evidence for Thompson to get a new trial and an acquittal. Evidence suggested that Deegan was not the only member of Connick's office who was involved in suppressing the evidence. That conduct led to Thompson spending 14 years on death row and a total of 18 years in prison.[68]

Not surprisingly, Thompson's lawyers filed a civil action on his behalf. They claimed a violation of § 1983. The admitted constitutional violation was the failure of DA's office to hand over exculpatory evidence, required under *Brady v. Maryland*.[69] The Court has held that an employer may be liable under § 1983, but not based on a theory of respondeat superior. The Court requires something more. As Thompson's attorneys alleged, Thompson's harm resulted from deliberate indifference to an obvious constitutional violation. Thus, they argued, Thompson should recover because Connick failed to put in place basic training for young DAs on the requirements under *Brady*. As the district court instructed the jury, the case turned on one issue: was "the nondisclosure caused by either a policy, practice, or custom of the district attorney's office or a deliberately indifferent failure to train the office's prosecutors[?]"[70]

The jury found that Connick failed to train prosecutors on how to follow *Brady*. It awarded Thompson $14 million in damages. The district court added another $1 million in attorneys' fees and costs. Post-verdict, Connick renewed the argument that he made on a motion for summary judgment that he could not be liable for a violation of § 1983 because Thompson failed to produce evidence of similar *Brady* violations. The district court reiterated its earlier finding when it rejected Connick's summary judgment motion: the need for *Brady* training was so obvious that the failure to provide the training showed the requisite indifference.[71]

---

68. *Id.* at 845–46.

69. Brady v. Maryland, 373 U.S. 83 (1963).

70. Connick v. Thompson, 563 U.S. 51, 57 (2011).

71. *Id.* at 57–58.

The Fifth Circuit affirmed. It held that Thompson need not prove a pattern of violations. Instead, it found that Connick was on notice of the need for *Brady* training because "attorneys, often fresh out of law school, would undoubtedly be required to confront *Brady* issues while at the DA's Office,"[72] and that such violations would result in serious constitutional violations.[73]

The Fifth Circuit granted en banc review. The court was evenly divided, thereby affirming the district court. The Supreme Court reversed the judgment of the Fifth Circuit, denying Thompson recovery.[74]

Unlike *Scott v. Harris*, *Connick v. Thompson* divided the Court along ideological lines, with the lead opinion written by Justice Thomas and a concurring opinion written by Justice Scalia and joined by Justice Alito.[75]

One can read Justice Thomas' opinion as a narrow decision, focused closely on existing case law. But as developed more fully in the dissent, the majority gave a begrudging reading to the full record. Along the way, the Court rejected a number of specific arguments on the plaintiff's behalf, but the most important argument was whether a plaintiff may recover against the state-actor employer when the plaintiff seeks to base liability on a single act of an employee.[76]

The Court has required that a plaintiff alleging a § 1983 violation must show more than illegal conduct by the state-actor employer. A plaintiff typically cannot prevail upon a showing of a single incident of misconduct. Despite pointing to multiple instances in which Louisiana appellate courts overturned convictions secured by Connick's office because of *Brady* violations, the plaintiff pursued a single violation theory before the Court.[77]

The Court has recognized that under some circumstances, a defendant may be liable for a failure to train even when liability is based on a single violation. In *Canton v. Harris*,[78] the Court held that a city may not be liable for the failure to train its employees unless that failure demonstrated deliberate indifference. But the Court also indicated that in

72. *Id.* at 58 (quoting Thompson v. Connick, 553 F.3d 836, 854 (2008)).

73. *Id.*

74. *Id.* at 59, 72.

75. *Id.* at 72 (Scalia, J., concurring).

76. *Id.* at 64, 68 (majority opinion).

77. *Id.*

78. Canton v. Harris, 489 U.S. 378 (1989).

some instances, the failure to train may be sufficient to make the employer liable:

> But it may happen that in light of the duties assigned to specific officers or employees the need for more or different training is so obvious, and the inadequacy so likely to result in the violation of constitutional rights, that the policymakers of the city can reasonably be said to have been deliberately indifferent to the need. In that event, the failure to provide proper training may fairly be said to represent a policy for which the city is responsible, and for which the city may be held liable if it actually causes injury.[79]

The *Connick* majority found that the need to train recent law school graduates about *Brady* violations was not within the narrow exception that the *Canton* Court had in mind. Thus, according to Justice Thomas, "Attorneys are trained in the law and equipped with the tools to interpret and apply legal principles, understand constitutional limits, and exercise legal judgment."[80] All new lawyers must have graduated from law school and passed the bar. As a result, "all new attorneys have learned how to find, understand, and apply legal rules."[81] At least in some states, attorneys must meet continuing legal education requirements. (Justice Thomas conveniently failed to mention that Louisiana did not have a CLE requirement in place at the time of Thompson's trial.) Attorneys who work with other lawyers, as was the case in Connick's office, get on-the-job training from more experienced attorneys. Hence, "recurring constitutional violations are not the 'obvious consequence' of failing to provide prosecutors with formal in-house training about how to obey the law."[82] Further, DAs in Connick's office knew about *Brady* in general terms.[83]

Justice Scalia's concurring opinion went further. He saw this case as involving a single rogue rotten apple, the deceased attorney Gerry Dee-

79. *Id.* at 390.

80. *Thompson*, 563 U.S. at 64.

81. *Id.*

82. *Id.* at 66.

83. *Id.* at 67.

gan, who acted in bad faith. Further, he saw no causal link between the failure to train and harm to the plaintiff.[84]

Especially given the frequent criticisms of how little law schools supposedly teach their graduates, Justice Thomas' view of young attorneys as practice-ready seems like a rosy picture of new law graduates. And as developed below, part of the problem with Justice Thomas' young-lawyers-get-on-the-job-training-from-senior-lawyers theory is that it ignores information in the record suggesting that Deegan was not an outlier in Connick's office. That also suggests that Justice Scalia's Deegan-was-a-rare-rotten-apple argument was not supported by the record either.[85]

Apart from those arguments, one might read this case quite simply as an instance in which the Court was merely deciding a narrow legal question: what is the scope of a state-actor employer's liability when the plaintiff's case turns on a single act by an employee? That is indeed a legal question and well within the clear role of the Court. In theory, the Court was interpreting § 1983, and the Court is unequivocally the right governmental body to interpret statutes. But, as Justice Ginsburg pointed out in her dissent, the distinctions that the Court has developed in its long line of cases are hardly supported by the simple language of § 1983.[86]

Alternatively, one might defend the majority by arguing that the Court was interpreting its case law on point. Of course, as this Court has done in so many other areas, *Connick v. Thompson* gave a very narrow reading to precedent. It continued a trend in place for many years making recovery for § 1983 violations extremely difficult. Individual actors have significant qualified immunity; their employers have won repeated major victories in narrowing the liability of governmental entities. The result is that many violations of citizens' constitutional rights go unpunished. But as indicated, read narrowly, *Connick* is a decision interpreting legal standards. That is not the role of other governmental entities and certainly is not the role for the jury in the run-of-the-mill case.[87]

At the same time, Justice Ginsburg's dissenting opinion provides a much different view of what the record demonstrated. She stated the

---

84. *Id.* at 72–78 (Scalia, J., concurring).

85. *Id.* at 75–76.

86. *Id.* at 79–109 (Ginsburg, J., dissenting).

87. *Id.* at 64–72 (majority opinion).

Court's view that the record showed only "an aberrant *Brady* violation" did not square with the record; "the conceded, long-concealed prosecutorial transgressions were neither isolated nor atypical."[88] Deegan was not working alone but was part of a four-attorney team that hid from the defense and the court the *Brady* material. The prosecution continued to withhold that information "despite multiple opportunities, spanning nearly two decades[.]"[89] The jury, in the dissenters' view, could "reasonably conclude that inattention to *Brady* was standard operating procedure at [Connick's] Office."[90] In addition, Justice Ginsburg recounted other information that the prosecution team withheld in Thompson's murder trial. According to her count, the prosecution team committed three other *Brady* violations.[91]

Justice Ginsburg also laid out in considerable detail Connick's failure to understand *Brady*'s requirements; indeed, he admitted that the U.S. Attorney had indicted him for having withheld a crime lab report. Two lawyers who were senior to Deegan and who were on the team prosecuting Thompson demonstrated a similar lack of awareness of *Brady*'s importance and a casual—perhaps callous—attitude toward their obligations. Ginsburg's opinion included a thorough examination of the record that rebuts point-by-point the majority's approach.[92]

As I discussed above, one might argue that Justice Thomas' opinion merely interprets § 1983 and relevant case law interpreting that statute. A close look at Justice Ginsburg's dissent suggests something else is afoot. The majority gave the record an exceedingly narrow and begrudging reading. In some instances, Justice Thomas clearly inaccurately stated what appears in the record and ignored other facts that appeared there. So what may be afoot?

Think back to the discussion of Professor Roosevelt's criteria for evaluating when the Court acts illegitimately. As was the case with *Scott v. Harris*, the Court effectively took this case from the jury. By finding that the district court should have granted summary judgment, *Scott* was more explicit in doing so. *Connick* ended up doing so by the majority's

88. *Id.* at 79 (Ginsburg, J., dissenting).

89. *Id.*

90. *Id.* at 79–80.

91. *Id.*

92. *Id.* at 79–109.

begrudging reading of the record—by ignoring facts in the record, the Court could conclude that Thompson's evidence revealed only one *Brady* violation. Because I see *Connick* as an instance where the majority viewed itself better able to assess whether Connick's office violated § 1983, whether the Court or the jury was in fact a better decision maker is a fair question.

Arguments may support limiting § 1983. Imposing liability on prosecutors and other actors in the criminal justice system without some qualified immunity may make them too timid in prosecuting guilty parties. Finding municipalities liable based only a respondeat superior theory is not consistent with the Court's understanding of the legislative history. Making recovery against local governmental entities too easy may deprive that entity of the resources to improve the very services under attack. But the Court's holdings on issues like qualified immunity for police and prosecutors address those concerns. So too do the Court's holdings requiring a showing of employers' indifference. That does not explain why the majority read the record so narrowly, taking the case from the jury here.[93]

Individuals' views of juries often vary depending on whether they agree with the jury's decision in a particular case. O.J. Simpson's acquittal certainty demonstrated that. So too did the acquittal of Emmett Till's killers so many years ago. Cases expanding and then limiting jury trials precede the Roberts Court, so the justices on the right wing have had limited occasions to express their views about juries' virtues and vices. But taking the case away from the jury in *Connick* suggests that the justices in the majority did not share the same set of values as did the jurors who found for Thompson.[94]

Why not? As I wrote in my essay about the case, "Shortly after the Supreme Court published *Connick v. Thompson*, reaction among legal commentators was almost unanimously unfavorable. Even the anonymous posts on various Web sites joined the condemnation."[95] And yet, the justices on the right wing of the Court lack that same empathy. Here, I do not mean that the justices should decide cases based on a desire to feel good about the case: they should follow the law. But as I argued

93. *Id.* at 60–63 (majority opinion).

94. *Id.* at 54, 71–72.

95. Vitiello, *supra* note 59, at 217.

above, the Court read the case law narrowly. Even more damning, the Court ignored facts in the record that supported Thompson's position. Justice Alito was a former prosecutor. He may have some empathy for prosecutors who have made mistakes and now face liability for their misconduct. Although during the nomination hearings he claimed limited memory about his activities as a member of Concerned Alumni of Princeton, the organization opposed Princeton's use of affirmative action. Justice Scalia made statements suggesting callousness towards individuals on death row, even opining that we have not executed innocent defendants. Indeed, he pointed to cases like Thompson's as evidence that the system works. Despite or because of his race, Justice Thomas seems to hold in contempt other African-Americans who do not succeed. What seems to be missing is much empathy towards Thompson.[96]

Return to the discussion of values and introduction where I discussed the brouhaha over Judge Sotomayor's nomination to the bench. Her critics raised concerns that she would decide cases based on her own values. The idea that justices' values and ideology do not influence their decisions is frivolous. As I have argued above, *Scott* and *Connick* demonstrate the ways in which the justices on the right wing of the Court may have decided those cases consistent with their values and ideologies. But then, the fact that justices cannot divorce themselves from their values and ideologies should surprise no one.[97]

But think back to the overarching theme in this book: cases like *Scott* and *Thompson* provide more evidence that the right wing of the Court—consciously or otherwise—is closing the courthouse door. No matter which way you viewed Harris' conduct, you must see that Connick's lawyers gravely and unjustifiably harmed John Thompson. Yet a five justice majority slammed the courthouse door in his face.

---

96. *See, e.g., id.* at 219.

97. *See supra* Parts B and C.

SEVEN

Transfer of Venue and Limiting Access to Court

A. Introduction

A unanimous decision resolving a narrow statutory construction issue would not seem to fit into the theme of this book. Indeed, when I first read *Atlantic Marine Construction Co. v. U.S. District Court*,[1] I missed its significance. Upon closer reading, I got it: at one level, the decision is narrow and technical; but it represents another instance in which the Court favors defendants, often large corporate actors, over plaintiffs who are seeking to sue in a convenient forum.

This chapter first discusses *Atlantic Marine* and relevant case law. Thereafter, it examines critically the decision's flawed analysis. It also focuses on the negative effects of the decision for plaintiffs. Thereafter, the discussion focuses on some of the lower court case law since the Court decided *Atlantic Marine*.

1. Atl. Marine Constr. Co. v. U.S. Dist. Ct., 134 S. Ct. 568 (2013).

B. *Atlantic Marine Construction Co. v. U.S. District Court*

Atlantic Marine, a Virginia corporation, entered into a contract with the United States Corps of Engineers to build a facility at Fort Hood in western Texas. It entered into a contract with J-Crew Management, Inc., a Texas corporation, to work on the facility. That contract included a forum-selection clause, requiring the parties to litigate all claims in state or federal court in Norfolk, Virginia.[2]

When the deal soured, J-Crew filed an action against Atlantic Marine in the Western District of Texas. Atlantic Marine filed a motion to dismiss under Rule 12(b)(3),[3] contending that venue was improper. Alternatively, Atlantic Marine asked for a transfer of venue under § 1404(a).[4] The district court denied the motions. It did so largely based on the analysis under the Supreme Court's holding in *Stewart Organization, Inc. v. Ricoh Corp.*[5] There, the Court held that the forum-selection clause was only one factor determining whether the court should transfer venue. Atlantic Marine sought a writ of mandamus in the Fifth Circuit Court of Appeals. It asked for a dismissal under § 1406(a)[6] or transfer under § 1404(a). The Fifth Circuit rejected Atlantic Marine's argument and found that it failed to carry its burden for the issuance of a writ of mandamus. It also found that the district court did not abuse its discretion. Further, it also concluded that the proper rule for a challenge was Rule 12(b)(3).[7]

At the outset, the Court decided that venue was proper in the Western District of Texas. Thus, it rejected Atlantic Marine's claim that venue was improper. Although not without doubt, the Court's explanation is relatively straightforward: § 1391 (defining proper venue in federal courts) states "this section shall govern the venue of all civil actions brought in district courts of the United States."[8] It found that the literal

2. *Id.* at 575–76.
3. Fed. R. Civ. P. 12(b)(3).
4. 28 U.S.C.S. § 1404(a).
5. Stewart Org., Inc. v. Ricoh Corp., 487 U.S. 22 (1988).
6. 28 U.S.C.S. § 1406(a).
7. Fed. R. Civ. P. 12(b)(3).
8. 28 U.S.C.S. § 1391.

reading of § 1391(b)[9] applied and that the Court had rejected Atlantic Marine's argument in dicta in *Stewart Organization*.[10]

Atlantic Marine is not the final chapter in this area. For example, before *Atlantic Marine*, some scholars and courts disagreed with that reading of the venue and transfer of venue statutes. Professor Stephen E. Sachs believes that the proper motion was a Rule 12(b)(6) motion, because when a plaintiff files an action in a court other than the contractually indicated forum, the plaintiff did not have a claim for relief in that forum. Professor Sachs submitted an amicus brief arguing that position. But the Court left the question open because the parties did not advance that position.[11]

Alternatively, some courts have found that a Rule 12(b)(1) motion was the proper vehicle to challenge the action because any court other than the selected forum did not have subject matter jurisdiction over the claim. The Court did not address that question. From my perspective, were the Court to decide the case on either of those grounds, forum-selection clauses would have even more power than the parties have likely considered.[12]

The Court, however, did not stop after resolving that venue was proper.[13] The important question before the Court was whether the district court should honor the forum-selection clause. In a footnote, Justice Alito observed, "Our analysis presupposes a contractually valid forum-selection clause."[14] Apparently, J-Crew did not contest the validity of the provision. In light of that concession, the Court found that the district court should transfer the case consistent with the clause. That is

9. 28 U.S.C.S. § 1391(b).

10. *Stewart Org.*, 487 U.S. 22.

11. *Atl. Marine*, 134 S. Ct. at 580; Stephen E. Sachs, *Forum Selection After* Atlantic Marine: *Five Questions After Atlantic Marine*, 66 Hastings L.J. 761, 763 (2015).

12. *See, e.g.*, Lim v. Offshore Specialty Fabricators, Inc., 404 F.3d 898, 901 (5th Cir. 2005) ("Circuits are split on the issue of whether Rule 12(b)(1) or 12(b)(3) is the proper motion for seeking dismissal based on a forum selection or arbitration clause.").

13. The Court resolved a second question that is beyond the scope of the discussion in this chapter. Atlantic Marine argued that because the contract included as an alternative forum at state court in Virginia, § 1404(a) did not apply. That provision allows transfer only to another federal court, not a state court. The Court recognized, however, that the district court retained power to grant a forum non conveniens motion, premised on the fact that the original was correct, but sufficiently inconvenient.

14. *Atl. Marine*, 134 S. Ct. at 581 n.5.

the case absent "extraordinary circumstances unrelated to the convenience of the parties...."[15] The case before the Court did not present such circumstances.[16]

Had the controlling law not honored forum-selection clauses, the Court's analysis would have proceeded under *Stewart Organization*. There, the plaintiff filed the action in Alabama, instead of New York as required by the forum-selection clause. The defendant moved the court to transfer the venue to New York, consistent with the forum-selection clause. The case presented a vertical choice of law problem. Alabama courts found such clauses to violate public policy and were, therefore, unenforceable. Instead, the Supreme Court found that federal law controlled. It found a conflict between federal and state law (federal law provided a more flexible approach to the question in conflict with the state law). It held that § 1404 represented a valid exercise of Congress' constitutional power and, therefore, controlled.[17]

By contrast, Justice Alito found that *Stewart Organization* was not controlling because the controlling law[18] was, by hypothesis, valid. Thus, the Court found that the plaintiff's choice of the forum carried no weight. Further, unlike the situation in *Stewart Organization*, the district court should not give weight to private factors weighed in transfer and forum non conveniens motions. The plaintiff waived such objections as convenience. The district court should refuse to enforce a forum-selection clause only in an instance in which the public interest justifies the denial. That, according to the Court, will seldom happen.[19]

Because J-Crew selected a proper venue, one would have expected that upon transfer, Texas choice of law would have traveled with the suit. The Court so held in *Van Dusen v. Barrack*[20] and *Ferens v. John Deere Co.*[21] But the Court found that the policies leading to the result in *Van Dusen* were inapplicable to *Atlantic Marine*. *Van Dusen* rejected the defendant's efforts to forum shop by changing courthouses. But by signing

15. *Id.* at 581.

16. *Id.*

17. *Stewart Org.*, 487 U.S. at 24–25, 30–32 (1988).

18. The contract involved a dispute arising on federal law and presumably, federal law governed the validity of a forum-selection clause.

19. *Atl. Marine*, 134 S. Ct. at 581–83.

20. Van Dusen v. Barrack, 376 U.S. 612 (1964).

21. Ferens v. John Deere Co., 494 U.S. 516 (1990).

the forum-selection clause, J-Crew waived its rights to seek "state-law advantages."[22] As it has done elsewhere, the Court premised that conclusion on the notion that the parties bargained for that result: "A forum-selection clause, after all, may have figured centrally in the parties' negotiations and may have affected how they set monetary and other contractual terms; it may, in fact, have been a critical factor in their agreement to do business together in the first place."[23] As a result, upon transfer, the Court directed that the Virginia district court must apply Virginia choice of law rules.[24]

C. A Closer Look

As indicated at the outset, at first blush, this case looks unobjectionable. Two corporations entered into an agreement. The Court honored the agreement and gave J-Crew no benefits from its attempt to circumvent the agreement. At some level, that seems fair. Why should J-Crew be able to forum shop at Atlantic Marine's expense? What's not to like?

On the facts of the case, the Court's central premise that the forum-selection clause was a bargained-for provision is plausible, even if incorrect. Online research suggests that the two parties were of roughly equal bargaining power. At least if my search is correct, J-Crew does about $2 million of business a year, while Atlantic Marine does between $2.5 and $5 million. But even as pointed about by some business lawyers, Atlantic Marine may have offered the contract including that provision on a take-it-or-leave-it basis.[25]

Almost certainly more typical than a dispute between relative equals are cases involving one much larger party to the contract. Consider a real case involving a friend who opened a business in a western state shortly before the recession. He and his business partner bought an ex-

22. *Atl. Marine*, 134 S. Ct. at 583.

23. *Id.* at 584.

24. *Id.*

25. *Atlantic Marine Construction*, MANTA, http://www.manta.com/c/mmdrljs/atlantic-marine-construction (last visited June 28, 2016); *J-Crew Management Inc.*, MANTA, http://www.manta.com/c/mm2znsq/j-crew-management-inc; *see* Linda Mullenix, *Gaming the System: Protecting Consumers from Unconscionable Contractual Forum-Selection and Arbitration Clauses*, 66 HASTINGS L.J. 719, 758 (2015).

pensive machine from a manufacturer in a state on the east coast. At the onset of the recession, my friend's business failed. The manufacturer sued him in its home state. My friend soon learned that the contract contained boilerplate language binding him to suit in the manufacturer's home state. He had a counterclaim for fraud on the grounds that the salesperson misrepresented the suitability of the product for my friend's business. I referred my friend and his east coast lawyer to *Stewart Organization*. Before the Court decided *Atlantic Marine*, he filed a § 1404 motion to transfer the case to his home state. He argued in his memorandum that his home state was the more convenient forum because witnesses to the fraud lived in his home state. He lacked resources to litigate fully in the east because of his precarious financial situation. The parties settled the case before the district court ruled on the motion to transfer venue.

Almost certainly, my friend would have won the motion to transfer venue. No doubt, that was a significant factor leading to the settlement of the case. But the result would differ today: at least if the east coast state law upheld forum-selection clauses, the court would give no weight to the obvious inconvenience to the plaintiff and his witnesses. Presumably, because state law did not do so, the court would not consider the unequal bargaining power of the two parties.

The result might have differed, had the forum state not honored forum-selection clauses. Then, presumably, *Stewart Organization* would control. That also points out an anomaly that may exist after *Atlantic Marine*. Had my friend beaten the manufacturer to the courthouse and filed in his home state, whether the court had to transfer under § 1404(a) would turn on his home state's approach to forum-selection clauses. If it honored them, the court would have to transfer the case east without regard to the inconvenience.

The example suggests that many entering business contracts lack bargaining power, contrary to the Court's assumption that the parties bargained over the forum-selection clause. One other aspect of the example undercuts the Court's blithe assumption: not only was the forum-selection clause in the boilerplate language in the contract, but also, he did not hire counsel to represent him in negotiating the sizeable contract (for him, not the manufacturer). Corporations typically have in-house counsel or hire outside counsel to prepare legal documents. Small businesses or sole proprietors are not likely to have ready access to counsel.

But even if they do, especially in light of the likely take-it-or-leave-it approach of many large companies, hiring counsel might have made little difference.[26]

One might still object to my example: my friend was entering into a significant business arrangement. He should go in with his eyes open. But how does *Atlantic Marine* apply in a case involving consumers in non-business settings? If someone buys a vehicle or other expensive consumer item, she is not likely to hire counsel to enter into a sales contract. Would a court, post-*Atlantic Marine*, really uphold a forum-selection clause in such a case?

Almost immediately, some lower courts have found ways to avoid the Court's holding, with divided results among those courts.[27] Commentators have identified a number of issues unresolved by the Court's opinion. But elsewhere, the Court has routinely upheld forum-selection clauses. As Professor Linda Mullenix has observed, "The Supreme Court loves forum-selection clauses. It has told us so at least four times."[28] Most relevant to this discussion, the Court has done so in a case involving a consumer transaction where the injured plaintiffs had little reason to know that they had accepted such a contract term.

Specifically, a couple bought tickets for a cruise on a Carnival Cruise Lines ship from a travel agent in Washington. While they were in international waters near Mexico, Mrs. Shute fell during a tour of the ship. The Shutes filed their action in federal district court in Washington. Carnival Cruise Lines moved to dismiss on the grounds of a forum-selection clause in the contract that specified that the plaintiffs had to sue in Florida. The Ninth Circuit reversed the district court's dismissal of the complaint on the ground that the clause was not "freely bargained for."[29] The Supreme Court reversed. While the Court suggested that it might not uphold all such contracts, *Carnival Cruise Lines* demonstrates how seriously the Court takes such clauses. Almost certainly, Carnival Cruise

---

26. Mullenix, *supra* note 25, at 758.

27. Diane Fleming Averell & Pamela R. Kaplan, *Location, Location, Location: Drafting Enforceable Forum-Selection Clauses under* Atlantic Marine, 82 Def. Counsel. J. 335 (July 2015); *see also* Melanie Kalmanson & Emily Plakon, Atlantic Marine *After Ten Years*, 42 Franchise L.J. 399 (2023). *See* discussion *infra* Section D.

28. Mullenix, *supra* note 25, at 720.

29. Shute v. Carnival Cruise Lines, 897 F.2d 377, 388–89 (9th Cir. 1990).

Lines would not have bargained with the Shutes for a different provision, even if the Shutes had any idea that the provision was in the contract.[30]

Given the Court's "love" for forum-selection clauses (in Professor Mullenix's words),[31] *Atlantic Marine* analytically should apply in numerous settings where the Court's assumption about the parties bargaining for the provision is a pure fiction.

The effect of the decision seems to impair injured parties, most likely plaintiffs. Given the application of the decision to many consumer contracts, the net effect is to increase the cost of litigation for injured parties who may lack the resources to pursue a remedy against a tortfeasing defendant. At a minimum, the effect of the decision is to reduce the settlement value of the case for an injured party lacking resources to launch her case in a faraway venue.[32]

I can only speculate as to why no member of the Court dissented in *Atlanta Marine*. At least some of the more liberal justices seem to object to forum shopping. As Chapter Three developed, that may explain the late-Justice Ginsburg's interpretation of general jurisdiction.

As I discussed there, however, the Court has yet to explain what is wrong with forum shopping. Commentators have correctly recognized that efforts to reduce forum shopping are ineffective. Smart lawyers find ways to select favorable forums through a variety of devices. *Erie Railroad, Inc. v. Tompkins*[33] identified intra-jurisdictional forum shopping as the evil to be avoided. The Court explained its holding—that federal courts lacked the power to create general federal common law—in part, based on avoiding that policy. In *Klaxon Co. v. Stentor Electric Mfr. Co.*,[34] the Court held that a federal court sitting in diversity must apply the choice of law rules of the state where the court sits because of the same policy of avoiding intra-jurisdictional forum-shopping. But those cases did not end forum shopping. As *Ferens v. John Deere, Inc.*[35] demonstrates, plaintiffs can forum shop between jurisdictions, if not within the same jurisdiction.

---

30. Carnival Cruise Lines v. Shute, 499 U.S. 585 (1991).
31. Mullenix, *supra* note 25, at 720.
32. *Id.* at 759.
33. Erie R.R. v. Tompkins, 304 U.S. 64 (1938).
34. Klaxon Co. v. Stentor Elec. Mfg. Co., 313 U.S. 487 (1941).
35. *Ferens*, 494 U.S. 516.

And also as I discussed in connection with personal jurisdiction, apart from whether forum shopping is good or bad, the Court's decisions limiting plaintiffs' abilities to forum shop increases defendants' abilities to forum shop. That is evident in *Atlantic Marine*. Counsel for Atlantic Marine obviously recognized that inclusion of a forum selection clause in the contract forced the smaller party to come to Virginia.[36] That added to the plaintiff's costs, for example, by forcing the plaintiff to transport witnesses to Virginia if the case went to trial. Further, Atlantic Marine established home court advantage. As one article observed, litigants recognize the advantages of staying close to home, just as do major leagues sports teams.[37] No doubt, a large corporation may be able to rely on goodwill in its home venue. It may be a major employer and otherwise be visible there. Diversity, of course, is supposed to limit bias against out-of-state litigants, but trying a case in a federal court or state court within the same region does little to level the playing field.

Beyond those home court advantages, competent corporate counsel may also have done her homework: the chosen forum may have laws that favor the corporation. Corporations and other large donors have clout in state legislatures, often leading to favorable substantive law. Limitations on pain and suffering in tort cases, like medical malpractice, offer one example. Corporate money has flown into state judicial elections in recent years, often influencing the development of local law.[38]

If one doubts that forum selection clauses, as reinforced in *Atlantic Marine,* favor large corporate defendants, consider some of the supporters of the Court's decision. Harvard Law Professor Stephen Sachs, a prominent member of the Federalist Society, wrote an amicus brief in favor of enforcement of such provisions.[39] Contrast with Sachs' view that of left-leaning Professor Mullenix's views developed in her Hasting Law Journal article cited above. There, she expressed concern that the Court has failed to distinguish between forum-selection clauses between large corporate parties and consumer contracts. By doing so, the Court has

---

36. Mullenix, *supra* note 25, at 729–30.

37. Eric V. Travers & Peter A. Berg, *Forum-Selection Clauses After* Atlantic Marine, 34-SUM CONSLAW 6, 14 (2014).

38. *See supra* Chapter 3, n.93 and accompanying text.

39. *See* Brief of Professor Stephen E. Sachs as Amicus Curiae in Support of Neither Party, Atl. Marine Constr. Co. v. U.S. Dist. Ct., 134 S. Ct. 568 (No. 12-929) (2013), https://papers.ssrn.com/sol3/papers.cfm?abstract_id=2284517.

allowed corporate defendants to exploit their position to their economic benefit. According to Mullenix, *Atlantic Marine* furthers their ability to do so.[40]

One can find more evidence of that reality when one considers the effect that the Court's decision has had in overriding some states' progressive statutes. For example, California's Business Code provides franchisees protection against such provisions, reflecting the reality that the typical franchisee lacks the bargaining power to prevent inclusion of such provisions on their franchise agreements.[41] Whether *Atlantic Marine* signals that in the future courts will ignore such state laws, absent a very strong showing that the public interest outweighs enforcement of such clauses, is up for grabs.[42] The next section picks up on that point.

D. Uncertainty in the Lower Courts

As indicated above, the Court's analysis left open several questions. In reliance on Melanie Kalmanson and Emily Plakon's article reviewing ten years of litigation since the Court's decision,[43] this section examines ways that lower courts have analyzed the *Atlantic Marine* framework. It also examines some of the issues that divide lower federal courts.

Lower courts have grappled with the Court's modified forum non conveniens analysis that gives controlling weight to the forum selection clause unless enforcing the clause "would actually deprive the opposing party of his fair day in court."[44] With regard to the first change, courts

---

40. Mullenix, *supra* note 25, at 719.

41. *See, e.g.*, CAL. BUS. & PROF. CODE § 20040.5 (1994) ("A provision in a franchise agreement restricting venue to a forum outside this state is void with respect to any claim arising under or relating to a franchise agreement involving a franchise business operating within this state.").

42. Dominic V. Signorotti & Roger J. Brothers, *CASE ALERT*: Atlantic Marine Construction Company v. United States District Court—*The Beginning of the End of the California Franchise Relations Act?*, BUCHMAN PROVINE BROTHERS SMITH LLP (2014), https://www.primerus.com/legacy-files/wp-content/uploads/2014/01/Alert-Vol-XIV-No-II-Case-Alert-Atlantic-Marine-Construction-Co-v-U-S-D-C-The-Beginning-of-the-End-of-the-California-Franchise-Relations-Act.pdf.

43. *See* Kalmanson & Plakon, *supra* note 27.

44. Marc Jones Constr., L.L.C. v. Scariano, 2021 U.S. Dist. LEXIS 44614, at *21 (E.D. Ark. Mar. 10, 2021).

have found enforcement of a forum selection clause unreasonable where (1) inclusion of the clause was the product of fraud or overreaching, (2) the party wishing to repudiate the clause would effectively be deprived of his day in court if the clause is enforced, or (3) enforcement would contravene a strong public policy of the forum in which suit is brought.[45]

While the Court made no such distinction explicitly in *Atlantic Marine*, lower courts have distinguished between mandatory and permissive forum selection clauses.[46] The difference between the two, in some cases, is the deciding factor on whether to enforce the clause. A mandatory forum selection clause requires a case to be brought in the specified venue, generally including language indicative of the parties' intent to permit jurisdiction only in the selected venue. Words like "exclusive," "only," and "must" suggest exclusivity to courts.

A permissive forum selection clause, on the other hand, is "nothing more than a consent to jurisdiction and venue in the named forum."[47] Here, the clause does not exclude jurisdiction or venue in any other forum, so a permissive clause does not mandate a transfer or change of venue. Courts have stated that, in effect, the *Atlantic Marine* framework usually applies only to cases involving mandatory forum selection clauses.[48] It is therefore an important first step for a court to determine whether it is dealing with a mandatory or permissive clause.

Kalmanson and Plakon also explore state franchise laws protecting against forum selection clauses and how courts have dealt with them. California's Business and Professional Code § 20040.5 has been litigated in several federal districts. In *Baird v. OsteoStrong Franchising, LLC*,[49] the Eastern District of California voided a forum selection clause and held that § 20040.5 prohibits "enforcement of a forum selection clause that would require a franchisee to litigate matters related to the operation of a California franchise out of state."[50]

45. Minhong Inv., Inc. v. Felix Chac Chuo, 2022 U.S. Dist. LEXIS 120452, at *11 (C.D. Cal. Mar. 9, 2022).

46. *Marc Jones*, 2021 U.S. Dist. LEXIS 44614, at *23.

47. *Id.* at *24.

48. *Id.*

49. 2022 U.S. Dist. LEXIS 66098 (E.D. Cal. Apr. 8, 2022).

50. *Id.* at *3.

Other districts have found otherwise. In *Postnet International Franchise Corp. v. Wu*,[51] the District of Colorado held § 20040.5 is preempted by federal law and a forum selection clause in a franchise agreement is enforceable. In *Yiren Huang v. FutureWei Technologies, Inc.*,[52] the Northern District of California enforced a forum selection clause, noting that federal law governs enforceability of a contractual forum selection clause in a diversity case. Through the lens of federal law, "forum selection clauses 'are prima facie valid and should be enforced unless enforcement is shown by the resisting party to be unreasonable under the circumstances.'"[53]

Prior to the Court's *Atlantic Marine* decision, in *Jones v. GNC Franchising, Inc.*,[54] the Ninth Circuit recognized that § 20040.5 "expresses a strong public policy of the State of California to protect California franchisees from the expense, inconvenience, and possible prejudice of litigating in a non-California venue."[55] Although the Ninth Circuit has yet to take up § 20040.5 again, an Idaho case has suggested that it would enforce § 20040.5 and find a forum selection clause in a franchise agreement void as against public policy. An Idaho statute similar to California's was enforced by the Ninth Circuit, overriding a forum selection clause in a franchise agreement, reasoning that forum selection clauses contravened the strong public policy of Idaho.[56] Thus, it seems the Ninth Circuit would hold as they did in *Jones* in 2000 regarding § 20040.5.

Several other states have similar statutes. Federal courts around the country have divided in their interpretations of those laws post-*Atlantic Marine*.[57] At a minimum, the conflicting approaches taken by lower courts suggest differing views concerning access to the courts.

Thus far, the Court has not revisited its test, despite the emerging splits among lower federal courts. One can only speculate whether the Court will do so in the near term. An issue that might test the premise that the Court uses procedure to impair substantive rights that it disfavors may come before the Court. Some civil rights statutes include spe-

51. 521 F. Supp. 3d 1087 (D. Colo. 2021).

52. 2018 U.S. Dist. LEXIS 235769 (N.D. Cal. Sept. 24, 2018).

53. *Id.* at *8; *see also* Pinnacle Foods of California, LLC v. Popeyes Louisiana Kitchen, Inc., 2021 U.S. Dist. LEXIS 154266 (C.D. Cal. Apr. 21, 2021).

54. 211 F.3d 495 (9th Cir. 2000).

55. *Id.* at 498.

56. Gemini Techs., Inc. v. Smith & Wesson Corp., 931 F.3d 911, 917 (9th Cir. 2019).

57. Kalmanson & Plakon, *supra* note 27, at 406–410.

cial venue provisions. Title VII's special venue provision provides such an example.

In 2017, the Second Circuit noted that while "several district courts have held forum selection clauses unenforceable where they conflict with Title VII's special venue provision," no circuits have addressed the issue.[58] Ultimately, the Second Circuit weighed the Court's guidance in *Atlantic Marine* heavily, finding that the plaintiff's case was not the kind of exceptional case in which a forum selection clause should not be enforced.[59] Still, the court preserved the possibility that a conflict with Title VII's special venue provision, combined with other factors, may render a forum selection clause unenforceable.[60] Since that decision, no other circuit addressed the issue, and that is still true today. District courts that have faced the issue have adopted a case-by-case approach to determining whether Title VII's special venue provision impacts enforceability of a forum selection clause. Thus, it remains to be seen whether a special venue provision trumps an enforceable forum selection clause.

E. A Few Closing Thoughts

As developed in this chapter, enforceability of forum selection clauses seems at first blush to be the driest of topics. Even some proceduralists might fail to see the significant policy implications of a decision like *Atlantic Marine.* Two corporations seem capable of bargaining at arms' length. Or so it would seem.

This chapter has argued, however, that upon closer inspection, a seemingly minor procedural decision can have significant substantive policy consequences. Here, again, the Court's ruling favors large corporate litigants over parties who are likely to deal with them with little bargaining power. In *Atlantic Marine*, the Court ruled in a case where few members of the public are likely to respond with more than a shrug of the shoulders. That is especially true because the Court was unanimous. And yet, it is one more example where the Court's procedural case law deprives litigants of their full day in court.

---

58. DeBello v. VolumeCocomo Apparel, Inc., 720 F. App'x 37, 40–41 (2d Cir. 2017).

59. *Id.* at 41.

60. *Id.*

EIGHT

Class Actions and More

A. Introduction

Imagine corporate employees under pressure to increase profits engaging in an elaborate scheme to defraud consumers. The scam added about $40 to each consumer's annual bill for utilities, but resulted in billions of dollars of illicit gains for the corporation. Or imagine a company adding small charges to each consumer's bill amounting to a few dollars a year for each consumer, but again resulting in significant additional revenue for the company. Or imagine a corporation engaged in illegal discharge of toxic chemicals, resulting in damage to a community's water supply. The pollution was the result of a conscious decision to release the chemicals rather than paying for more expensive disposal as required by federal environmental protection regulations. That corporations engage in such conduct is beyond dispute.[1]

Why do corporate officials engage in such behavior despite the obvious criminality of their conduct? Doesn't the federal government regulate such conduct? The obvious answer is that governmental resources

1. *See, e.g.*, *Examples of Corporate Fraud Investigations—Fiscal Year 2015*, IRS, https://www.irs.gov/uac/examples-of-corporate-fraud-investigations-fiscal-year-2015 (last visited June 29, 2016); *Attorney General Kamala D. Harris Announces $23.8 Million Settlement with AT&T for Environmental Violations*, State of California Department of Justice (Nov. 20, 2014), https://oag.ca.gov/news/press-releases/attorney-general-kamala-d-harris-announces-238-million-settlement-att.

are limited. Indeed, right-wing activists have worked hard to limit resources for enforcement agencies. During the 2016 Presidential campaign, some Republican candidates urged for further gutting of those agencies. Senator Ted Cruz notably campaigned on a promise to kill the Environmental Protection Agency, an enforcement agency that has long been in the crosshairs of extreme right-wingers like the Koch brothers.[2]

Donald Trump's reelection in 2024 promises even greater efforts to gut oversight of corporations and to erode the EPA's enforcement powers (short of defunding the agency). Trump's various cabinet officials and involvement of Elon Musk in the government suggest a form of crony capitalism seldom seen in the modern era.[3] It is far from certain that even a Republican controlled Congress will have the votes to scrap major legislation. But the current climate seems to invite further erosion of consumer protections and other plaintiff friendly laws designed to limit improper conduct by powerful organizations.[4]

For many years, advocates for reform have argued that class action plaintiffs serve as private attorneys general, able to enforce laws where public resources are inadequate. Indeed, the joinder mechanism is well-suited to enforcing such laws. In the examples cited above, no single plaintiff or small group of plaintiffs could find a lawyer willing to bring suit against the defendant on a contingency fee basis. And few plaintiffs, if any, could fund litigation in light of the miniscule potential recovery.[5]

What about class actions? As discussed in this chapter, they are powerful medicine for addressing social harm caused to large numbers of individuals when each individual's damages are small. Not surprisingly, however, corporate America is dead set against class action suits and has worked to limit their effectiveness. As with other areas of the law discussed in this book, the right wing of the Court obliged.

---

2. Jane Mayer, Dark Money 274–75 (2016).

3. Frank Vogl, *The Trump Era of Crony Capitalism*, https://www.theglobalist.com/united-states-donald-trump-trump-clan-crony-capitalism/.

4. Indeed, as the edition of the book is going to press, the Trump administration is trying to shut down the Consumer Financial Protection Bureau, created by the Dodd-Frank bill to address some of the conditions that led to the economic debacle at the end of the second George W. Bush presidential term.

5. Abraham L. Pomerantz, *New Developments in Class Actions—Has Their Death Knell Been Sounded?*, 25 Bus. Law 1259, 1259 (1970).

Over a several year period, the Roberts Court was very active in reviewing cases involving class actions. Indeed, the Court's active role garnered academic attention. For example, the Akron Law Review hosted a symposium in 2015 on the Roberts Court's class action jurisprudence. Commentators observed that the Court's record was mixed, with several victories for plaintiffs and several for defendants. Some defense oriented commentators in that symposium and elsewhere claimed that pro-plaintiff commentators overstated the Court's hostility to class actions.[6] In part, they argued that the Roberts Court was unanimous in many of the cases, even when it limited class actions. But as developed below, the right wing of the Court limited class actions in very significant ways. Further, while some liberal commentators may have overstated the extent to which the Court gutted class actions, the Court's important limitations fit into an overall pattern developed in this book: too often, the Court is closing the courthouse door in ways that favor powerful corporate interests over the interests of injured plaintiffs.[7]

This chapter explores briefly the advantages of class actions, not only for plaintiffs and their lawyers, but also for the public at large. That discussion also focuses on why corporate America hates class actions and examines some of its efforts to circumvent them. Most commonly, big business has inserted arbitration clauses into standard form contracts. Those provisions waive a consumer's right to sue. Elsewhere, business interests have convinced legislatures to limit the use of class actions. The chapter then turns to a surprising Supreme Court decision, *Shady Grove Orthopedic Associates, P.A. v. Allstate Insurance, Co.*,[8] that seems to contradict my overall thesis that the right wing of the Court has led the procedural revolution that has closed the courthouse door. There, the justices aligned in an unusual way, defying easy stereotypes. Justice Scalia wrote the plurality opinion that upheld the applicability of Federal Rule of Civil Procedure 23 in a case favoring plaintiffs over corporate defendants. That section also explores a possible explanation for the un-

6. Paul G. Karlsgodt & Dustin M. Dow, *The Practical Approach: How the Roberts Court Has Enhanced Class Action Procedure by Strategically Carving at the Edges*, 48 Akron L. Rev. 883 (2015); Andrew J. Trask, *The Roberts Court and the End of the Entity Theory*, 48 Akron L. Rev. 831 (2015).

7. *See, e.g.*, Daimler AG v. Bauman, 571 U.S. 117 (2014); Goodyear Dunlop Tires Operations, S.A. v. Brown, 564 U.S. 915 (2011).

8. Shady Grove Orthopedic Assocs., P.A. v. Allstate Ins. Co., 559 U.S. 393 (2010).

usual alignment. Thereafter, however, this chapter turns to the more predictable case law, where the right wing of the Court has limited class actions in consumer cases.

B. Class Actions

Although originally included in the Federal Rules of Civil Procedure, the 1966 amendment to Rule 23 invigorated class action practice. Abraham Pomerantz, a prominent plaintiffs' class action lawyer, described the benefits of class actions in a short article in 1970. As suggested above, the economics of class actions are straightforward: if no individual suffers a sufficiently serious injury, the social harm is real and the only effective way to redress the harm is through a class action. According to Pomerantz, the class action is "one of the most socially useful remedies in history."[9] Alternative remedies, like administrative or criminal proceedings against perpetrators of consumer fraud, often amount to slaps on the wrist of wrongdoers.[10]

Early opposition to class actions focused on the fact that a person who did not pursue her legal remedies should not be able to recover those damages when someone else pursued the action. That argument largely ignored the reality that some damages, although real, did not justify the plaintiff pursuing a remedy. Of course, in such a world, defendants had little reason to comply with the law as long as the risk of civil suits was small and administrative penalties or criminal fines were minor.

Class action proponents argued persuasively that Rule 23 served a "prophylactic purpose."[11] As Pomerantz argued, "[T]he wrongdoer must be made to disgorge. Permitting the wrongdoer ... to retain the fruits of their wrong would encourage preying on the public."[12] Even in cases where recovery does not go to harmed plaintiffs, the judgment serves as a deterrent to illegality. In effect, class plaintiffs and their lawyers serve as private attorneys general.[13]

---

9. Pomerantz, *supra* note 5, at 1259.

10. *Id.* at 1260.

11. *Id.*

12. *Id.*

13. *Id.* at 1261 n.4.

No one can doubt that some corporations cause significant social harm through illegal conduct. Writing in 1970, Pomerantz cited a class action brought by states and municipalities against pharmaceutical companies for fixing the prices of antibiotics. The companies settled for $120,000,000, an extraordinary sum in the 1960s.[14] Examining the kinds of cases where plaintiffs use class actions most frequently suggests their importance: consumer rights, securities fraud violations, antitrust, environmental harm, mass torts, and civil rights, including school desegregation, prisoners' rights cases, voting rights, and employment discrimination.[15]

What's not to like about such a powerful procedural device? Wrongdoers obviously object to being held liable for harm caused, but an objection from a proven wrongdoer whom the law has forced to pay back improperly acquired funds is not likely to resonate. But given the impact on the business community, not surprisingly, pro-corporate advocates began a counter-narrative at least as early as the 1970s. As summarized by Columbia Law Professor Milton Handler, class actions amount to "legalized blackmail."[16]

In defending class actions in a 1979 Harvard Law Review article, Professor Arthur R. Miller described the counter-narrative: "For most than a decade segments of the bench and bar have been waging a holy war over rule 23 of the Federal Rules of Civil Procedure."[17] Miller listed many of the claims made by opponents of class actions, including the claim that a class action is a "Frankenstein Monster."[18] In addition,

> They also have charged widespread abuse of the rule by lawyers and litigants on both sides of the "v.," including unprofessional practices relating to attorneys' fees, "sweetheart" settlement deals, dilatory motion practice, harassing discovery, and misrepresentations to judges. Finally, some have questioned

---

14. *Id.* at 1259.

15. *Id.* at 1259–60; Janet Cooper Alexander, *Contingent Fees and Class Actions*, 47 DePaul L. Rev. 347, 351 (1998).

16. Milton Handler, *The Shift from Substantive to Procedural Innovations in Antitrust Suits*, 71 Colum. L. Rev. 1, 9 (1971).

17. Arthur R. Miller, *Of Frankenstein Monsters and Shining Knights: Myth, Reality, and the "Class Action Problem,"* 92 Harv. L. Rev. 664 (1979).

18. *Id.* at 664.

> the wisdom of imposing the burdens of class actions on an already overtaxed federal judiciary. They assert that many rule 23 cases are unmanageable and inordinately protracted by opposing counsel, creating a certain millstone or dinosaur character that diverts federal judges from matters more worthy of their energies.[19]

As remains the case today, for example, when critics claim that attorneys engage in abusive discovery practices, commentators often rely on little empirical data.[20]

Miller's study of a decade's worth of cases, from the amendments to Rule 23 in 1966 through 1978, led him to conclude that "much of the debate has been based on erroneous assumptions."[21] Many class actions achieved the goal of achieving economies of scale. Instances of professional misconduct existed, but did not appear widespread. He acknowledged that some class actions were "beyond anything previously seen in Anglo-American courts in terms of size, complexity, and longevity."[22] They often require a much greater managerial role for trial court judges than what was typical at that point.[23]

The amendments to Rule 23, Miller argued, were not the primary reason for modern big cases. Instead, he identified a variety of changes in American law that resulted in larger cases than in the past. Prior to the Civil Rights Act of 1964[24] and the Voting Rights Act of 1965,[25] civil rights plaintiffs often filed test cases as individual plaintiffs, not as class plaintiffs. Statutes like the Civil Rights Act and Voting Rights act, along with other expanded rights based on gender and age, meant that new classes of rights holders increased the number of potential plaintiffs seeking access to federal court. These statutes passed at a time when the Supreme Court was also expanding rights protected under the Four-

---

19. *Id.* at 665–66.
20. *Id.* at 666 n.13.
21. *Id.* at 666.
22. *Id.* at 667.
23. *Id.* at 667–68.
24. Civil Rights Act of 1964, 78 Stat. 241.
25. Voting Rights Act of 1965, 79 Stat. 437.

teenth Amendment. Thus, concluded Miller, expansion of substantive rights, not the liberalization of Rule 23, resulted in the influx of cases.[26]

Fast-forward to the more contemporary debate. Class actions have remained controversial. In 1991, Stanford Law Professor Janet Cooper Alexander published an empirical study of class action suits. Her study focused on "a group of securities class actions alleging similar claims of fraud in the initial public offerings of computer-related companies in the first six months of 1983."[27] As she stated,

> The remarkable similarity of the companies and the claims reduces possible non-merits-related causes of variance in the cases' outcomes. Moreover, because suits were filed against every company in the industry whose stock declined significantly in the months following its initial stock offering, it is likely that the cases included a range of strength on the merits. Nevertheless, the cases settled for approximately one quarter of the potential damages according to the allegations of the complaint.[28]

Her data are certainly troubling for supporters of class actions, but are counterintuitive. Traditional theory suggests that a settlement reflects, at least in part, the merits of the case.[29]

The class action literature includes other empirical studies, but none that I could find focused on the same question addressed by Professor Alexander. Some scholars question whether a subset of securities fraud cases is representative of class action settlements generally. In addition, in 1995 and again in 1998, Congress enacted securities legislation intended to reform some of the perceived excesses of the plaintiffs' class action bar. Despite those reforms, business groups continued to call for reforms to securities class actions. According to those groups, securities class actions place U.S. capital markets at a disadvantage to foreign markets.[30]

---

26. Miller, *supra* note 17, at 674–75.

27. Janet Cooper Alexander, *Do the Merits Matter? A Study of Settlements in Securities Class Actions*, 43 STAN. L. REV. 497, 500 (1991).

28. *Id.*

29. *Id.* at 502.

30. James D. Cox, Randall S. Thomas & Lynn Bai, *There Are Plaintiffs and ... There Are Plaintiffs: An Empirical Analysis of Securities Class Action Settlements*, 61 VAND. L. REV. 355 (2008); Brian T. Fitzpatrick, *An Empirical Study of Class Action Settlements and Their Fee Awards*, 7 J. EMPIRICAL LEGAL STUD. 811 (2010).

Class actions are not without problems. They are complex. Especially in cases where the substantive law allows for treble or punitive damages, defendants may feel compelled to settle the litigation rather than risking rolling the dice with juries. Plaintiffs' attorneys may have a conflict of interest with class members; for example, a defendant may offer a settlement lucrative to the plaintiffs' attorney or attorneys, but one that leaves the injured class members with inadequate remedies. The plaintiffs' attorney may fear taking the case to trial because losing the case leaves the attorney with no fee and potentially a loss for litigation costs. Commentators point to "sweet heart deals" between the attorneys, deals largely benefiting the lawyers at the expense of the class members.[31]

Many of those issues are beyond the scope of this chapter. Suffice it to say that remedies are available that are less extreme than gutting class actions. Greater judicial supervision in approving class settlements can and often does prevent sweet heart deals between the attorneys. Greater use of Rule 11 may remedy the problem of marginal cases resulting in coerced settlements: demonstrating that the case is frivolous should provide leverage for defendants. Either the defendant should be able to get the case dismissed as so lacking in merit or to reduce the settlement value of the case to cents on the dollar of claimed harm.[32] Thus, marginal reforms may be able to prevent some of the perceived harm caused by class actions. But much of the debate about the harm that class actions do to the U.S. economy is misdirected. That needs closer attention.

One should question whether class actions are responsible for placing U.S. capital markets, for example, at a competitive disadvantage. Many observers believe that the collapse of the financial industry occurred because the U.S. financial markets were out of control, with investment bankers and others engaging in foolish and, at times, illegal activities. Apart from that obvious concern, the cost of compliance with existing regulations, not class actions, is the source of the problem.[33]

Examine the financial crisis closely. Many banks engaged in mortgage fraud, lending money to buyers who were not creditworthy. Many

31. Janet Cooper Alexander, *Contingent Fees and Class Actions*, 47 DePaul L. Rev. 347, 358 (1998).

32. Cox, Thomas & Bai, *supra* note 30, at 356 n.6.

33. *See* Paul Krugman, *Economics in the Crisis*, New York Times (Mar. 5, 2012), http://krugman.blogs.nytimes.com/2012/03/05/economics-in-the-crisis/.

also engaged in credit default swaps, which proponents claimed reduced risk, while creating risks that few understood. Market advocates among both political parties (but especially among Republicans) were convinced that the unregulated free market was, in effect, omniscient.[34] The George W. Bush administration adopted that view and allowed erosion of banking regulation during his presidency. A loose enforcement environment allowed banks to sell toxic mortgage-back securities, often fraudulently. That is a partial list of causes of the economic crisis. I have not found any serious economist who lists class action suits as a cause for the financial crisis. Greed placed the United States at risk of a second Great Depression.[35]

As importantly, even in an otherwise healthy economic environment, compliance with state and federal law, not the enforcement of those laws through class actions, may make companies less competitive. Indeed, many business groups claim that compliance with the post-collapse Dodd Frank Wall Street Reform and Consumer Protection Act makes U.S. companies uncompetitive.[36] One could make the same argument about compliance with environmental regulations: they add to the cost of doing business. Many companies want to shift the cost to individuals who must breathe bad air or drink tainted water. The risk of a class action suit does not raise those companies' costs: compliance with the law does. Many of those laws protect members of the public against real substantive harms.

As with efforts to impair discovery, business groups unable to secure reform of substantive provisions of laws like Dodd Frank or environmental regulations see procedural reform as effective in protecting corporate America. Gutting class actions leaves injured plaintiffs with no

---

34. For a recent book that debunks many myths about the free market, see NAOMI ORESKES & ERIK M. CONWAY, THE BIG MYTH: HOW AMERICAN BUSINESS TAUGHT US TO LOATHE GOVERNMENT AND LOVE THE FREE MARKET (2023).

35. *The Origins of the Financial Crisis: Crash Course*, THE ECONOMIST (Sept. 7, 2013), http://www.economist.com/news/schoolsbrief/21584534-effects-financial-crisis-are-still-being-felt-five-years-article.

36. *See, e.g.*, Gregg Greenberg, *Dodd-Frank Making U.S. Banks Uncompetitive, Says White & Case Partner*, THESTREET (July 24, 2015, 4:49 PM), https://www.thestreet.com/story/13231113/1/dodd-frank-making-us-banks-uncompetitive-says-white-case-partner.html.

effective remedy. Especially during Republican administrations, the threat of criminal or administrative sanctions remains weak.[37]

Can corporate America erode substantive law? Reforming federal regulations is difficult. Even when Republicans control Congress, Senate procedures, including the filibuster, may prevent direct frontal attacks on regulatory statutes. In addition, as developed in Chapter One, the American people understand frontal attacks on their rights. Pushback from the electorate makes procedural reform that much more tempting: typically, such reforms slip under the radar of the American people. As this section has argued, the attack on class actions is just such a case study.

C. State Reforms and an Odd Lineup in the Supreme Court

Corporate America may have difficulty effectuating congressional reform, as suggested immediately above, but it has often succeeded in state legislatures. Beginning in the 1970s, pro-defendant organizations have lobbied successfully for tort reform legislation. Those efforts have continued into the twenty-first century. State legislatures have been more receptive to those reforms than Congress has been.[38]

Not only have state legislatures been receptive to laws, for example, limiting pain and suffering in a variety of cases, but many have also adopted laws limiting class actions. At least two states have disallowed all class actions. More typical is a law like one in effect in New York.[39]

At the urging of the New York Court of Appeals, the New York legislature enacted a class action provision in 1975, designed to be comparable to Federal Rule of Civil Procedure 23.[40] But the Empire State Cham-

37. *See, e.g., Gutting Class Action*, New York Times (May 12, 2011), http://www.nytimes.com/2011/05/13/opinion/13fri1.html.

38. *See* Mark M. Hager, *What's (Not!) in a Restatement? ALI Issue-Dodging on Liability Apportionment*, 33 Conn. L. Rev. 77, 94–95 (2000).

39. Linda S. Mullenix, *Federal Class Actions: A Near-Death Experience in a Shady Grove*, 79 Geo. Wash. L. Rev. 448, 450 (2011).

40. Moore v. Metropolitan Life Ins. Co., 33 N.Y.2d 304 (1973); Thomas A. Dickerson, *New York State Class Actions: Make It Work—Fulfill the Promise*, 74 Alb. L. Rev. 711, 714 (2010).

ber of Commerce persuaded the legislature to add § 901(b). That subsection provides, "Unless a statute creating or imposing a penalty, or minimum measure of recovery specifically authorizes recovery thereof in a class action, an action to recover a penalty, or a minimum measure of recovery created or imposed by statute may not be maintained as a class action."[41] As developed below, whether that section applied in a suit that the plaintiff brought in federal court produced an unusual alignment in the Court.

After Sonia Galvez was involved in an accident, she sought medical treatment from Shady Grove Orthopedic Associates. Ms. Galvez assigned her insurance claim to Shady Grove. It sought payment from Allstate Insurance Company, Ms. Galvez's insurer. According to Shady Grove, Allstate failed to make a timely payment as required under New York insurance law. Specifically, that law provides that an insurer has 30 days after submission of a claim either to pay or to deny the claim. Allstate paid the claim late but refused to pay statutorily determined interest, amounting to $500 in this case.[42]

Ms. Galvez and Shady Grove filed a class action complaint in federal court in New York. The complaint alleged that Allstate routinely flouted its obligation to pay interest due on late payments. Allstate moved to dismiss and argued that the district court was bound by § 901(b). The district court granted the motion to dismiss and the United States Court of Appeals for the Second Circuit affirmed. The Supreme Court granted certiorari.[43]

Students and lawyers can readily see what is at stake. No lawyer would bring an individual's claim to recover $500, at least not based on a contingency fee. And no sane plaintiff would pay an attorney an hourly fee to recover $500. By comparison, if the plaintiffs' class action was proper, the value of the case exceeded $5,000,000. While students and lawyers can see what is at stake, they are less likely to be excited by the battle that took place in the Supreme Court. When announcing his plurality opinion, even Justice Scalia seemed to acknowledge that fact when he quipped, "Eyes have glazed over already."[44] But in the words of one commentator,

---

41. N.Y. C.P.L.R. Law § 901(b) (2016).
42. Shady Grove Orthopedic Assocs., P.A. v. Allstate Ins. Co., 559 U.S. 393, 397 (2010).
43. *Id.* at 397–98.
44. Mullenix, *supra* note 39, at 448.

> As a policy matter, the Court's decision in Shady Grove will have a wide-ranging impact on the future of class action litigation in both federal and state courts. In essence, a slim plurality of the Supreme Court saved the federal class action from death by a thousand cuts through state-limiting provisions on class litigation.[45]

What is most interesting from my perspective is the unusual alignment of the justices. The right wing of the Court split; Justices Kennedy and Alito joined Justice Ginsburg's dissent, but the Chief Justice and Justice Thomas joined Justice Scalia's plurality opinion. As I have argued throughout this book, Justices Roberts, Scalia, and Thomas frequently vote against plaintiffs and in close alignment with corporate interests. At a minimum, their realignment suggests that the various *Shady Grove* opinions merit attention.

In Chapter One, I discussed the *Erie* doctrine. That chapter explained how the press failed to understand the larger significance of a case that seemingly announced a technical procedural rule. As Justice Scalia's comment from the bench about eyes glazing over suggests, many students and lawyers approach the study of the *Erie* doctrine with about as much as enthusiasm as they would a dental appointment: one that may involve a good bit of pain, but even at best, one that presents little chance for excitement. At least, in approaching *Shady Grove*, students can see what is at stake; they can tell the difference between recovery of a claim of $500 and $5,000,000.[46]

Erie ultimately is a case about vertical choice of law: does federal or state law apply in federal diversity actions when those two sources of law are in conflict? At issue in *Shady Grove* was whether § 901(b) conflicted with Rule 23 and if so, whether state or federal law governed in federal court.

Years earlier in the progression of post-*Erie* cases, the Court struggled with conflicts between state and federal law when the conflict was not purely one of substance. In 1945, the Supreme Court held that a state statute of limitations applied when the plaintiff invoked a federal court's equitable jurisdiction in a diversity action. Had the district court been

45. *Id.*

46. *Shady Grove*, 559 U.S. at 408.

able to invoke the equitable doctrine of laches, the plaintiff's claim might not have been time-barred. Instead, in *Guaranty Trust, Co. v. York*,[47] the Court held that a state rule, even if fairly characterized as procedural, would apply in a diversity action as long as the application of federal as opposed to state law would have a substantial effect on the outcome of the case.

York's outcome determinative test posed significant problems as a matter both of application and policy. Determining when an avowedly procedural rule may "substantially" affect the outcome creates a great deal of uncertainty. Any procedural rule, under some circumstances, may affect a suit's outcome. Law professors often use a shopworn example to make that point: on the day before the statute of limitations will run on a plaintiff's claim, the plaintiff's lawyer attempts to file her complaint in a form acceptable under state law, but not under federal law. If the plaintiff cannot file the complaint, the case is over. But if the court clerk accepts the complaint, the plaintiff gets her day in court. Surely, the federal system does not have to bend to state law in such a case.[48]

One might argue that the result in that hypothetical would not be substantially different in most cases and therefore, a deviation in results in an unusual case would have to be tolerated. But that simply suggests the imprecision of *York*'s test.

In addition, requiring federal courts to follow state law overrides decisions by federal rulemakers to create a procedural system applicable throughout the federal system. The problem of deference to state law is especially acute with regard to the Federal Rules of Civil Procedure. Passage of the Rules Enabling Act came about after many years of effort. Drafting the rules was an involved and time-consuming project, involving the Advisory Committee, the Supreme Court, and Congress. The Rules' drafters aimed for the uniform application of the Federal Rules of Civil Procedure and for the just, speedy, and inexpensive adjudication of every case. Allowing a litigant to argue that state law trumps a federal rule undervalues the importance of the federal interest in its system of rules. It also adds unnecessary satellite litigation that creates delay and

47. Guaranty Trust Co. v. York, 326 U.S. 99 (1945).

48. Stephen N. Subrin, Martha L. Minow, Mark S. Brodin, Thomas O. Main & Alexandra D. Lahav, Civil Procedure: Doctrine, Practice, and Context 931 (4th ed. 2012).

expense for the party opposing application of state law. A trilogy of cases decided in 1949 suggested that the Federal Rules of Civil Procedure were, in fact, subject to a case-by-case challenge.[49]

As with so many procedural decisions, *Hanna v. Plumer*[50] appears to be yet another brain-numbing case. There, a plaintiff filed a diversity action in federal court and served process on an estate executor consistent with federal Rule 4. Rule 4 allows abode service rather than in-hand service if certain conditions are met. The defendant contended that the court should dismiss the action because state law governed and required in-hand service on an estate representative. Failing to serve process in-hand, if state law governed, meant that the statute of limitations had run.[51]

Chief Justice Warren's majority opinion established a framework for analysis when a state law conflicts with a Federal Rule of Civil Procedure. As indicated above, *York* created satellite litigation when a state and federal rule conflicted. The Chief Justice saw the obvious need to limit challenges to the applicability of the Federal Rules of Civil Procedure. Importantly, federal judge-made rules or congressionally created rules are different from the Federal Rules of Civil Procedure: the latter come about through an unusual process. The Advisory Committee acts pursuant to the Rules Enabling Act, whereby Congress gave the Court the power to create rules of practice and procedure. The act also instructed the Court not to modify, enlarge, or abridge substantive rights. The Court also has a role in drafting the rules: it must sign onto the proposed rules or amendments to the rules. Congress then can act to reject proposed changes; its inaction allows the rules to take effect.[52]

Hanna's analysis starts by determining whether a conflict exists between federal and state law. Absent a conflict, presumably, both federal and state law can co-exist. But if a Federal Rule of Civil Procedure does conflict with a state rule, the federal rule trumps unless the rule violates the Rules Enabling Act. In other words, is the particular rule a rule of

49. Woods v. Interstate Realty Co., 337 U.S. 535 (1949); Ragan v. Merchants Transfer, 337 U.S. 530 (1949); Cohen v. Beneficial Industrial Loan Corp., 337 U.S. 541 (1949).

50. Hanna v. Plumer, 380 U.S. 460 (1965).

51. *Id.* at 461–62.

52. *Id.* at 464, 471–72.

practice and procedure, or does it modify, enlarge, or abridge a substantive right?[53]

As Chief Justice Warren observed, involvement of the Advisory Committee, the Court, and Congress in effect creates a prima facie case that the rules do not violate the Rules Enabling Act or the Constitution. Rephrased, when the Advisory Committee and the Court promulgated the rules (and Congress allowed their adoption), one can assume that they acted in compliance with their obligation under the Rules Enabling Act.[54]

Hanna's analysis creates a level of certainty that the Federal Rules of Civil Procedure apply in diversity actions. That provides a disincentive for a party to engage in satellite litigation concerning the applicability of federal or state law.

Hanna's clarity may be more theoretical than real. A series of Supreme Court cases demonstrate that the first question—are federal and state law in conflict—is not always apparent. *Walker v. Armco Steel Corp.*[55] is a classic case: there, a plaintiff filed the complaint within the statute of limitations period in a diversity action, but failed to serve the defendant with process until after the statute of limitations ran, if state law applied. The plaintiff attempted to rely on what otherwise appears to be clear language: Rule 3 states that an action commences upon filing of the complaint.[56] That is, the plaintiff contended that Rule 3 tolled the statute of limitations.

The Court was unanimous in *Walker*: state law governed. One would have thought that Rule 3's language was unequivocal and controlling. Indeed, in a footnote, the Court stated what it would later hold: in an action based on a federal question, Rule 3 does toll the statute of limitations. Oddly, that same language does not toll an action in state court.[57]

The Court denied that it was giving Rule 3 a labored reading. Outsiders suggested that the obvious pretzel-like reading of the rule reflected the Court's concern that, were it to rule that Rule 3 did toll the statute of limitations, it might face a serious question whether Rule 3 violated the Rules Enabling Act. Literally, on *Walker*'s facts, the plaintiff's claim

53. *Id.* at 471–73.

54. *Id.* at 476–77.

55. Walker v. Armco Steel Corp., 446 U.S. 740 (1980).

56. *Id.* at 745–46.

57. *Id.* at 751 n.11.

would have been enlarged: the statute of limitations barred the claim if state law applied; the plaintiff's claim remained alive if Rule 3 tolled the statute of limitations.[58]

Prior to *Shady Grove*, a closely divided Court acknowledged that it gave a narrow reading to Rule 3 and would do so when a narrow reading avoided a conflict with important state substantive policies. Justice Ginsburg wrote the 5–4 opinion in *Gasperini v. Center for Humanities, Inc.*[59] Justice Scalia dissented in *Gasperini*.

Fast-forward to *Shady Grove*. Consistent with her majority opinion in *Gasperini v. Center for Humanities, Inc.*, Justice Ginsburg read Rule 23 narrowly to avoid a conflict with state law. According to Justice Ginsburg, when a state rule implicated important substantive policies, the Court's obligation is to read the federal law narrowly to avoid the conflict. For the four *Shady Grove* dissenters, New York's law embodied a regulatory policy to limit excessive damages. Absent a conflict, New York law applied and the district court rightly dismissed the class action.[60]

As one commentator observed, had Justice Ginsburg's view prevailed, class actions would have died "a death by a thousand cuts."[61] Corporate business interests and right-wing groups have worked hard over past decades to gain a foothold in state legislatures. (By 2010, for example, when states reapportioned districts for congressional seats, Republicans captured almost 60% of all governorships and made significant progress in taking over state legislatures. As of 2025, Republicans still control more state governments than do Democrats.) Deference to state laws like § 901(b) would erode federal court diversity class actions and give business groups incentive to get legislatures elsewhere to adopt class-action denying statutes.[62]

Analytically, Justice Ginsburg's position creates an anomaly: as Justice Scalia pointed out, her approach would force the Court to read Rule 23 narrowly in New York; but if, for example, New Jersey had no similar

58. *Id.* at 741–44.

59. Gasperini v. Center for Humanities, Inc., 518 U.S. 415 (1996).

60. Shady Grove Orthopedic Assocs., P.A. v. Allstate Ins. Co., 559 U.S. 393 (2010).

61. Mullinex, *supra* note 39, at 449.

62. *See id.* at 448.

statute or whatever statute it had in place reflected no important substantive policies, the Court would give Rule 23 a more natural reading.[63]

Justice Scalia's *Shady Grove* opinion addressed a number of issues. Most importantly, he argued why Rule 23 applied based on the facts of the case before the Court and rejected various arguments posed by Allstate. Because Rule 23 was on point and in conflict with state law, the Court could avoid application of Rule 23 only if it violated the Rules Enabling Act or the Constitution. Justice Scalia relied largely on *Hanna*'s analysis: if a rule is on point, it applies absent a violation of the Rules Enabling Act or the Constitution. And if a rule is rationally capable of being characterized as procedural, the rule does not violate the Rules Enabling Act or the Constitution.[64]

Justice Stevens concurred. Because his vote determines if the plurality or dissent can prevail, it takes on special importance.[65] The best way to understand Justice Stevens' differences with Justice Scalia is to focus on the two sections of the Rules Enabling Act. Section 2072(a) provides that the Court "shall have the power to prescribe rules of practice and procedure," and § 2072(b) provides, "Such rules shall not abridge, enlarge or modify any substantive right."[66] Commentators have noted an ambiguity in Chief Justice Warren's *Hanna* opinion: in effect, what is the relationship between the two sub-provisions of the statute?[67]

One reading of the two sub-provisions suggests that compliance with § 2072(a) means that the rule does not violate § 2072(b). As long as the rule can rationally be characterized as procedural, then the rule is valid. In effect, § 2072(a) and § 2072(b) are mirror images. That is the best way to understand Justice Scalia's opinion.[68]

Justice Stevens disagreed. In effect, he argued that compliance with § 2072(a) leaves open a second question: even if the rule meets § 2072(a), does it nonetheless conflict with § 2072(b)? As a matter of history, he may have the better argument: *Hanna* created a prima facie case that the

63. *Shady Grove*, 559 U.S. at 405–06.

64. *Id.* at 406–08.

65. Absent a new ruling by the Supreme Court superseding *Shady Grove*, lower courts have to assess how the *Shady Grove* Court would resolve similar issues.

66. Rules Enabling Act, 28 U.S.C.S. § 2071 (2016).

67. *See* Stephen Burbank, *Proposals to Amend Rule 68—Time to Abandon Ship*, 19 U. Mich. J. L. Reform 425, 440 n.81 (1986).

68. *Shady Grove*, 559 U.S. at 406–07.

rules violated neither the Rules Enabling Act nor the Constitution. That suggests a party might be able to carry the heavy burden of overcoming the prima facie case. Reframed, compliance with § 2072(a) creates a rebuttable presumption that the rule is valid. But rebuttable presumptions can be overcome. Justice Stevens joined in the result in *Shady Grove* because the defendant did not meet its burden.[69]

Viewed from the political lens that I have used in this book, though, Justice Ginsburg's dissenting opinion and Justice Stevens' opinion would invite states to gut class actions based on state law claims. Individual plaintiffs would have to bring claims against defendants like Allstate on their own, perhaps in small claims courts. That result would give Allstate little incentive to comply with New York's statute requiring prompt payment of claims. Justice Scalia's approach leaves class actions in place in many cases that would otherwise die on the vine.[70]

That leaves an important question: does Justice Scalia's plurality opinion undercut my thesis concerning the right wing of the Court's use of procedure to close the courthouse door? Here the effect seems to the contrary. Professor Linda Mullenix has written that *Shady Grove*'s ideological alignments are entertaining.[71] She offers the following explanation for why the three pro-business conservatives (Justices Scalia and Thomas and Chief Justice Roberts) voted as they did: they are aware of other developments in federal class action practice. Congress enacted the Class Action Fairness Act in 2005 with a clear intent to rein in class actions.[72] In part because of that Act, federal courts have been slower in recent years to certify classes.[73] That may be.

To some degree, their votes conflict with federalism concerns that the three right-wing justices sometimes espouse. Here, their votes override what appears to be a strong state interest in a statute that seems akin to a damages cap. At least Justice Scalia's commitment to federalism was lukewarm.[74]

---

69. *Id.* at 424–26 (Stevens, J., concurring).

70. Mullenix, *supra* note 39, at 452.

71. *Id.* at 480.

72. Class Action Fairness Act of 2005, 119 Stat. 4.

73. Mullenix, *supra* note 39, at 463–64.

74. *Id.* at 477.

Beyond Professor Mullenix's suggestion, I see Justice Scalia's plurality opinion as another instance of his commitment to textual analysis. His textual analysis of Rule 23 makes a more than plausible case for his view that the Rule is on point. As many scholars have observed, his view of statutory construction—its close textual readings with little or no deference to legislative history—may be one of his abiding legacies. The idea that a justice might come to a conclusion that seems contrary to his overall political philosophy in any given case is hardly an unusual one. Perhaps, Justice Scalia's opinion in *Shady Grove* reflected his commitment to textualism, despite the pro-plaintiff result in that case.[75]

And go back to Professor Mullenix's point: Justice Scalia no doubt was more than familiar with other developments that have narrowed class actions. Not only was he aware of such developments, but also, he and the rest of the right wing of the Court were instrumental in that process. That is the next topic in this chapter.

D. Narrowing Class Actions

As developed above, one can find examples that do not neatly fit into the overall theme of this book. That was the case with the Court's alignment in *Shady Grove*. Indeed, while the Roberts Court has reviewed numerous class action cases in its first decade, not all of those cases have been hostile to the class action format. A number of those cases have strengthened the joinder mechanism.[76] As a result, arguing that the Court has killed class action litigation is naïve. But elsewhere, the right wing of the Court has eroded class actions in several important rulings. This section focuses on some of those examples. In addition, it focuses on *Campbell-Ewald Co. v. Gomez*, which, had the Court found for the defendant, would have dealt plaintiffs' class actions a major blow. Fi-

---

75. *See* Craig Green, *Supreme Court Review: Black-and-White Judging in a World of Grays*, 46 Tulsa L. Rev. 391, 407 (2011). Interestingly, Justice Brandeis' decision in *Erie* advanced policies that he favored, including limiting the Court from overturning progressive legislation. He did so in a case that seemed to violate his commitment to injured plaintiffs. The result of the Court's decision was to deny a seriously injured plaintiff an ample judgment.

76. Bernadette Bollas Genetin, *Back to Class: Lessons from the Roberts Court Class Action Jurisprudence*, 48 Akron L. Rev. 697, 700 (2015).

nally, this section reviews the overall impact of the Roberts Court's class action case law and concludes, along with Professor Rich Freer, that the pro-defendant cases will have "the most far-reaching effects."[77]

(1) *Genesis HealthCare Corp. v. Symczyk*[78] and *Campbell-Ewald Co. v. Gomez*[79]

Laura Symczyk was a nurse who worked for Genesis HealthCare. She brought an action under the Fair Labor Standards Act, challenging the way in which her employer calculated her wages. Specifically, her employer automatically docked each employee's paycheck for a half-hour as a meal break, without regard to whether the employee took the break.[80]

Symczyk did not bring her action under Rule 23, dealing with class actions generally. Instead, her action, brought on behalf of herself and other employees who were covered by the Fair Labor Standards Act, was recognized under that statute.[81]

Along with its answer, the defendant offered a settlement to Symczyk. The offer of settlement was for her unpaid wages and any of her litigation costs. Symczyk did not respond to the offer. Thereafter, the defendant moved to dismiss for lack of subject matter jurisdiction. The defendant argued that, because it had offered full compensation, the plaintiff's action was moot. The district court agreed. The Third Circuit reversed, and the Supreme Court granted the writ of certiorari.[82]

The Supreme Court reversed the decision of the Third Circuit. The Court divided 5–4, with all of the members of the right wing of the Court in the majority. The Court relied on differences between Rule 23 class actions and collective actions allowed under the Fair Labor Stan-

77. *Id.* at 721–24. In *Tyson Foods, Inc. v. Bouaphakeo*, 577 U.S. 442 (2016), the Court upheld a class action brought by a group of workers who sued Tyson Foods for violations of the Fair Labor Standards Act of 1938. In a 7–2 opinion, Justice Kennedy upheld the Eighth Circuit's determination that workers could use an expert's determination based on a statistical sample to show the amount of time each worker spent donning and removing protective gear. Unclear is whether *Tyson* signals a more pro-class action sentiment within the current Court.

78. Genesis HealthCare Corp. v. Symczyk, 133 S. Ct. 1523 (2013).

79. Campbell-Ewald Co. v. Gomez, 136 S. Ct. 663 (2016).

80. *Genesis HealthCare*, 133 S. Ct. at 1527.

81. *Id.*

82. *Id.* at 1527–28.

dards Act[83] and rejected Symczyk's efforts to extend Rule 23 precedent to that law.[84]

Decided in 2013, *Symczyk* led to considerable speculation whether the Court would extend its holding to Rule 23 class actions. Further, some of its language invited attorneys defending class action suits to argue that should be the result. Defense oriented websites advocated for counsel to argue *Symczyk*'s application in such cases. Typical is an article entitled *A Strategy for Defeating Auto Industry Class Actions.*[85] There, the author argued that *Symczyk* opened the door to argue that an unaccepted offer of settlement to the class representative mooted the class action. She also noted that since the decision, circuit courts had divided on that question.[86]

Defendants would have gained enormous power had the Court extended *Symczyk* to Rule 23 class actions. The Court resolved that question in *Campbell-Ewald Co. v. Gomez.*[87] Justice Ginsburg wrote for a five justice majority; Justice Thomas concurred on different grounds. Justices Scalia and Alito joined the Chief Justice's dissent.[88]

There, the defendant, Campbell-Ewald, violated the Telephone Consumer Protection Act, a statute giving consumers protection from certain unwanted phone calls. The plaintiff, Jose Gomez, filed a class action complaint, on behalf of individuals nationwide who had received but not consented to receive messages from the defendant. Prior to the time in which the plaintiff was to file for class certification, the defendant offered to settle the plaintiff's claim and filed an offer of judgment consistent with Rule 68. The plaintiff rejected the offer. After the requisite time elapsed, the defendant filed a motion to dismiss for lack of subject matter jurisdiction. The district court denied the motion.[89]

83. Fair Labor Standards Act of 1938, 52 Stat. 1060.

84. *Genesis Healthcare*, 133 S. Ct. at 1529–30.

85. Kara F. Kennedy, *A Strategy for Defeating Auto Industry Class Actions*, LAW360 (June 2, 2014), http://www.alston.com/files/Publication/7a8b67e3-ca14-44d6-8adf-4ec6d4203eb5/Presentation/PublicationAttachment/7bf2c8cc-e8fc-4c86-bd33-50e0ba9f5ffb/Kennedy%20Publication.pdf.

86. *Id.*

87. Campbell-Ewald Co. v. Gomez, 136 S. Ct. 663 (2016).

88. *Id.*

89. *Id.* at 666–68.

The district court later granted a motion for summary judgment on other grounds. The Ninth Circuit reversed that judgment and remanded the case to the district court. Instead, the defendant sought a writ of certiorari, which the Court granted to resolve the conflict among the circuits on the effect of an unaccepted offer of settlement. The Court found that an unaccepted settlement offer does not render a case moot. A contrary result would have done great damage to class action litigation, giving defendants the power to scuttle class action suits by offering the class representative a settlement of that party's claim.[90]

Even Justice Ginsburg's opinion leaves open future efforts to circumvent the Court's holding. In *Campbell-Ewald*, the defendant's offer did not give the plaintiff what he precisely asked for. As a result, the Court left open how it would have resolved the case, had the defendant entered the precise amount requested by the plaintiff in a dedicated account and the court entered a judgment for the plaintiff in that amount.[91]

The Chief Justice's dissent has invited defendants to litigate the question left open in Justice Ginsburg's opinion. He stated that the majority opinion was limited to its facts and suggested that the case would come out differently had the defendant offered full relief.[92]

Since Justice Ginsburg's death and the Court's further move to the right, the right wing of the Court may prevail at some future date. Under the Chief Justice's approach, defendants may be able to control the litigation by offering a full settlement to a class representative in order to force dismissal of the case. Presumably, unless time-barred, a new plaintiff might come forward to refile. But at a minimum, it offers defendants a new tool. At best, lower courts will have to sort out how to resolve that question and almost certainly will come to conflicting decisions, forcing another trip to the Supreme Court. One might ask the Chief Justice what interests are served if he gains a majority. Such a practice, dilatory at best, seems in flagrant disregard of Rule 1 and invites a good bit of unnecessary delay and satellite litigation.[93]

The Chief Justice's position also ignores the reality of class action practice: a plaintiff's role in class actions is more formal than in non-

90. *Id.* at 668–69.

91. *Id.* at 683–85 (Alito, J., dissenting).

92. *Id.* at 682–83 (Roberts, J., dissenting).

93. *Id.* at 677–83.

class action litigation. Far more important is whether counsel is able to represent the class effectively. That is an issue especially in cases where individual class members have small stakes in the outcome. In such cases, the class representative and, more importantly, counsel for the plaintiffs' class, serve as private attorneys general to ensure enforcement of substantive legal principles.[94]

(2) *Wal-Mart Stores, Inc. v. Dukes*[95]

According to the class plaintiffs in *Wal-Mart Stores, Inc. v. Dukes*, Wal-Mart had in place a method of determining pay and promotion that resulted in discrimination against female employees in violation of Title VII. The district court granted class certification for a nationwide class of over 1,500,000 female employees. The Ninth Circuit agreed and found that certification was proper under Rule 23(b)(2) (dealing with cases in which "final injunctive or corresponding declaratory relief is appropriate respecting the class as a whole").[96]

The Supreme Court reversed. The Court was unanimous with regard to the applicability of Rule 26(b)(2). Commentators largely agree that the Court's result on that issue was correct because "the back pay ... did not flow naturally from the injunctive relief that was being sought."[97] But the Court divided along ideological lines, with Justice Scalia writing a decision for the right wing of the Court in which it held that the class failed to satisfy Rule 23(a)(2). Specifically, the class failed the commonality requirement of that sub-section of the rule.[98]

The majority's holding on commonality ratchets up the requirements for class actions. As Professor Freer has written, "Commonality had never been much of a factor. It was all but impossible to find cases in which courts denied certification because of a failure to satisfy Rule 23(a)(2)."[99]

---

94. *See id.*

95. Wal-Mart Stores, Inc. v. Dukes, 564 U.S. 338 (2011).

96. *Id.* at 345–46.

97. Genetin, *supra* note 76, at 728.

98. Richard D. Freer, *The Class Action After a Decade of Roberts Court Decisions: Front-Loading, Avoidance, and Other Features of the Recent Supreme Court Class Actions Jurisprudence*, 48 Akron L. Rev. 721, 728 (2015).

99. *Id.* at 730.

The plaintiffs' theory was that Wal-Mart's policy of allowing local supervisors make important wage decisions subjected all women working for Wal-Mart to a discriminatory policy. Justice Scalia rejected that as the controlling question. Instead, the plaintiffs had to identify "a common method of exercising discretion that pervades the entire company."[100] At the pleading stage, the plaintiffs tried to overcome that problem with a sociologist's expert opinion about the effects of the policy. But the majority rejected the expert's opinions as worthless because the expert could not testify about individual decisions. Justice Scalia also rejected reliance on statistical data because those data did not show anything about "specific employment practice[s]."[101]

Not surprisingly, lower courts have differed on how much more demanding the Court's new standard is. Some lower courts have continued to rely on pre-*Wal-Mart* precedent. But again as Professor Freer has pointed out, "[T]he case makes life more difficult for plaintiff classes by injecting various procedural hurdles" into class actions.[102]

Federal law provides various groups with protection against discrimination. The Court cannot abandon such a statute as long as it is constitutional. But setting up increasingly burdensome procedural hurdles makes enforcement of such substantive rights far less meaningful. Justice Scalia had to acknowledge that statistical data demonstrated a pay disparity between male and female employees at Wal-Mart and that the disparity was greater than at other retail companies. The Court has held in the past that a plaintiff cannot recover without more. But one would have thought demonstrating that something more would have been what discovery was about and, after discovery, what a trial would be about. Instead, setting a high bar at the outset prevented the plaintiffs' class from getting past class certification.[103]

---

100. *Wal-Mart Stores*, 564 U.S. at 356.

101. *Id.* at 357.

102. Freer, *supra* note 98, at 734.

103. *Id.* at 754–55.

(3) *AT&T Mobility LLC v. Concepcion*[104] and *American Express Co. v. Italian Colors Restaurant*[105]

The next chapter returns to the topic of arbitration. As discussed there, unlike most of the developments discussed in this book, compulsory arbitration did suddenly make the front pages of the *New York Times* and got public attention (although events since the first edition of this book suggest that liberal reforms to the Court's holding will not occur).[106] This section focuses on *AT&T Mobility LLC v. Concepcion*, yet another case in which the Court has disallowed a class action. Instead, the right wing of the Court read the Federal Arbitration Act broadly to prevent plaintiffs from seeking an effective remedy for their claims. As with other procedural rulings, the Court's arbitration decisions favor corporate America over injured plaintiffs.

Enacted in 1925, the Federal Arbitration Act[107] overcame judicial hostility to enforcement of arbitration agreements. At least in some business contexts, allowing parties with equal bargaining power to enter a contract providing for an alternative to litigation makes sense. But as developed in this section, expansive reading of the Act raises serious questions for injured plaintiffs, often without any realistic bargaining power. Further, ironically, one empirical study demonstrates that corporations are more likely to include mandatory arbitration clauses in consumer contracts where those clauses are buried in boilerplate language than when they enter contracts with non-consumer business peers. The reason why corporations prefer arbitration clauses in consumer contracts is obvious: apart from avoiding litigation expenses, corporations are repeat players in arbitration; individual consumers are not. As a result, defendant-corporations do well in arbitration, where they win outright or have lower than expected damage awards entered against them.[108]

---

104. AT&T Mobility LLC v. Concepcion, 563 U.S. 333 (2011).

105. Am. Express Co. v. Italian Colors Restaurant, 133 S. Ct. 2304 (2013).

106. As developed in Chapter 9, the hope that Congress might overrule Supreme Court holdings dealing with some aspects of the FAA did not come to fruition since the first edition of this book. Also as discussed there, chances that such reforms will occur during the current Trump administration seem slim to none.

107. Federal Arbitration Act, 43 Stat. 883.

108. Freer, *supra* note 98, at 742.

Over the past decades, the Court has often read the Act broadly. That has encouraged corporations to include arbitration clauses in a host of consumer contracts, including cellular phone service, credit card, discount brokerage, and now even medical services contracts. In many of those instances, even if consumers are aware of the arbitration clause and understand its significance, opting out of the clause is a virtual impossibility. Imagine, for example, refusing to sign such a clause when you next need medical care. And if you doubt how ubiquitous such clauses are, take a look at all of the consumer contracts that you have signed in recent years. Almost certainly, you have waived your opportunity to sue in most of those contracts.[109]

AT&T Mobility LLC v. Concepcion demonstrates the right wing of the Court's broad reading of the Act. As with so many other areas of the law, the Court's reading favors corporations and leaves many plaintiffs without effective remedies.[110]

In *AT&T Mobility LLC v. Concepcion*, class members signed up for a phone plan that included a free phone. But AT&T billed their customers' sales tax on the transaction (amounting to $30.22 per customer). Certainly, the plaintiffs believed that the advertising was false and possibly fraudulent and brought suit claiming a violation of California's consumer fraud laws.[111]

The contract included an arbitration clause among its other provisions. Despite that, the Concepcions joined with other members of a putative class. The district court denied AT&T's motion to compel arbitration, and the Ninth Circuit affirmed.[112]

The lower courts and the four dissenting Supreme Court justices focused on language in the Act. The Act provides that arbitration agreements are valid "save upon such grounds at law or in equity for the revocation of any contract."[113] California law makes a class action waiver in any contract unenforceable if certain circumstances are met. Further, the California Supreme Court held that such waivers of the right to collective arbitration are unconscionable in cases like the one before the court.

109. *Id.* at 745–46.

110. *See id.* at 742–45.

111. AT&T Mobility LLC v. Concepcion, 563 U.S. 333, 337–38 (2011).

112. *Id.*

113. *Id.* at 339.

The Supreme Court reversed. Writing for the Court's right wing, Justice Scalia held that federal law preempted state law. That was the case because the state law "stand[s] as an obstacle to the accomplishment of the FAA's objectives."[114]

One might justify the majority's approach: allowing a class action suit creates litigation because each individual's claim is so small that the claimants will not sue individually. The California Supreme Court summarized the counterargument: the defendant is attempting to exempt itself from its own fraud or willful injury to the consumers.[115]

AT&T Mobility LLC v. Concepcion was not without ambiguity. There, Justice Scalia assumed that the individual plaintiffs would pursue their claims because of some reasonably generous provisions in the contract. That invited a question: was the Court's holding limited to such cases? That question was answered in *American Express Co. v. Italian Colors Restaurant.*[116]

In *American Express Co. v. Italian Colors Restaurant*, restaurant owners sued American Express for a violation of federal antitrust laws. The plaintiffs alleged American Express forced them to pay the company higher interest rates than its competitors, based on its monopoly power. The problem for the class plaintiffs was that they signed an agreement that included an arbitration requirement.[117]

The plaintiffs' claims might be significant. Counsel argued that, unlike the plaintiffs in *AT&T Mobility LLC v. Concepcion*, individual plaintiffs could not pursue litigation individually. The cost of hiring an economic expert, able to explain the complex issues in the case, would preclude individual suits. The Second Circuit agreed and found that only through class litigation could the antitrust laws be vindicated.[118]

Once again, Justice Scalia wrote an opinion for a five justice majority, including all of the members of the Court's right wing. *AT&T Mobility LLC v. Concepcion* did not turn on whether suits by individual plaintiffs were economically feasible at least on the facts of the case. Justice Scalia recognized that public policy may invalidate such an agreement if it

114. *Id.* at 343.

115. *Id.* at 357–58 (quoting Discover Bank v. Sup. Ct., 36 Cal. 4th 148, 162–63 (2005)).

116. Am. Express Co. v. Italian Colors Restaurant, 133 S. Ct. 2304 (2013); Freer, *supra* note 98, at 746–47.

117. *Am. Express Co.*, 133 S. Ct. at 2307–08.

118. *Id.* at 2308.

truly prevented pursuit of a statutory remedy. But federal antitrust law existed long before the adoption of Rule 23. Thus, the antitrust law did not turn on availability of liberal joinder as a necessary enforcement mechanism.[119]

Justice Kagan's dissent summarized the majority's position as follows:

> Here is the nutshell version of this case, unfortunately obscured in the Court's decision. The owner of a small restaurant (Italian Colors) thinks that American Express (Amex) has used its monopoly power to force merchants to accept a form contract violating the antitrust laws. The restaurateur wants to challenge the allegedly unlawful provision (imposing a tying arrangement), but the same contract's arbitration clause prevents him from doing so. That term imposes a variety of procedural bars that would make pursuit of the antitrust claim a fool's errand. So if the arbitration clause is enforceable, Amex has insulated itself from antitrust liability—even if it has in fact violated the law. The monopolist gets to use its monopoly power to insist on a contract effectively depriving its victims of all legal recourse.
>
> And here is the nutshell version of today's opinion, admirably flaunted rather than camouflaged: Too darn bad.[120]

As she argued, nothing in the Court's precedent dictated the majority's conclusion. Consistent with the Second Circuit's opinion and with the Ninth Circuit's decision in *AT&T Mobility LLC v. Concepcion*, Justice Kagan laid bare what is at stake in these cases: can a powerful corporate defendant immunize itself from the law? As has so often been the case with the Court's right wing, the answer is yes.[121]

The next chapter picks up with more recent cases involving arbitration clauses decided since the first edition of this book. Despite efforts by the plaintiffs' bar to work around the Court's decisions enforcing arbitration clauses, the Court has continued to favor those clauses. Consistently, the effect has been to deny injured parties the ability to bring class actions in such cases, the far more realistic way to bring defendants to bar.

---

119. *Id.* at 2309–10.

120. *Id.* at 2313 (Kagan, J., dissenting).

121. *Id.* at 2320.

E. Concluding Thoughts

Class actions have been a powerful device for enforcing an array of state and federal laws. Public agencies may lack resources to pursue those violations. Even in cases where individual plaintiffs lack sufficient injuries to bring suit, class plaintiffs become private attorneys general. But as developed above, the Supreme Court has curtailed the availability of class action suits in a variety of settings.

Powerful financial interests have spent billions of dollars to gut various federal laws. Many members of the libertarian right wing would like to gut environmental laws. Many oppose a host of federal regulations, including antitrust, minimum wage, and workplace safety laws. Overturning many of those laws outright has not been feasible. For example, even after significant efforts to convince members of the public that climate change is not a man-made problem, the right wing is unlikely to get Congress to overrule many environmental laws (one reason why President Trump is trying to use executive orders to limit the power of the EPA). A compliant Supreme Court has reduced the need for doing so.

As argued throughout this book, the Court's war on procedure achieves many of the goals of the right wing. Closing the courthouse door is almost as effective as simply denying a plaintiff a substantive right. And to date, the public usually does not understand the impact of the Court's procedural decisions. That is not surprising. Even many law students and lawyers fail to see the power of procedure. My hope is that you understand the point after reading this book.

NINE

Arbitration Clauses and Concluding Thoughts

A. Introduction

When I was writing the first edition of this book, Justice Scalia died unexpectedly. As I worked on that edition of the book during the summer of 2016, former President Obama's selection of Justice Scalia's replacement produced multiple headlines. His replacement might have had a major impact on the law, especially in high profile cases.[1] Then Senate Majority Leader Mitch McConnell succeeded in frustrating efforts to provide nominee Merrick Garland with a hearing before the Senate. With the election of Donald Trump, hope for a significant shift in the Court's direction faded. Further, then-Senate Majority Leader Mitch McConnell's success in ramming through Amy Coney Barrett's nomination at the end of President Trump's first term shifted the Court further to the right.

Prior to those developments, there was some hope that Congress would reverse some of the Court's case law upholding arbitration agreements at the expense of injured plaintiffs. For example, a series of articles in the *New York Times* offered hope for constructive change in the trend that I have documented in the previous chapter and that I explore in

1. *See, e.g.*, Daniel Fisher, *How Scalia's Death Affects 9 Big Cases at Supreme Court*, Forbes (Feb. 14, 2016), http://www.forbes.com/sites/danielfisher/2016/02/14/scalias-death-scrambles-all-the-calculations-on-big-cases/#3566e7e42861.

more detail below. Beginning in late 2015, the *Times* ran a series of articles highlighting the effects of the Court's decisions upholding arbitration clauses in consumer contracts. Unlike many of the areas of the law described in this book, narrowing access to our courts through the use of arbitration clauses seemed to have resonated at least with the media, some liberal lawmakers and, some of us hoped, with the public. In 2016, reformers were attempting to reverse the Court's arbitration decisions through formal rulemaking and legislation.[2] As developed in this chapter, those hopes failed to come to fruition.

This chapter focuses on the Supreme Court's arbitration case law, revisiting some of the cases discussed in Chapter 8, dealing with class actions. That section also discusses related contract clauses providing forum selection or choice of law provisions. Afterwards, it reviews the *New York Times* articles that brought this issue to the attention of the public. Thereafter, it discusses some of the efforts to reverse the Court's restrictive case law. Those efforts included proposed legislation and proposed rules that were working their way through the Consumer Financial Protection Bureau's rulemaking procedures. Those efforts failed early in the first Trump administration.[3] Despite changes to some administrative rules that limited some arbitration agreements, the most important rules changes were short-lived. With a Republican-led Congress, Trump signed legislation undoing the administrative rules changes. Even during Joe Biden's presidency, Congress was unable to pass reformist legislation that would have limited arbitration clauses.

Unlike hopes for reform that existed in 2016, the chapter also updates more recent Supreme Court cases that have continued the enforcement

---

2. Michael Corkery & Jessica Silver-Greenberg, *In Religious Arbitration, Scripture Is the Rule of Law*, New York Times (Nov. 2, 2015), http://www.nytimes.com/2015/11/03/business/dealbook/in-religious-arbitration-scripture-is-the-rule-of-law.html; Jessica Silver-Greenberg & Michael Corkery, *In Arbitration, a 'Privatization of the Justice System,'* New York Times (Nov. 1, 2015), http://www.nytimes.com/2015/11/02/business/dealbook/in-arbitration-a-privatization-of-the-justice-system.html; Jessica Silver-Greenberg & Robert Gebelof, *Arbitration Everywhere, Stacking the Deck of Justice*, New York Times (Oct. 31, 2015), http://www.nytimes.com/2015/11/01/business/dealbook/arbitration-everywhere-stacking-the-deck-of-justice.html; *see, e.g.*, *Eliminating Forced Arbitration*, Alliance for Justice, http://www.afj.org/our-work/issues/eliminating-forced-arbitration.

3. *See* Zachary Warmbrodt, *Pence Breaks Tie in Senate Vote to Ax Arbitration Rule*, Politico (Oct. 24, 2017, 11:25 PM), https://www.politico.com/story/2017/10/24/consumer-protection-arbitration-senate-pence-244140.

of arbitration clauses in ways that prevent many individuals from enforcing their rights in any meaningful forum and that prevent states from enforcing progressive policies aimed at limiting enforcement of overreaching arbitration clauses invoked against consumers in one-sided agreements.

Returning to the introduction where I mentioned Professor Mullinex's suggestion that the first edition of this book was too pessimistic, I revisit that theme at the end of this chapter. Sadly, from my perspective, the hope that existed briefly between Justice Scalia's death and Mitch McConnell's success in preventing then-President Obama from appointing Merrick Garland to the Court has long since faded. We now face many years of a Court dominated by far right wing Justices who seem ready to continue efforts to close the courthouse door to many aggrieved litigants.

B. The Power of Arbitration

During the summer of 2016, while writing the first edition of this book, I needed to have a medical procedure. After scanning the consent form, I dutifully signed the agreement, which included a clause requiring that I submit any malpractice claim to arbitration. One might ask, if arbitration clauses are so bad, why would a law-trained consumer sign such a form? The answer is straightforward: I needed the procedure and had no realistic alternatives.

When I teach or lecture on subjects like this or on other similar contractual provisions like forum selection or choice of law provisions, I challenge audience members to check how often they have signed away their rights without being aware that they have done so. And even for those who are aware, I ask them how often they have been able to negotiate an alternative to the contract's boilerplate language. I have yet to find anyone who has been able to do so.[4]

This section initially reviews the Supreme Court's case law upholding forum selection provisions. That case law, in effect, invited corporate litigants to take the questionable underlying principle that such clauses

4. *See* Silver-Greenberg & Corkery, *supra* note 2; Silver-Greenberg & Gebelof, *supra* note 2.

were the product of bargaining between the parties and to extend the principle to arbitration clauses. Thereafter, this section turns to the Supreme Court's arbitration case law.

(1) Forum Selection Clauses

For much of our history, state and federal courts have disfavored forum selection provisions. Often, those courts rejected such provisions out of populist sentiment, fear that out-of-state corporations forced local residents to litigate in inconvenient fora. Perhaps, such concerns lessened over time as the nation modernized its communication and transportation systems.[5]

No doubt, arbitration clauses, along with forum selection or choice of law provisions, have their place in business contracts. For example, in 1972, the Supreme Court described one such provision in *The Bremen v. Zapata Off-Shore Co.*,[6] a case involving an agreement between a Houston and a German corporation. The German corporation agreed to tow one of the Houston corporation's drilling rigs from Louisiana to Italy. The Houston corporation's rig was damaged during the towing operation as a result of a severe storm.[7]

The contract included a provision requiring suit to be tried in the London Court of Justice. The Houston corporation filed suit in a federal district court in the United States in an effort to avoid litigation in London. The District Court enjoined the German corporation from litigating in London; the United States Court of Appeals for the Fifth Circuit agreed. The Supreme Court disagreed and found that the lower courts had given too little weight to the forum selection agreement.[8]

Chief Justice Burger recognized the historical hostility toward forum selection clauses. He emphasized the increased globalization of trade and the need in that context for such agreements. Most importantly, on the facts of the case, the Houston corporation could not show that the

5. *See, e.g.*, The Bremen v. Zapata Off-Shore Co., 407 U.S. 1, 9–10 (1972) ("Forum-selection clauses have historically not been favored by American courts.").

6. *The Bremen*, 407 U.S. 1.

7. *Id.* at 2–6.

8. *Id.* at 4–9.

clause was unreasonable. Indeed, the parties bargained over the forum selection provision during the course of their negotiations.[9]

Many commentators assumed that the Court's holding in *The Bremen* would not apply to consumer contracts. Most consumers lack bargaining power when they are faced with form contracts containing boilerplate language. Indeed, that language may often be in small print and consumers may have little appreciation for the significance of such language.[10]

Despite that, the Court upheld a forum selection provision in *Carnival Cruise Line, Inc. v. Shute.*[11] There, the Shutes, Washington State residents, signed up for a Carnival Cruise Line cruise. They boarded the ship in Los Angeles, and Ms. Shute was injured when the ship was in Mexican waters. The Shutes sued in a federal district court in Washington State. At issue was whether the district court should enforce a forum selection clause included on the face of the tickets issued to the Shutes. The district court dismissed, but the Court of Appeals for the Ninth Circuit reversed. The Supreme Court agreed with the district court.[12]

The divided Court emphasized the facts of the case before it. The ticket issued by Carnival Cruise Lines stated in bold type that the purchaser should read other specified provisions, which included the forum selection clause. The Shutes conceded that they were aware of those provisions. Despite that, they argued that, unlike the situation in *The Bremen*, they did not in fact negotiate for the forum selection provision.[13]

The Shutes argued that the reasoning in *The Bremen* supported their case: there, the Chief Justice emphasized the importance of such provisions in modern international business transactions and the importance of the bargained-for provision in the specific contract. As the Court described in *Carnival Cruise Lines*, in *The Bremen*, the Chief Justice also observed that the Court "was not 'dealing with an agreement between two Americans to resolve their essentially local disputes in a remote alien forum,' and that in such a case, 'the serious inconvenience of the

9. *Id.* at 16–19.

10. *See* Kia Franklin, *Screwed by the Fine Print*, The Nation (Feb. 10, 2009), https://www.thenation.com/article/screwed-fine-print/.

11. Carnival Cruise Lines v. Shute, 499 U.S. 585 (1991).

12. *Id.* at 587–90.

13. *Id.* at 591–93.

contractual forum to one or both of the parties might carry greater weight in determining the reasonableness of the forum clause.'"[14]

Despite those arguments, the Court found that the provision signed by the Shutes was reasonable. It rejected the need for any bargaining between the parties concerning the forum selection clause. It found such clauses beneficial because they may clarify uncertainty about where a suit is proper. The Court also concluded that such provisions no doubt lead to lower fares for consumers. Further, the forum selected was not inconvenient for the parties; as a result, it did not deny the Shutes their day in court. Thus, they did not meet their heavy burden to show that the clause was unreasonable.[15]

The Court has not revisited the particular question in *The Bremen* and *Carnival Cruise Lines*. Its test, focusing on unreasonableness, leaves lower courts with room to avoid unfair provisions.[16] But *Carnival Cruise Lines* also demonstrates the Court's willingness to ignore the reality of consumer transactions where individuals are unlikely to understand the significance of their choices and have little, if any, meaningful bargaining power if they prefer not to accede to the drafter's choice of forum. Professor Linda Mullenix has identified *Carnival Cruise Lines* as one of the Court's worst non-constitutional decisions in forceful language:

> The Court's decision is a corporate rogue wave, hurling unsuspecting, ordinary people overboard without a flotation device or life raft. Too bad.
>
> Moreover, the decision is based on injudicious, insupportable rationales that irrationally and erroneously extend inapplicable prior precedent. The decision is untouched by any empirical proof. If this were not bad enough, the Court's *Carnival Cruise* decision tacitly has encouraged further judicial endorsement of two similar perils (the Scylla and Charybdis of forum selection): the choice-of-law clause and the manda-

---

14. *Id.* at 592.

15. *Id.* at 593–95.

16. *See* Richard L. Barnes, *Rediscovering Subjectivity in Contracts: Adhesion and Unconscionability*, 66 LA. L. REV. 123, 172 (2005).

> tory arbitration clause, which collectively scr*w [sic] folks of ordinary understanding in their everyday lives.[17]

But as bad as is *Carnival Cruise Line*'s holding, extending it to arbitration clauses takes it well beyond the harm created by forum selection clauses.

Think back to the Shutes. Although Florida was a far less convenient forum than Washington would have been, they could have litigated their claim in a court with a full panoply of procedural rights, including rights to discovery and a jury. Arbitration provides a litigant with far fewer rights than traditional litigation does and, as developed below, plaintiffs seldom benefit from the more relaxed procedures available in arbitration.[18]

(2) Extending the Rationale and the Explosion of Arbitration Clauses

Imagine consumers who claim to have been overcharged or dealt with fraudulently by a large corporate defendant. Their claims may amount to small sums, so small that no sane lawyer would handle their cases individually. One option might be the pursuit of a class action. Alternatively, according to proponents of arbitration, consumers might welcome arbitration as a cost-effective alternative to traditional litigation. That may be the case if a potential plaintiff has options.

Giving consumers the option between arbitration and traditional litigation, however, does not sufficiently advance corporate interests. As developed in Chapter 8, corporate and business representatives usually detest class actions.[19] The challenge for defense oriented, corporate groups, however, was whether they could overcome state and federal courts' hesitance to enforce arbitration agreements. As it turns out, the Roberts Court has been more than accommodating to those interests.[20]

---

17. Linda Mullenix, Carnival Cruise Lines, Inc. v. Shute: *The Titanic of Worst Decisions*, 12 NEV. L.J. 549, 549–50 (2012).

18. *Id.* at 551–52.

19. *See, e.g.*, Kara F. Kennedy, *A Strategy for Defeating Auto Industry Class Actions*, LAW360 (June 2, 2014), http://www.alston.com/files/Publication/7a8b67e3-ca14-44d6-8adf-4ec6d4203eb5/Presentation/PublicationAttachment/7bf2c8cc-e8fc-4c86-bd33-50e0ba9f5ffb/Kennedy%20Publication.pdf.

20. *See* Silver-Greenberg & Gebeloff, *supra* note 2.

As discussed in more detail below, corporations began inserting arbitration clauses in standard form contracts over two decades ago. That was part of a strategy developed, in part, by a group of Wall Street lawyers and credit card companies. Before his appointment to the bench, Chief Justice Roberts was instrumental in getting the Supreme Court to grant review in a case involving his client, Discover Card, in an effort to limit class actions and to enforce arbitration as its alternative.[21]

The previous chapter explored the two most important cases decided by the Roberts Court that upheld such clauses at the expense of ordinary consumers. The first of those cases was *AT&T Mobility LLC v. Concepcion.*[22] There, class members signed up for a phone plan that included a free phone. But AT&T billed their customers sales tax on the transaction (amounting to $30.22 per customer). The plaintiffs brought suit claiming a violation of California's consumer fraud laws.[23]

Although the contract contained an arbitration clause, the Concepcions joined with other members of a putative class. AT&T filed a motion to compel arbitration, which the district court, affirmed by the Ninth Circuit, denied.[24]

The lower courts and the four dissenting justices focused on language in the Act, which provides that arbitration agreements are valid "save upon such grounds at law or in equity for the revocation of any contract."[25] California law makes a class action waiver in any contract unenforceable if certain conditions are met, and the California Supreme Court had held that such waivers of the right to collective arbitration are unconscionable in cases like this one. Justice Scalia wrote the majority opinion for the right wing of the Supreme Court, reversing the decision on preemption grounds. He wrote that the state law stood "as an obstacle to the accomplishment of the Federal Arbitration Act's objectives."[26]

Unclear in Justice Scalia's opinion was whether the case turned on the plausible alternative to traditional litigation. His opinion focused on some of the generous provisions in the contract that gave individual

21. *Id.*

22. AT&T Mobility LLC v. Concepcion, 563 U.S. 333 (2011).

23. *Id.* at 337–38.

24. *Id.*

25. *Id.* at 339.

26. *Id.* at 343.

litigants incentive to arbitrate their cases. The open question was whether the Court would read the Federal Arbitration Act (FAA) to limit a litigant to arbitration if the litigant's possible award in arbitration made it unlikely that the consumer would pursue that remedy.[27]

The Court answered that question in *American Express Co. v. Italian Colors Restaurant*,[28] where restaurant owners sued American Express for a violation of federal antitrust laws. The plaintiffs alleged American Express took advantage of its monopoly power to force them to pay higher interest rates than its competitors charged. As in *AT&T Mobility LLC v. Concepcion*, class members had signed an agreement including an arbitration clause. Unlike *AT&T Mobility LLC v. Concepcion*, however, individuals were unlikely to pursue litigation individually because the cost of hiring an economic expert, able to explain the complex issues in the case, would preclude individual suits.[29]

Justice Scalia wrote the majority opinion, again for the five-justice right wing. On the facts of the case at least, it was not dispositive in *AT&T Mobility LLC v. Concepcion* whether it was economically feasible for individual plaintiffs to file suit. Justice Scalia did recognize that an agreement could be invalidated by public policy if the agreement actually prevented relief under a statutory remedy. However, because federal antitrust law existed long before the adoption of Rule 23, it did not turn on availability of liberal joinder as a necessary enforcement mechanism.[30]

Justice Kagan's dissent focused on two important points: she disputed whether the Court's precedent dictated the result in the case. She also emphasized the reality: powerful corporate interests were immunizing themselves from liability.[31]

Yet another case demonstrates the Court's willingness to enforce arbitration clauses, although it produced a somewhat unusual division in the Court. In *DirecTV, Inc. v. Imburgia*.[32] the plaintiffs objected to early termination fees imposed by DirecTV. They filed suit in California state court and contended that the termination fees violated state law. Di-

27. *Id.* at 357–58.

28. Am. Express Co. v. Italian Colors Restaurant, 133 S. Ct. 2304 (2013).

29. *Id.* at 2307–08.

30. *Id.* at 2309–10.

31. *Id.* at 2313 (Kagan, J., dissenting).

32. DirecTV, Inc. v. Imburgia, 136 S. Ct. 463 (2015).

recTV moved to have the case sent to arbitration. The California trial court and court of appeal refused to do so.[33]

The issue before the Supreme Court focused again on the language of the FAA that deals with the enforceability of arbitration agreements and provides that such agreements are enforceable "save upon such grounds as exist at law or in equity for the revocation of any contract."[34] The Supreme Court rejected the California court of appeal's conclusion that the provision was unenforceable. Writing for six justices, Justice Breyer found that the court of appeal's decision did not give "due regard ... to the federal policy favoring arbitration."[35] As a result, federal law preempted state law as interpreted by the court of appeal.[36]

Justice Thomas dissented. He relied on his previous view that the FAA does not apply to state court proceedings.[37] Justice Ginsburg, joined by Justice Sotomayor, agreed with the state court's conclusion. She believed that ambiguity in the contract written by a powerful economic interest should be read in favor of the consumer, not the drafter.[38]

While the issue in *DirecTV, Inc. v. Imburgia* was not as sweeping as the decision in, say, *American Express Co. v. Italian Colors Restaurant*, it is yet another instance in which the Court has given a corporate-friendly reading to the FAA. In addition, it did so in a case that frustrates state policies opposed to enforcement of such agreements.

While corporate interest representatives continued to work to expand enforcement of arbitration agreements, members of the plaintiffs' bar also found ways around the Court's limiting case law. In a 2018 Fordham Law Review article, Professor Myriam Gilles observed that any hopes of legislative action to undo cases like *Concepcion* were likely futile. But she argued that one method that might work is "concerted state/private enforcement solutions."[39] As she explained, "[a]s we careen toward the cliff's edge—'the virtual death of the class action in employment cases and consumer contracts involving the sale of goods and services'—new

33. *Id.* at 466–67.

34. *Id.* at 465–66.

35. *Id.* at 471.

36. *Id.* at 466–67.

37. *Id.* at 471 (Thomas, J., dissenting).

38. *Id.* at 471–78.

39. Myriam Gilles, *The Politics of Access: Examining Concerted State/Private Enforcement Solutions to Class Action Bans*, 86 Fordham L. Rev. 2223, 2223 (2018).

coalitions of public interest lawyers and nonprofit entities have formed in search of state-based solutions to the dilemma of class action bans."[40] Her article explored various efforts that amounted to partnerships between state attorneys general and consumer advocate attorneys. In effect, those efforts involved making the private attorneys into private attorneys general. As such, private parties could pursue class actions to advance a state's policy against enforcement of arbitration agreements. As has been the case with so many other efforts to circumvent the Court's enforcement of arbitration agreements, at least some of the efforts described by Professor Gilles in 2018 have been unavailing.[41]

As indicated, historically, many states disfavored arbitration agreements when those were imposed on consumers, who most often lack any meaningful bargaining power. Many states continue to try to circumvent the Court's expansive reading of the FAA. California has been a leader in the field. For example, as it became increasingly clear that the Court was on a mission to limit consumer protection class actions by reading the FAA expansively, the California legislature enacted the Private Attorney General's Act of 2004 (PAGA).[42]

PAGA sought to address problems with the enforcement of the state's Labor Code. PAGA sought protection for employees whose employers violated their rights under the Labor Code. Because those violations typically did not justify individual employees suing their employers and because many employers require employees to sign arbitration agreements, PAGA adopted an approach to circumvent the arbitration route. PAGA made an aggrieved employee the state's agent or proxy to enforce the state's attorney general's right to sue the employer. In effect, the employee was filing the action on behalf of the government, the real party in interest.[43]

PAGA contained other requirements before the suit could advance. It also included provisions for providing a successful plaintiff's attorney with attorney's fees and an allocation of an award against an employer.[44] In theory, because the real party in interest is the state and because the

---

40. *Id.* at 2226.

41. *Id.* at 2233–34.

42. Cal. Lab. Code §§ 2698–2699.5.

43. Gilles, *supra* note 39, at 2231 n.34.

44. Cal. Lab. Code § 2699(g)(1).

state was not a party to an agreement with the employer to submit its claims to arbitration, the FAA would not apply.[45] Or so prospective plaintiffs and their lawyers would have hoped.[46]

In 2016, Angie Moriana began working as a sales representative for Viking River Cruises, Inc. She signed a bilateral arbitration agreement.[47] As commentators like Professors Gilles and Mullenix[48] have observed, business groups and corporate attorneys have continually worked to expand the effect of arbitration agreements.[49] After California adopted PAGA, employers like Viking began to insert expanded arbitration clauses in their employee agreements.[50]

The contract that Ms. Moriana signed included a provision that stated that she would use an individualized arbitration proceeding to resolve a labor dispute rather than class, collective, representative, or private attorney general action proceedings. Ms. Moriana did have the option of opting out of that provision of her contract but did not do so.[51]

After she left her employment with Viking, she filed a PAGA action in state court. Her complaint alleged several violations of the state's Labor Code. Viking moved to compel arbitration and to stay the proceedings. The lower court ruled against Viking because consistent with precedent, PAGA was not preempted by the FAA. After the California appellate court affirmed the trial court and the state Supreme Court declined to grant review, Viking filed a writ of certiorari, which the Supreme Court granted.[52]

45. United States Arbitration Act, Pub. L. 68-401, 43 Stat. 883, codified at 9 U.S.C. Ch.1 (1925).

46. Gilles, *supra* note 39, at 2231 ("So for now at least, it seems fair to conclude that in the wake of *Concepcion*, state attorneys general and other officials remain free to bring cases on behalf of large groups of injured citizens—even if those individual citizens are themselves subject to arbitration clauses that preclude collective litigation.").

47. Viking River Cruises, Inc. v. Moriana, 596 U.S. 639, 647 (2022).

48. Linda S. Mullenix, *Class Action Waivers in Arbitration Agreements: The Twenty-First Century Arbitration Battleground and Implications for the E.U. Countries*, 38 Emory Int'l L. Rev. 785 (2024).

49. Gilles, *supra* note 39, at 2227–2228; *see also* Mullenix, *supra* note 48 at 785.

50. Mullenix, *supra* note 48, at 797 ("PAGA actions had increased defendants' risks for those sued under the statute.").

51. *Viking River Cruises, Inc.*, 596 U.S. at 647; *see also* J.A. 76 (Jan. 31, 2022), https://www.supremecourt.gov/DocketPDF/20/20-1573/211810/20220131134258276_2022-01-31%20Viking%20JA%20FINAL.pdf.

52. *Viking River Cruises, Inc.*, 596 U.S. at 643.

In light of other recent Supreme Court cases like *Concepcion* and two other more recent decisions that came after *Concepcion*,[53] the Court's holding in *Viking* should not have come as a surprise. The Court upheld Viking's authority to enforce the arbitration agreement. The Court found that PAGA's built-in mechanism for claim joinder conflicted with the FAA. As a result, the FAA controlled.[54]

In a recent article in the Emory International Law Review, Professor Mullenix observed that,

> With each successive Court opinion, and to immunize themselves from having to engage in any form of collective arbitration or litigation, corporate counsel have expanded and elaborately defined the list of arbitration exclusions (other than bilateral arbitration). On the other hand, plaintiffs' attorneys have proven equally adept at devising means to pursue collective relief notwithstanding carefully crafted arbitration language specifically designed to describe and prohibit every possible collective procedure.[55]

The plaintiffs' bar may have other options that would circumvent the enforcement of arbitration agreements.[56] Some commentators, including Professor Mullenix have observed that the Court has yet to rule that qui tam actions, suits brought purely on behalf of the government by

---

53. In *Epic Systems Corp. v. Lewis*, 584 U.S. 497 (2018), the Court in a 5–4 decision found that the FAA required enforcement of arbitration agreements regardless of collective action provisions in the National Labor Relations Act and the Fair Labor Standards Act of 1938. In *Lamps Plus, Inc. v. Varela*, 587 U.S. 176 (2019), the Court, again in a 5–4 decision, held that the FAA preempted traditional common law contract doctrines governing ambiguous language. Under traditional contract law, ambiguous language is read against the drafter's position. Rejecting that traditional rule, the Court again found that the FAA controlled, reversing the court of appeals.

54. *Viking River Cruises, Inc.*, 596 U.S. at 659–62. The Court engaged in an extensive discussion of specific policy questions raised by the parties. For purposes of this discussion, however, the crux of the case was the Court's willingness yet again to frustrate efforts to protect individuals and to give a broad reading to the FAA.

55. Mullenix, *supra* note 48, at 803.

56. As the Court explained in a footnote in *Vermont Agency of Natural Resources v. United States ex rel. Stevens*, 529 U.S. 765 (2000), "qui tam" is an abbreviated Latin phrase with the meaning "'who pursues this action on our Lord the King's behalf as well as his own.'"

private citizens, may circumvent the FAA.[57] But a consistent theme during this century has been that the Court has found for defendants over and over again.

For a short moment about a decade ago, the Court's arbitration cases seemed to be different from other decisions discussed in this book. Those cases seemed to produce a public backlash, creating hope that Congress would reverse the course taken by the Court and would give injured potential plaintiffs greater protection. That is the next topic of this chapter, including a discussion of how hoped-for change has not taken place.

C. Getting the Public's Attention

The Court's arbitration line of cases has generated a good deal of scholarly attention. That is not surprising. Many law professors, especially proceduralists, recognize the importance of access to the courts.[58] Indeed, they often write about the ascendant importance of procedure. But usually, that scholarship is in academic journals. About a decade ago, the Court's arbitration cases gained broader attention. For example, Dean Erwin Chemerinsky writes not only scholarly articles and books, but has written books aimed at a wider public than members of the academy and legal profession. Thus, in one of his books, *The Case Against the Supreme Court*, he identified this line of cases as part of the Roberts Court's pro-business bias. The Court's arbitration cases also gained attention in the national media.[59]

Beginning in 2015, the *New York Times* published a series of articles about the law and realities of arbitration. There, authors Jessica Silver-Greenberg and Robert Gebelof described the spread of the use of arbitration clauses. As they observed, "Over the last few years, it has become

---

57. Mullenix, *supra* note 48, at 802.

58. *See, e.g.*, Janet Cooper Alexander, *Do the Merits Matter? A Study of Settlements in Securities Class Actions*, 43 STAN. L. REV. 497 (1991); Michael Vitiello, *Limiting Access to U.S. Courts: The Supreme Court's New Personal Jurisdiction Case Law*, 21 U.C. DAVIS J. INT'L L. & POL'Y 210 (2015).

59. *See* ERWIN CHEMERINSKY, THE CASE AGAINST THE SUPREME COURT (2014) (discussing how the Roberts Court's pro-business bias can be perceived in its rulings in several areas, including arbitration and class action laws).

increasingly difficult to apply for a credit card, use a cellphone, get cable or Internet service, or shop online without agreeing to private arbitration. The same applies to getting a job, renting a car or placing a relative in a nursing home."[60]

The authors contended that the strategy was the brainchild of a coalition of credit card companies and retailers, aided by lawyers like John Roberts, Jr. The net and, no doubt, intended effect was to disable consumer challenges to predatory lending practices, wage theft, and discrimination. As cited in the *Times*, one Reagan appointee to the bench summed it up as follows: "Ominously, business has a good chance of opting out of the legal system altogether and misbehaving without reproach."[61] In addition, at some of the meetings, the lawyers who developed the arbitration strategy expressed the desire to destroy class actions "and send plaintiffs' lawyers to the 'employment lines.'"[62]

In a letter to the editors at the *Times*, Lisa A. Rickard, the President of the U.S. Chamber Institute for Legal Reform, an arm of the U.S. Chamber of Commerce, criticized the three part series with the standard justification for arbitration. She challenged the assumption that class action suits do a good job of protecting consumers from corporate wrongdoing. In the overwhelming majority of such suits, members of the class other than the named plaintiff do not receive financial compensation. She dismissed class actions as existing primarily for the benefit of plaintiffs' lawyers. By comparison, she contended, "Arbitration provides consumers with a fairer, simpler, cheaper and faster way of resolving disputes, and one with greater potential benefits to individual customers."[63]

Ms. Rickard's response largely ignored much of the teaching of the Silver-Greenberg and Gebelof series. Her claim that class actions are not needed because arbitration is the better alternative did not withstand close scrutiny. The authors found that, "Once blocked from going to court as a group, most people dropped their claims entirely."[64] They ex-

60. Silver-Greenberg & Gebelof, *supra* note 2.

61. *Id.*

62. *Id.*

63. Lisa A. Rickard, *The Virtues of Arbitration*, New York Times (Nov. 14, 2015), http://www.nytimes.com/2015/11/14/opinion/the-virtues-of-arbitration.html.

64. Silver-Greenberg & Gebelof, *supra* note 2.

amined thousands of court records and conducted hours of interviews with those involved in the judicial and arbitration process.[65]

The authors found that the stakes for companies were quite high. Small banking fee cases, where banks overcharged consumers or duped them into taking on obligations that were largely useless, generated billions of dollars of profits for the banks. Denying class status and forcing arbitration in such cases immunized the conduct because, unlike Ms. Rickard's claim, most consumers simply did not pursue their cases. As the *Times* article noted, "[B]etween 2010 and 2014, only 505 consumers went to arbitration over a dispute of $2,500 or less."[66] In addition, Verizon, a company with over 125 million customers, arbitrated only 65 consumer cases in that period; Time Warner Cable, with 15 million customers, arbitrated only seven claims.[67]

The *Times* series also included a series of anecdotes, describing individuals who sought relief but faced obstacles when arbitration is the only option. For example, one plaintiff filed suit on behalf of Sprint customers whom the company billed for roaming charges that the plaintiff claimed were illegal. After the trial court dismissed the suit in reliance on an arbitration clause, the plaintiff faced this reality: "The cost of arbitration was far more than the $20 charges [the plaintiff] was contesting. And his lawyer... advised him that winning would require high-tech experts at a six-figure bill."[68] In addition, his attorney told him that if he lost, he might have to pay for Sprint's lawyers. Examples like this one and several others included in the article rebut claims made by business groups and defense lawyers that arbitration benefits consumers with small claims.[69]

The authors also questioned whether plaintiffs win in arbitration. Data show that plaintiffs win financial awards in only about a third of the cases brought to arbitration. Scholarly research has demonstrated the litigation bias in favor of corporate defendants. Obviously, arbitrators make their livings only if parties select them to arbitrate disputes. Individual plaintiffs are seldom repeat players; large corporations are repeat players. Favoring corporate litigants assures a steady stream of work,

---

65. *Id.*
66. *Id.*
67. *Id.*
68. *Id.*
69. *Id.*

creating a clear pro-defendant bias. Some arbitrators admitted that they felt obligated to companies out of a fear of losing business if they found for plaintiffs too often. The second article in the series recounted a story of a particular arbitrator who found in favor of a plaintiff in an age discrimination case and entered a substantial award in the case. He was never hired again in an employment case.[70]

The *Times* series focused on problems related to the "privatization" of the legal system. Arbitration, for example, deprives injured parties' rights like the right to appeal. Further, the rules of evidence do not apply. As the authors summarized, "Little is known about arbitration because the proceedings are confidential and the federal government does not require cases to be reported. The secretive nature of the process makes it difficult to ascertain how fairly the proceedings are conducted."[71] In addition, arbitration is largely a private event with no precedential value and no public record that may serve as precedent in similar cases. Indeed, the authors described how one plaintiff who sought treatment for drug and alcohol abuse signed an arbitration agreement with a Christian treatment program. The arbitrator resolved the case in light of the Holy Scripture, not domestic law. Not only does religious law (including Scientology) apply in such cases, but the litigant, who may be a nonbeliever, is bound by religious principles.[72]

Any claim that public agencies, including law enforcement, are available to deter such conduct fails too. Many state attorneys general expressed concern that the bans on class actions would lead to increased unlawful business practices. No doubt, they see class action plaintiffs and lawyers as private attorneys general.[73] Of course, if plaintiffs cannot pursue class actions, they cannot serve as private attorneys general.

The *Times* series also focused on how the Supreme Court has repeatedly ruled in favor of businesses. Many states remain hostile to forced arbitration, viewing such rules as contrary to important public policies. As indicated above, the Supreme Court's decisions have had the effect of preempting contrary state laws.[74] Also, as discussed above, in cases like

70. Silver-Greenberg & Corkery, *supra* note 2.

71. *Id.*

72. Corkery & Silver-Greenberg, *supra* note 2.

73. Silver-Greenberg & Gebeloff, *supra* note 2.

74. *Id.*

Viking, the Court has continued to frustrate efforts by progressive states to circumvent the Court's pro-business arbitration decisions.

The *Times'* articles seemed notable for two reasons. As discussed in Chapter 1, the media seldom recognize the significance of legal rulings dealing with procedure. If the media report at all, the stories do not appear on the front page. Even if they do, few readers appreciate the implications that such decisions have on access to justice. By comparison, the *Times* series was front-page news. The series was ongoing, with three major sections and several follow-up stories. That suggested significant interest in the topic.

Not only did the *Times* provide in-depth coverage to a procedural issue, but the authors also captured an issue that seemed to have legs. Consumer advocates and liberal lawmakers took up the issue and pushed for reforms.[75] For a time, one could be optimistic that those efforts would succeed. That is the subject of the next section.

D. Legislation and Rulemaking

The *Times* articles coincided with significant efforts to reform the law governing mandatory arbitration. Indeed, at least for some lawmakers, the *Times* articles were a wakeup call. When I wrote the first edition of this book, I noted that it remained an open question whether reform efforts would succeed. Not surprisingly, groups that brought about the arbitration revolution pumped resources into a campaign to defeat reform efforts. During 2016, a major bill was working its way through Congress; it did not pass in a Congress controlled by Republicans.[76] Trump's victory in 2016 and the Republicans' retention of both houses of Congress signaled the end of reform efforts.[77]

A proposed federal regulation of the financial services industry was also working its way through the Consumer Financial Protection Bu-

75. *See, e.g.*, Ron Lieber & Tara Siegel Bernard, *From Card Fees to Mortgages, a New Day for Consumers*, New York Times (June 25, 2010), http://www.nytimes.com/2010/06/26/your-money/26money.html?pagewanted=all&_r=0.

76. Arbitration Fairness Act, S. 1133, 114th Cong. (2015).

77. *See* David Lazarus, *Republicans Cook Up Plan to Cripple Consumer Agency*, LA Times (June 14, 2016), http://www.latimes.com/business/lazarus/la-fi-lazarus-dodd-frank-20160614-snap-story.html.

reau. Although the provision was limited to that industry, it would have limited arbitration agreements and forced greater transparency about the arbitration process. Unlike the proposed legislation, the agency regulation did not require congressional approval.[78]

This section describes some of the proposals that were working their way through Congress and the Consumer Financial Protection Bureau. Despite hopes almost a decade ago that those reforms might work, the next section describes their failure.

(1) Legislative Proposals

Former Senator Al Franken and others sponsored reform legislation over several years a decade ago. For example, Franken put the Arbitration Fairness Act of 2015 in the hopper that year. It included several key provisions.[79]

At root, the proposed legislation would have limited the Federal Arbitration Act to commercial agreements between parties with comparable bargaining power. In recognition of problems like those identified above (lack of fair procedures, frustration of the development of important federal laws, and problems of "repeat-player bias"), the legislation would have restored the Act's original intention by limiting the scope of the Act. The proposal would have invalidated arbitration agreements requiring employment, consumer, antitrust, or civil rights disputes to be submitted to arbitration when those agreements are entered prior to a dispute arising between the parties. In effect, that would have left open the option of arbitration if the parties agree to it, but only if they did so at the onset of litigation.[80]

In a memo explaining the proposed reform, Franken responded to an argument often advanced by proponents of arbitration that it is faster

---

78. *CFPB Proposes Prohibiting Mandatory Arbitration Clauses that Deny Groups of Consumers Their Day in Court*, Consumer Financial Protection Bureau (May 5, 2016), http://www.consumerfinance.gov/about-us/newsroom/consumer-financial-protection-bureau-proposes-prohibiting-mandatory-arbitration-clauses-deny-groups-consumers-their-day-court/.

79. Ashlee Kieler, *Arbitration Fairness Act Would Reinstate Consumers' Right to Sue in Court*, Consumerist (April 30, 2015), https://consumerist.com/2015/04/30/arbitration-fairness-act-would-reinstate-consumers-right-to-sue-in-court/.

80. *Id.*

and cheaper than litigation. If the parties believed that to be the case, they were free to arbitrate their disputes. Restoring the Act to its original meaning, however, would have required that any such choice was voluntary. The proposed legislation would have overruled *AT&T Mobility LLC v. Concepcion* and *American Express Co. v. Italian Colors Restaurant*. Indirectly, it would have overruled the result in *DirecTV, Inc. v. Imburgia*. That would have been the case because state policy disfavoring arbitration agreements in consumer and other similar contracts would no longer violate the FAA.[81]

The Arbitration Fairness Act of 2015 tapped into a populist sentiment that one can still see among states that are hostile to the Supreme Court's expansive reading of the FAA. Not only do state courts like the California court in *DirecTV, Inc. v. Imburgia* demonstrate hostility to the Court's broad application of the FAA, but some state legislatures sought ways to dissent from the Court's holdings. For example, New Jersey's Assembly proposed Resolution No. 145 that laid out the argument against the Court's arbitration case law and urged Congress and the President to enact The Arbitration Fairness Act of 2015.[82]

As indicated above, a Republican controlled Congress did not enact the Arbitration Fairness Act of 2015. Too many Republican donors lined up against such reforms.[83] Since then, even though one could see the emerging doubts about the fairness of arbitration agreements in a bipartisan bill introduced in the Senate, Congress has failed to enact any reform bill.

Senate Bill 2331 provides another example of a failed reformist proposal.[84] It was similar to the Arbitration Fairness Act of 2015 in that it would have invalidated arbitration agreements entered into before disputes arise. However, the bill was far more narrowly focused and protected only members of the Armed Forces.[85] Numerous veterans' groups

---

81. *See id.*

82. Assemb. Res. 145, 217th Leg. (N.J. 2016).

83. *See, e.g.*, Jared Bennett, *Who is killing the CFPB's arbitration rule?*, Center for Public Integrity (July 28, 2017) ("To fight the CFPB, the financial industry has spent millions cultivating relationships with lawmakers such as Rep. Keith Rothfus, R-Pa., who sponsored the resolution to undo the CFPB arbitration rule."), https://publicintegrity.org/inequality-poverty-opportunity/who-is-killing-the-cfpbs-arbitration-rule/.

84. SCRA Rights Protection Act, S. 2331, 114th Cong. (2015).

85. S. 2331.

endorsed the legislation.[86] Such a focused bill had a greater chance of passage, especially because protection of service members often generates bipartisan cooperation.[87] (Of course, one might question proponents of protecting service members but not members of the public: one should ask why the same arguments of unfairness would not apply.) Even with bipartisan support, passage of Senate Bill 2331 was not a sure thing. As observed in the *New York Times*, the bill "faces an uphill battle. A similar measure never made it out of committee last year after lobbying by the U.S. Chamber of Commerce and Wall Street's major trade group...."[88] Not surprisingly, Congress did not pass S.B. 2331.[89] Other attempts have failed as well, even during the Biden years. Indeed, proponents of reform introduced the Forced Arbitration Injustice Repeal (FAIR) Act in 2019, 2022, and 2023 with no success.[90]

As indicated above, reforming the law governing arbitration did not happen under the first Trump or the Biden administration. Given the pro-business stance of the Trump administration, reform is not likely in

---

86. *See* Press Release, Elizabeth Warren, Senator, Sen. Warren Cosponsors Servicemembers Civil Relief Act Rights Protection Act (July 25, 2014) ("Tens of national military organizations have endorsed the Servicemembers Civil Relief Act Rights Protection Act."), https://www.warren.senate.gov/newsroom/press-releases/sen-warren-cosponsors-servicemembers-civil-relief-act-rights-protection-act.

87. *See, e.g.*, Jennifer Steinhauer, *Republicans and Democrats Unite on at Least One Issue: Oversight of the V.A.*, New York Times (Dec. 10, 2018), https://www.nytimes.com/2018/12/10/us/politics/veterans-affairs-congress.html.

88. Jessica Silver-Greenberg & Michael Corkery, *Bipartisan Bill Would Protect Service Members' Right to Avoid Arbitration*, New York Times (Nov. 20, 2015), http://www.nytimes.com/2015/11/21/business/dealbook/bipartisan-bill-would-protect-service-members-right-to-go-to-court.html.

89. S. 2331. The Library of Congress web page shows the bill was merely introduced and referred to the Committee on Veterans' Affairs. *All Info: S.2331—114th Congress (2015–2016)*, Congress.Gov (last visited Mar. 2, 2025), https://www.congress.gov/bill/114th-congress/senate-bill/2331/all-info.

90. The FAIR Act passed the House in 2019. *H.R.1423—116th Congress (2019–2020)*, Congress.Gov (last visited Mar. 2, 2025), https://www.congress.gov/bill/116th-congress/house-bill/1423. It also passed the House in 2022. *H.R. 963—117th Congress (2021–2022)*, Congress.Gov (last visited Mar. 2, 2025), https://www.congress.gov/bill/117th-congress/house-bill/963. But it was doomed in 2023 after being referred to the House Judiciary Committee. *All Actions: H.R.2953—118th Congress (2023–2024)*, Congress.Gov (last visited Mar. 2, 2025), https://www.congress.gov/bill/118th-congress/house-bill/2953/all-actions.

the near term. Nonetheless, reform may be possible in the long-term future. But underscore "long-term."

When I wrote the first edition of this book, I could argue without exaggeration that, "Even without legislative action, however, reform may still be in the cards. Efforts to use agency rulemaking may provide a solution." That too has not panned out, as developed below.

(2) Agency Rulemaking

The Dodd-Frank Wall Street Reform and Consumer Protection Act of 2010 created the Consumer Financial Protection Bureau. Section 1028(a) of Dodd-Frank mandated that the bureau study "the use of agreements providing for arbitration of any future dispute... in connection with the offering or providing of consumer financial products or services."[91]

In compliance with § 1028(a), the agency spent three years studying such agreements. In March 2015, the agency published its findings in a document entitled *Arbitration Study: Report to Congress*, pursuant to Dodd-Frank Wall Street Reform and Consumer Protection Act Section 1028(a). After making some important findings, the massive report included two major proposed regulations.[92]

The report's findings were consistent with much of the literature critical of arbitration. It found that in many areas, like mobile wireless services and payday loan contracts, arbitration agreements were virtually universal. Almost all arbitration clauses also preclude class action suits. Most consumers are unaware that they are agreeing to submit their claims to arbitration.[93]

The Consumer Financial Protection Bureau published two proposed regulations. The first would have banned providers of some consumer financial products from binding consumers to agreements to arbitrate future disputes or precluding participation in class action suits. The sec-

---

91. Dodd-Frank Wall Street Reform and Consumer Protection Act, 124 Stat. 1376 (2010).

92. Bureau of Consumer Financial Protection, Arbitration Study: Report to Congress (2015).

93. *Id.*

ond regulation would have required covered providers to submit certain records to the agency.[94]

The argument for the first regulation seemed obvious considering the earlier discussion in this chapter and in Chapter 8. Class actions are a powerful tool for vindicating plaintiffs' rights; in many cases, individual arbitrations are not sufficient to protect consumers. Further, public resources are not sufficient to protect consumers, and, as a result, our system relies on private enforcement of those rights through class actions.[95]

As summarized in a letter submitted by a group of law professors in support of the regulations, the second proposal would have required covered providers to submit to the agency two kinds of information: "(a) claims, clauses, and judgments (if any) relating to consumer arbitration filings; and (b) any determinations by arbitrators or arbitration providers to the effect that a particular arbitration agreement does not comply with relevant fairness principles."[96]

The second regulation would have created transparency in an area traditionally hidden from public view. That degree of privacy has made understanding of the process difficult, including, among other things, understanding the kinds of defenses raised, rates of settlement, and rates at which claimants prevail. Proponents of arbitration argued that it provides an effective and affordable alternative to litigation, and the regulation would have allowed researchers to test the accuracy of such claims more meaningfully.[97]

The first regulation would not have prohibited parties from agreeing to arbitration after a dispute arose. Indeed, if proponents are correct that arbitration is consumer friendly because of cost, some parties could have chosen to submit their cases to arbitration. Requiring data collection and the study of those data would have given litigants a more meaningful insight as to whether arbitration is a good alternative to an individual suit or a class action.[98]

---

94. Arbitration Agreements, 81 Fed. Reg. 100 (proposed May 24, 2016).

95. *Id.*

96. 210 Professors, Comment Letter on Proposed Rule on Arbitration Agreements (May 24, 2016), https://www.regulations.gov/document?D=CFPB-2016-0020-0003. Not surprisingly, given what I have written in this chapter and in Chapter 8, I was one of the many law professors who signed the letter.

97. *Id.*

98. *Id.*

For a short period of time, those administrative rules were the law.[99] More evidence of the fact that the Trump administration was (and, of course, remains) pro-business and anti-consumer can be found in the short and bitter life of the proposed agency rules that disallowed the use of arbitration agreements if they precluded class actions. The agency's rules went into effect on September 18, 2017. But the Republican controlled Congress passed legislation removing the provision, a resolution that President Trump signed in November 2017.[100]

As I complete this chapter in early 2025, the Trump Administration has announced radical changes in the way the government will do business. One would be hard-pressed to find any pro-consumer changes in any of those announcements.[101]

E. Justice Scalia's Death

In the first edition of the book, I included a discussion of what might have been if Mitch McConnell had not prevented Merrick Garland from being confirmed to the open seat on the Supreme Court. At stake was a significant shift in the Court for the first time in years: a majority of the justices would have been appointed by Democratic Presidents for the first time since President Nixon got to make four appointments between 1969 and 1971.[102] Prominent Republican Senators understood that reality. In voicing their objections, those Senators focused on changes to

---

99. Arbitration Agreements, 82 Fed. Reg. 33210 (Sept. 18, 2017) (codified at 12 C.F.R. pt. 1040).

100. Action Removing Part 1040, 82 Fed. Reg. 55500 (Nov. 22, 2017). Lower federal courts are divided on the interpretation of some aspects of the Dodd-Frank law. For example, there is a circuit split whether the law prohibits agreements to arbitrate whistleblower claims. *Compare* Santoro v. Accenture Fed. Servs., LLC, 748 F.3d 217, 222 (4th Cir. 2014) (finding that Dodd-Frank prohibits agreements to arbitrate whistleblower claims), *with* Daly v. Citigroup Inc., 939 F.3d 415, 424 (2d Cir. 2019) (finding that "Congress did not intend to preclude arbitration of Dodd-Frank whistleblower claims"), *and* Khazin v. TD Ameritrade Holding Corp., 773 F.3d 488, 492–95 (3d Cir. 2014) (finding that Dodd-Frank does not prohibit agreements to arbitrate whistleblower claims).

101. The White House, President Trump's America First Priorities (Jan. 20, 2025), https://www.whitehouse.gov/briefings-statements/2025/01/president-trumps-america-first-priorities/.

102. S. Sidney Ulmer & John A. Stookey, *Nixon's Legacy to the Supreme Court: A Statistical Analysis of Judicial Behavior*, 3 Fla. St. U. L. Rev. 331, 331 (1975).

substantive rights. For example, Senator Chuck Grassley, Chair of the Senate Judiciary Committee, explained his party's refusal to hold hearings, in part, as follows: "A lifetime appointment that could dramatically impact individual freedoms and change the direction of the court for at least a generation is too important to get bogged down in politics."[103] Then-Presidential candidate Ted Cruz commented similarly that Obama's candidate, Merrick Garland, would "undermine Second Amendment gun rights, legalize late-term abortions and empower 'overreaching bureaucratic agencies.'"[104] Typical of other commentators on Justice Scalia's replacement to the Court, both Grassley and Cruz focused on the possible impact on substantive rights with little, if any, attention to the effect his replacement would have on procedure and access to justice. As is quite typical, the public and commentators focus on substantive rights, without appreciating the importance of procedural rights.[105]

In the original edition, I identified areas where a new more liberal majority might make an impact in reversing the right wing's use of procedure to close the courthouse door.

That discussion considered some of the cases discussed in earlier chapters in which the Court divided 5–4 with Justice Scalia in the majority. That included some of the Court's specific jurisdiction cases. For example, Justice Scalia joined Justice Kennedy's extremely begrudging opinion in *J. McIntyre Machinery, Ltd. v. Nicastro*,[106] a case in which the Court divided 4–2–3. A more liberal justice might have joined a coalition including the three dissenters and one of the concurring justices to keep in place personal jurisdiction when a product arrives in state via the stream of commerce.[107]

---

103. Josh Vorhees & Leon Neyfakh, *How Washington and Everyone Else Is Reacting to President Obama's SCOTUS Pick*, Slate (Mar. 16, 2016), http://www.slate.com/blogs/the_slatest/2016/03/16/republican_reaction_to_obama_s_scotus_nomination_of_merrick_garland.html.

104. *McConnell Tells Obama's Nominee to Supreme Court that the Senate Won't Consider His Nomination*, US News (Mar. 16, 2016), http://www.usnews.com/news/politics/articles/2016-03-16/the-latest-obama-praises-merrick-garland-for-high-court.

105. *See supra* Chapter 1.

106. J. McIntyre Machinery, Ltd., v. Nicastro, 564 U.S. 873 (2011).

107. *See* Vitiello, *supra* note 58.

Another decision that the Court might have rethought was *Ashcroft v. Iqbal*,[108] another 5–4 decision in which Justice Scalia joined the right wing of the Court. It is vulnerable on a number of grounds: as discussed in Chapter 4, it flies in the face of the history of federal pleading. It has caused a good deal of confusion among lower courts, with many courts resisting its broad application. Even after *Iqbal*, the Court has decided cases that seem to return to the original meaning of Rule 8(a)(2). Under such circumstances, the Court could easily have narrowed *Iqbal*, for example, by emphasizing the unusual facts of the case (including the high bar that the plaintiff had to overcome when suing public officials entitled to qualified immunity).[109]

Chapter 6 focused on the Court's 5–4 decision in *Connick v. Thompson*,[110] a case in which the majority was willing to substitute its judgment for that of a jury that entered a substantial award in favor of a man unfairly convicted of murder. While *Connick v. Thompson* was fact-sensitive, the majority's willingness to substitute its judgment for the jury demonstrated a lack of empathy for some actors in the system and a preference for others.[111]

Many of the leading class action and arbitration cases were 5–4 decisions, with Justice Scalia in the conservative majority. Typical was *Wal-Mart Stores, Inc. v. Dukes*,[112] which narrowed the availability of class actions in wage discrimination cases. *AT&T Mobility LLC v. Concepcion*[113] was also a 5–4 decision, with the Court divided along its liberal-conservative lines. *American Express Co. v. Italian Colors Restaurant*[114] was a 5–3 decision. Justice Sotomayor did not participate in the decision, but she has sided with the liberal wing of the Court in other arbitration cases, including *Concepcion*.

One area in which the Court has not been deeply divided is in the reform of the discovery rules. For example, the liberal justices did not dissent from the amendments to Rule 26(b), designed to give judges more

108. Ashcroft v. Iqbal, 552 U.S. 662 (2009).

109. *Id.*

110. Connick v. Thompson, 563 U.S. 51 (2011).

111. *Id.*

112. Wal-Mart Stores, Inc. v. Dukes, 564 U.S. 338 (2011).

113. *AT&T Mobility*, 563 U.S. 333.

114. Am. Express Co. v. Italian Colors Restaurant, 133 S. Ct. 2304 (2013).

authority to limit discovery.[115] At the same time, the Rule is hardly self-defining, inviting challenges to its application. One can imagine the two wings of the Court dividing over how to read the rule, with the right wing of the Court favoring a discovery-limiting interpretation of the Rule.[116]

Thus, in several important areas discussed in this book, Justice Scalia's replacement might have made a significant impact in reopening the courthouse door. With Trump's appointment of three new right-wing justices, any hope that the Court would rebalance is idle at best.

F. Concluding Thoughts

Does access to justice matter? Without easy access to our court system, our panoply of substantive rights is meaningless. For those of us who grew up in the 1950s and 60s, the courts provided hope, for example, to African Americans seeking enforcement of their civil rights.[117] Women's groups followed suit.[118] In the 1980s and 90s and beyond, conservative groups used to the courts to advance their agenda.[119] Access to our courts is essential to upholding the rule of law. Although some commentators claim that the political process would have eventually worked to guarantee minority rights, for example, one might readily doubt such a claim. Indeed, proving such a thesis is problematic. And, of course, citizens routinely denied their rights while the political process eventually worked in their favor (if it did at all) would no doubt take a dim view of the promise that the process would eventually work to their advantage.

Does procedure matter? That, of course, is a rhetorical question and the central theme of this book. I have developed that theme by focusing on the kinds of biases demonstrated by the Court's right wing in its procedural holdings. Agree or disagree with my political perspective, my hope is that you agree that procedure is no dry subject. Instead, rules, like Rule 8(a)(2), seemingly dry stuff about the nature of pleading, are

---

115. *See supra* Chapter 5.

116. *Id.*

117. *See, e.g.*, Bailey v. Patterson, 369 U.S. 31 (1962).

118. *See, e.g.*, Frontiero v. Richardson, 411 U.S. 677 (1973).

119. *See, e.g.*, Richmond v. J.A. Croson, Co., 488 U.S. 469 (1989).

about who gets to prevail in litigation: injured parties may have no way to allege specific facts without access to discovery. The same is true of all of the subjects covered in this book: without liberal rules of procedure in place, our substantive rights are for show. Given the Court's further turn to the right, I suspect that many, including Professor Mullenix, would agree that progressive reformers are in for some lean years.

Index

D